I0643774

Making Better Flies

0 11557 01138 8

Making Better Flies

How to Design, Develop, and Improve Fly Patterns for Salt and Fresh Water

LOU TABORY

STACKPOLE
BOOKS

Published by
STACKPOLE BOOKS
5067 Ritter Road
Mechanicsburg, PA 17055
www.stackpolebooks.com

Printed in the United States of America

10 9 8 7 6 5 4 3 2 1

First edition

Cover design by Caroline Stover
Cover images by Barb Tabory
Photos by Barb and Lou Tabory except where noted

Library of Congress Cataloging-in-Publication Data

Names: Tabory, Lou.
Title: Making better flies : how to design, develop, and improve fly patterns for salt and fresh water / Lou Tabory.
Description: First edition. | Mechanicsburg, PA : Stackpole Books, 2016. | Includes index.
Identifiers: LCCN 2015033554 | ISBN 9780811711388
Subjects: LCSH: Fly tying. | Flies, Artificial.
Classification: LCC SH451 .T23 2016 | DDC 688.7/9124--dc23 LC record available at http://lccn.loc.gov/2015033554

To Barb

For keeping me sane when I was self-destructing in the technological jungle. For without your patience, hard work, and companionship, this book would never have been completed.

Contents

Acknowledgments xi

Introduction xiii

CHAPTER 1: Imitation and Design Characteristics 1

CHAPTER 2: Important Baits and Food Types 27

CHAPTER 3: Fly-Building Supplies 39

CHAPTER 4: Snake Fly 57

CHAPTER 5: Sand Eel Snake Fly 65

CHAPTER 6: Worm Hatch Snake Fly 69

CHAPTER 7: Long Saddle Snake Fly 75

CHAPTER 8: Mullet and Whitefish Snake Fly 81

CHAPTER 9: Slab Fly 85

CHAPTER 10: Badger Sand Eel 93

CHAPTER 11: Mole Nose Bunker 97

CHAPTER 12: Glow Squid 105

CHAPTER 13: Barracuda Fly 111

CHAPTER 14: Pop-Hair Bug 117

CHAPTER 15: Bonefish Fry 123

CHAPTER 16: Wide-Eyed Shrimp 127

CHAPTER 17: Blue Lady 135

CHAPTER 18: Glow Sand Eel 143

CHAPTER 19: Sea Rat 149

CHAPTER 20: Trout Rat 153

CHAPTER 21: Winged Weedless Rat 159

CHAPTER 22: Rat Chovy 169

CHAPTER 23: Rat Needlefish 177

CHAPTER 24: How to Set Up a Fly Box 181

Index 187

A
B
C
D
E
F

A Beaches, outflows, and the mouths of jetties can have big baitfish activity. This 40-pound-plus striper took a big fly fished where the jetty meets the beach.

B My wife, Barb, took this nice oceanic bonito on a small anchovy pattern south of Block Island. The fish were acting strangely, repeatedly rising to the surface and swimming in circles. In this case fly placement was as important as the pattern. BARB TABORY

C While fishing with Capt. Al Conti, we took school tuna like this one Al is holding. These tuna were feeding on squid spilling from dragger's nets. It was the best offshore fishing I will ever experience. We took fish all day long—I couldn't straighten my hand for a week.

D This striper took a dark-colored pattern in the wash along a Nantucket beach. It was a dark night with no moon.

E My first nice striper from rolling surf took a big Snake Fly along Madaket Beach on Nantucket Island. It was early October and the surf conditions were ideal for fly fishing. Jack Frech introduced me to this great island in the 1970s. JACK FRECH

F My first big trout came on a dark night fishing Duck Creek near West Yellowstone. The fish took a black marabou streamer. It was a good lesson—dark nights, dark flies. This was my first trip West, and my wonderful friend Pete Laszlo was my guide. This photo brings back fond memories. PETE LASZLO

G This is the first jack crevalle I took, and the biggest. Jack Frech, my long-time surf-fishing partner, joined me on the trip to Costa Rica. I was lucky to spend time with such a great surf angler. JACK FRECH

H A big Costa Rican snook that took a long, multicolored fly. I did not realize that at the time this 30-pound snook might have been a world record. Note the glass fly rod, a Great Equalizer—this was before graphite. JACK FRECH

Acknowledgments

Scott Bennett at Complete Angler, Darien, Connecticut—for all your help with tying materials. Every time I needed information on different fly-tying products, you had the answer. Thanks for all the tips on fly materials and pike fishing.

All my friends at Eldredge Bros. Fly Shop, Cape Neddick, Maine—Scott Eldredge, Jim Bernstein, Tom Cormier, Mark Drummond, and Jeff Faulkner—for years I have taught a two-day saltwater fishing class in the store. Each year we talked about fishing and fly-tying gear, and I always learned something new. Thanks.

Scott Wessels, Bear's Den, Taunton, Massachusetts—over the years when we talked your knowledge on fly materials was a great help.

Dave Rimmer—a longtime fishing buddy who paved the way with the Massachusetts Division of Marine Fisheries to get some great photos of river herring on Cape Cod. And for fun times we spent on the water.

Paul Diodati, Massachusetts Division of Marine Fisheries—who authorized permission for me to handle and photograph river herring and gave me the contacts of state biologists who helped me in researching these great baitfish.

John Sheppard and Ray Jarvis, Massachusetts Division of Marine Fisheries—for helping to get photos of river herring.

Mike O'Conner and Dick Hilmer, Eastham, Massachusetts Department of Natural Resources—for allowing me to take part in the annual release of river herring into Cape Cod Bay.

John Engstrom, Eastham, Massachusetts—who lives near the herring run and helped in my picture-taking.

Enrico Puglisi, owner of EP Flies—as always, thank you for your support and your great knowledge of synthetic materials.

Dave Skok—a great angler, top-notch photographer, and builder and designer of excellent flies. Thanks for all your advice and knowledge and for all the great days on the water.

Eric Peterson—a wonderful fishing partner and builder of great flies. Over the years I keep learning from our talks. Thanks.

D. L. Goddard—for many years I have marveled at your effortless techniques for building flies. Thanks for your insights into creating different fly patterns and how to make them work.

John Posh—for all the great times together and for all the help that you have given me. Your years on the water and your knowledge of fishing have helped me become a better angler. Your knowledge about fly tying is priceless.

Paul Fuller—we had two exciting Alaskan fishing trips together when we caught some great fish. And thanks for your wonderful support at all the shows where I was given a chance to do talks and casting demos. You help jump-start a kid into the outdoor business.

Capt. Frank Catino—a top-notch guide. Your help and information about Southern fishing and fly design gave me great insight about a fishery that I need to learn more about. Thanks for being a great friend and sharing your knowledge.

Lefty Kreh—just through our casual talks I keep learning so much. Your wisdom is priceless, but your friendship is worth even more. Over the years you were never too busy to share your wealth of fishing experience. Thanks, Pop.

Bob Popovics—the way you build flies has always fascinated me. Your precise, organized tying methods are a sharp contrast to my often scatterbrained approach to fly tying. But writing a book about fly design and building patterns requires structure, and that I learned from watching you work at the vise. Thanks, old buddy.

Chauncey Goodrich—for your help in developing flies for Western river trout fishing. But mostly for the good times we have spent on the water. Thanks.

Pete Laszlo and Jack Frech—two special, departed friends who bring back so many great times. Thanks for taking the time to take photos even when you should have been fishing.

John Cumisky—for testing some of my early Southern patterns. Without even knowing, you gave me great insight into building Southern patterns.

Spirit River Company—for their continuing support.

Steve Fournier and Dr. Slick Co.—thanks for all your support and help with fly-tying tools. You have made fly tying easier and helped to make this book better.

Jay Nichols—thanks for your knowledge and guidance about photography and for putting this book together. You are easy to work with and allowed me to change the book's focus to include different topics and broaden the subject matter.

Introduction

Fly fishing gives us so much enjoyment, so many rewards, and tying your own flies adds another pleasure to a great sport. Building your own flies provides many advantages. When you're traveling to some locations, replacing lost flies might be impossible, yet with a small kit, you can make flies to replenish the fly box or to make other patterns you need. Making flies at home allows you to choose the hook size and type and build a fly of a specific size and color. Part of the fun and enjoyment of making flies is experimenting—fooling with different materials or perhaps adding a different wing or tail. If you need a fly with a certain size eye or different head or tail, you can easily produce that fly at your vise with a few turns of tying thread. And you get the satisfaction of catching fish on a self-tied fly. However, nothing is more magical than

Sometimes fish feeding in groups or schools are not selective. Here, I'm fishing off a beach along outer Cape Cod in late September. This school of stripers had small bunker trapped in the drop-off along the shoreline. This kind of fishing is fun and often easy. Blitzing fish usually take anything that moves.

creating a new pattern, a design of your own that fools tough-to-take fish.

Fly tying has become too mystical. Many of today's patterns are complex, require special tying skills and elaborate materials, and are time consuming to make. For the skilled fly tier who is willing to take the time to create works of art, most of my patterns are easy to tie. I believe many anglers want to make flies that take less time to build, catch fish in many environments, and don't require special tying skills.

In our high-tech world, we need simplicity; we need to go back to the basics. But few anglers want to fish with Joe Brooks' Blonde or a single-winged streamer. They might catch fish, but they are perhaps too primitive. Still, with some imagination, you can improve even such basic patterns with little or no effort.

Not all the flies I use are basic patterns, but by mixing several materials they come to life, move well in the water, and are still relatively easy to tie. Sometimes developing a new pattern or altering materials can be time consuming, but the same is true the first time you cook an elaborate meal, build a doghouse, or carve a fish—anything new always takes longer until you develop a system.

Discovering the proper mix and amounts of materials to use for new fly patterns, and what hook size and type to use, plus where to place the different parts on the hook, requires time and patience. This is especially true when designing flies that must settle and sit properly on the bottom. Flies that are designed to flow through the water, fished up in the water column, and that use a moving retrieve, are often easier to develop. However, with most patterns, once you perfect the design and develop a tying routine, building flies should be straightforward.

My approach to fly tying is simple: I make flies that catch fish, not fishermen. Many patterns I use are easy to make, and once you are set up, they take little time to tie. Some of my flies take ten to fifteen minutes to make. Bonefish and permit patterns, for example, require more time because they need to look and act properly. Some of the bigger herring or bunker patterns take longer because they are large flies and have several types of materials and more parts. Adding weight or installing weedguards to patterns requires more steps and more time. And if you use epoxy to build precise patterns, or patterns that need a body coat to prevent tangling, it takes time for the material to harden. Simple fly patterns are one reason I enjoy saltwater fly

Too many anglers try to limit a fly for catching certain species of fish in one location. Trying to plan for every fishing event is impossible. This is why good fly patterns work for many different species—because they imitate a number of food sources. If a fly has nice action and is the general size and shape of a food type, it will catch fish anywhere. This fly is the size of most midsize saltwater patterns, yet this brown trout inhaled it.

fishing. I tell the students in my saltwater fly-fishing classes if you can eat with a knife and fork, you can tie most of my best patterns. When making flies, I tie materials in bunches or clumps and do not count hairs or strands of flash. Only if the fly needs to be thin will I mention strands of materials in numbers, and that is just to help make tying information clear.

I do most of my fishing in the Northeast, but I fish Southern waters frequently and spend enough time fishing fresh water to know that a few good patterns in different sizes can work for many species. Using patterns that were originally developed for the Northeast, I have had success with species like tarpon, snook, snapper, grouper, and barracuda and many freshwater species like trout, Alaskan salmon, and freshwater bass. Bigger saltwater patterns are ideally suited for pike and muskies because these are big gamefish that will feed on large foods. Also flies that are designed for trout work well for freshwater bass or vice versa, and some flies developed for freshwater species are effective in salt water, requiring only different types of hooks to match the conditions.

Tying flies is simply putting a blend of materials onto a hook to construct a fly that comes alive. No one material blend is best, and no single way to build a fly is perfect. You can always improve or change the blends of materials or change the shape or size of patterns to fit a particular need. Patterns like the original Snake Fly blend a tail of ostrich herl and a wing of marabou with a spun deer head to create an easy-to-tie and all-purpose pattern with ideal action. But modify this fly, changing the tail or wing or altering the size of the head, and the fly becomes a shrimp or worm imitation. That is what makes the Snake Fly a versatile pattern. I will always continue to use the original design because it worked so well, but from this pattern, other patterns are born.

Some flies are designed for special uses. They can be made in different sizes, but the construction needs to remain the same or similar for the fly to perform properly. These flies have a specific purpose and are often used in clear, shallow water for selective fish. Once you find a pattern that works in locations on tough-to-take fish, do not change it—only modify the color to fit the environment.

Gamefish around the world in both fresh and salt water feed on small fish, whether it's baitfish or immature gamefish. Any fly that imitates a small fish and has action will catch fish in most waters as long as it looks similar to a local food. Remember that a short, chunky baitfish pattern looks like a shrimp in some conditions, and a thin baitfish pattern with tail movement can look like an eel or worm.

I have never cared why a fish grabbed my fly—only that I fooled the fish to take that pattern. The only reason I would want to know why the fish hit is if I could learn a better way to build flies or to fish a fly using a better technique to fool more fish. I always believed that most fly patterns should be labeled by the food type they copy, not the fish they catch. I have used "bonefish flies" to catch stripers and "striper flies" to catch trout. And by altering material types and changing the length of the fly's tail or the bulk of the fly's body, I can use a pattern like the Snake Fly to mimic a baitfish, eel, shrimp, or worm. The one exception might be bonefish flies, which is a common term for many small, shrimp-type patterns. Often however, fly patterns target a gamefish like bonefish, but they will catch other species that feed on similar food types. Flies copy food types; a shrimp fly might be designed for bonefish, but it will catch other gamefish.

An Alaskan trip really sold the Snake Fly concept to me. I was walking along a high riverbank with Paul Fuller and Burt Bomhoff when we spotted a big bow holding below a sandbar. I crossed the river below the fish to get to a better, level casting location. As they watched, I tried several rainbow patterns, but this fish was not interested. I finally tied on a light-colored Snake Fly, casting it upstream and letting the fly drift so it swung several feet above the fish. To my amazement when the fish spotted the fly, it bolted upstream about five feet and crushed it. Here was a picky fish that that would not even follow other patterns, yet it rushed the Snake Fly and took it with no hesitation. The Snake Fly has become my go-to fly when fishing the Northeast for stripers. However, it was my first trip to Alaska where I saw how valuable this fly could be. After that trip I started building different size flies for all types of fishing. Throughout the week in Alaska, I started using the Snake Fly for not only rainbows, but for other species of Alaskan gamefish, with excellent results. The fly seemed to draw fish like a magnet.

Sometimes, any fly pattern within reason will fool a fish. When some gamefish are feeding aggressively, competing for food, they would probably grab a banana peel. Don't waste fancy flies on blitzing fish like bluefish when they are striking anything that moves. This is the proper time to fish easy-to-tie flies like Blondes or single-winged streamers; why destroy flies that take time to make when you can have great action with flies that are old? When fishing from a boat, I keep a box of old, reject flies—ones that didn't come out quite right, or ones with a mixture of materials that made the fly look like a ruptured pig in the water. However, they won't work with hardtails up north or when fishing clear, shallow water.

What I hope this book does is spark a feeding frenzy with anglers and start the creative juices flowing. Many creative fly tiers out there can look at how a fly is built and perhaps improve the fly or change materials to make the fly work in different environments.

About a third of the way through writing this book, I chose my favorite fish-getting flies from my fly boxes. I was looking at several fly-pattern books and wanted to be sure that some of my new flies were not copies of other patterns. With so many patterns today, most flies are adaptations of other flies. I wanted to select one group of flies that caught many types of fish in different conditions and another group that were for special conditions for a specific species. I organized my flies in different groups for the baits the flies copy, the types of gamefish they were usually used for, and the different species that they might catch. Some fit in several groups, others were for a specific type of fishing. I wanted to feature a given number of flies that I feel confident fishing.

Writing this book made me rethink the way I tied some patterns and made me look at some patterns differently. The Sea Rat, a somewhat forgotten pattern, came to life because I

My first big Alaskan rainbow, taken on a Snake Fly. This fish rushed and grabbed the fly after refusing other patterns. The way this fish attacked the fly told me that the Snake Fly pattern was a winner. PAUL FULLER thought about how, with some refinements, it would work as a weedless fly for Southern fishing and a fine trout fly. Also I worked on building better bonefish patterns, not so much to improve their appearance but to make them perform better in the water. And the old standby, the Snake Fly keeps ticking with several new additions.

This book is about the patterns I enjoy fishing, but perhaps more importantly, my purpose in writing it is to make fly tiers think about how flies are built and the different ways we can alter patterns to make them work in a number of waters to match other bait species. Throughout this book I feature flies for different species of gamefish in both fresh and salt water. Some of the flies were originally designed to fish for saltwater species in my home waters of the Northeast. However, I soon discovered that these patterns also worked for many different species in both fresh and salt water with little or no alteration.

Most fly design is not set in stone. Even the best patterns can be refined or modified to fit a special purpose or a specific need. It's not always that the fly requires a change to make it better, but rather the alteration makes the fly more effective in certain fishing environments. Most fly patterns should be *works in progress*. After looking at *Inshore Fly Fishing* and *Stripers on the Fly* and pattern books that featured my patterns, I saw that I had altered some of my patterns without realizing that I did. I finally recognized that in order to write this book, I needed to stop improvising the flies and finish the patterns I had so I could complete the project. It wasn't easy; there is still need for improvement. I always remember the great author Eric Leiser's sound advice: "A book you like writing will never be finished—there will always be more you want to say."

The first fly I designed as a young fly rodder was a primitive sand eel pattern. The fly was thin with a tail of brown bucktail and a dark, gray wool body. Lefty Kreh described the fly's appearance in his excellent book *Fly Fishing in Salt Water* as "unfinished"—an accurate description. It was a basic pattern that copied the thin body of a sand eel, the popular small, thin baitfish that appears along Northeast beaches in spring. The fly worked well fished under and around thick schools of this important baitfish. This pattern's basic design—a thin tail, no wing, and a thin, wrapped-on body—has been copied and

After spawning, the adult herring return to open water. These large, flat-sided baitfish can be over 10 inches long. Flies built for these big baits are usually 7 to 9 inches long, with a wide profile, blue to green backs, and light-colored undersides. These are bright-sided baits, so plan to mix in flash to match the bait's color. As juveniles begin to develop in their spawning location, they become a food source when reaching about an inch in length. They continue to grow, providing gamefish in the estuaries with a bonus food supply until they reach 3 to 5 inches and return to the sea, anytime from spring to late fall.

improved by many other fly tiers, producing a sand eel imitation that is far superior to my first pattern. This is why designers should be willing to alter a pattern to improve it. You might use different materials or a different eye or add a wing or tail.

My original Snake Fly still catches a number of different species of gamefish around the world, yet I continue to make variations when the need arises. I see how other fly tiers have altered this fly to fill a need in other fishing locations, and I learn from them. And in fact, the first Snake Fly was designed after Eric Leiser's Angus Fly. I copied the Angus' action, which was a breathable fly, but changed the way it was tied to make it quicker to tie and easier to build. And using the Snake Fly's design, I could easily change the fly's shape to make the body in different thicknesses and lengths. Later I used different materials to build a family of Snake Flies.

One reason for altering fly patterns is to keep up with changes from one year to the next. With the beginning of each season, different species of gamefish might be more or less active, or a major food type might be totally different from the previous year. Look at one baitfish type, river herring, which can be dominant one year and absent the next. These big baits migrate into fresh water in late winter for early spring spawning and then move back to the sea in late spring to early summer. When these big baits return to the sea, they provide an important food source for bigger fish. But they also provide an important food source in the ponds and lakes where they spawn. And when the young of the year move back into the sea, they become another food type and size in that location.

One bait type might require several different flies for the time that it is present. Weather and changing water conditions might do the same. Anglers should be willing to develop fly patterns that keep up with a changing fishery, both in size and type. Adaptable fly pattern are ones that remain *works in progress*.

I have some patterns that can be either simple or complex, depending on whether you put on a wing or tail that simply produces action versus layering or blending materials to create a tail that looks lifelike. Although, sometimes a lifelike fly might not be as difficult to tie as anglers think. It often requires learning different techniques. Patterns like a Snake Fly or Sea Rat tied conventionally are easy to make, but if you start to blend different synthetics with hair or feathers to form the wing and tail, then you have to test to see if the materials will blend. Also it often takes a few tries to perfect the pattern so it flows properly in the water. Both the Snake Fly and Sea Rat lend themselves to a variety of patterns, from a 2-inch trout fly to a large billfish fly. This book does not have enough space to cover all the possible varieties, but most fly tiers don't need step-by-step instructions for each. Just use your imagination and start tying.

Once you develop a routine, or a system, most fly building is repetitive. I marvel at professionals who sit down and tie 300 identical flies. But this is how they can produce a good product. They learn the most efficient, quickest ways to build the fly by developing techniques that work for them. When I develop a pattern or change the way a pattern is built, it takes much longer to make the first few flies. Once I develop a system, the time to make that fly is much less, and the flies keep looking better. I might build a fly differently than you do, so use my instructions only as a guide, not as the only way to build a certain pattern. We all borrow techniques from other anglers; this is how we learn. Never listen to a fellow tier who says there is only one way to build a fly. Certain techniques make fly tying easier, but if you prefer to use another method to tie a fly, follow your instincts.

CHAPTER 1

Imitation and Design Characteristics

Bonefish are one of the hardest fish to fool with a fly. In many places, fish that are well educated require a fly that is well designed and well balanced. The fly must match a local food source in color, size, and shape. And the fly must also be fished properly and placed in a position where the fish can see it.

The bonefish was tailing about 35 feet off my rod tip, pushing up a good mud. The fish was big and close, its huge tail waving in the light breeze, making my heart pound. It was feeding on a large flat that often has too much fishing pressure. I knew even with the ideal cast my odds were slim. There were several other fish nosing around the edges of the sand cloud. I had seen this before: these satellite fish, I call them, were smaller but still nice fish. I dropped a cast right in front of the fish, let it settle, and then slowly retrieved. Nothing. Two more casts and still nothing. With each cast I inched the fly closer to the fish. I knew that anything too close would blow the fish off the flat. The fly's design made almost no noise when it landed even with a light breeze, and each time it settled to the bottom, it was in an upright position. I had fished this location before and knew that as I tried to place the fly closer, there was a chance of spooking the fish. The fourth cast, which landed about 18 inches in front of the fish, caused an eruption as the big fish spun, turning in a tight circle, and then resumed its feeding position with its tail back up.

Everything occurred so fast that before I even knew what happened, I was hooked. My full concentration was on the big fish in the center. Apparently one of the satellite fish spotted the fly on the drop and took so aggressively that it hooked itself. The fish rushed toward the flat's edge, kicking up sand and water with its powerful tail. After two runs I worked the fish into shallow water, removed the fly, and the fish swam off the flat none the worse for wear and a little smarter. I guessed the weight at about 8 pounds and wondered how big the fish in the middle was. It was a concept and design that I had worked on for some time: getting a fly that would land softly and then settle and sit upright, looking like a living bottom creature. I still had some work to do, but the basic concept worked in practice.

A fly pattern may catch fish for several reasons. The general shape and size are important, and the color or blend of colors is sometimes significant too. Some anglers believe that for a fly to catch fish, it must look lifelike, matching the food source to a tee. If this were true, successful fly patterns like a Deceiver or Clouser Minnow would not be as popular. You need to think about four features when matching a food type: body shape, length, movement (action), and color. As a fly tier, you have to consider how materials behave in the water and also keep in mind the balance of the fly, especially for bonefish patterns. A good bonefish fly must settle to the bottom and sit upright—that is good balance.

Shape (Profile) and Length

Many years ago while fishing the small creeks on Shelter Island, New York, for weakfish, I learned how important matching a food type could be. During the prime weakfish years, Shelter Island was an ideal fly-fishing location. A number of small creeks flowed into Peconic Bay. Each one was different, and they emptied at different periods in the tide, allowing a large window of time to fish each one.

The sound of feeding weakfish at night is unmistakable—a loud pop that carries for some distance on a calm night. Often this sound is an indication that they are feeding on small shrimp floating on or near the surface. This night I had nothing to match what I saw in the water. Sand eel patterns or small, single-winged flies usually worked—but this night was different. After casting different baitfish patterns with no takes, I cut most of the tail off a tan Snake Fly and fished it just along the surface. That did the trick. It was close in size and shape to the shrimp and fairly buoyant. (For future trips I made floating shrimp, spinning deer body hair on a hook shank with a small tail that matched the shrimp well, and I had success.) Sadly this great fishing vanished due to overharvesting and never came back, but I learned a lesson about building flies to match food sources other than baitfish like the cinder worm swarm.

When you build a fly, consider its general body shape first. If you are making a squid, the fly needs to be cylindrical with a tapered tail and large eye. A herring fly has a wide, somewhat flat body with a tapered tail, while a fly matching a spearing needs to have a round, tapered body of medium width. Crab flies should look like a thick quarter to fifty-cent piece with legs, while bottom-dwelling shrimp look like small lobsters with tiny claws. Common shrimp are larger with a midbody shape something like a baitfish pattern with a slightly chunkier body.

Part of building flies is learning the proper spacing of the materials. On a new pattern, I often run out of space. An important rule when building new patterns is to leave more space for parts than you think you need. Small bonefish flies are a prime example of flies that don't have enough space for many parts. Often placing the eye first, on patterns with fixed eyes, helps you space the different parts so you don't run out of room. Every tier must develop a system to make different patterns easier to tie.

Length and size are two basic features that some fish key on when feeding. Other than general shape, length and size can be important when fish are feeding on one specific food type. Big baitfish like herring and bunker require large, flat-sided flies that can be tough to cast. Baitfish like spearing, smelt, or bay anchovies have a cigar shape and are similar in color, and often one pattern in several sizes will match all of these baits. Foods like squid, small shrimp, worms, or crabs in some conditions might require a special pattern in a specific color, but other times a general attractor pattern with good action will catch fish.

Most fly patterns are actually attractors that look like several food sources. The Snake Fly could be a worm, an eel, or a baitfish; a Deceiver looks like a small herring, menhaden, or spearing; and a mullet fly has a silhouette close to a squid. Even a fly intended to match a certain baitfish might actually mimic several food types. Many types of baitfish in different stages of their lives look similar, although baitfish change as they grow, sometimes looking much different when they mature. Examples of perhaps a dozen baitfish that look alike are the herring-shad-sardine families. Many of these baitfish could be copied with several patterns using a few variations. Matching freshwater aquatic insects using dry flies or nymphs is a much more precise science than matching baitfish in either fresh or salt water. Matching different foods in both fresh and salt water is actually simpler than many anglers believe. We spend too much time trying to make something look pretty rather than making

Here are two baitfish from the same small section of water in the Bahamas; the locals call these baits pilchards. They are actually scaled sardines—pilchard is a common name that groups them together with other, similar baitfish. Sometimes several baits are dominant in one location, but when they look alike, one pattern will often work as a good match. At the top are two small, thin baitfish patterns. In the other photo below, the handheld baitfish is thinner. This small fish is one of several different types of anchovies that reside in Southern waters. They all look similar. I snagged this baitfish while casting to cruising bonefish. The thin epoxy flies in the top photo caught bonefish even when they were feeding on pilchards. At times, a fly that suggests the bait but does not match it will still catch fish. In this case, I think that the bonefish were out of their element, chasing baitfish, and were not as cautious as they can be when feeding on shrimp and crabs along the bottom. When you do not have the ideal match, try a pattern that is as close as possible. Never be afraid to break the rules and try other patterns, even if they do not match the bait.

I took this weakfish earlier in the evening on a sand eel fly. But once the fish started to feed on shrimp, that fly was ineffective. Many small creeks on Long Island's north shore had nice runs of weakfish. Shelter Island was a favorite spot for small-creek fly fishing as darkness fell. In the spring as the tide began flowing out of these creeks, shrimp would move out with the tide. The weakfish would take up holding spots like trout, feeding on the small shrimp as they floated out. Often you would hear a pop that sounded like a cup being slapped face down on the water's surface.

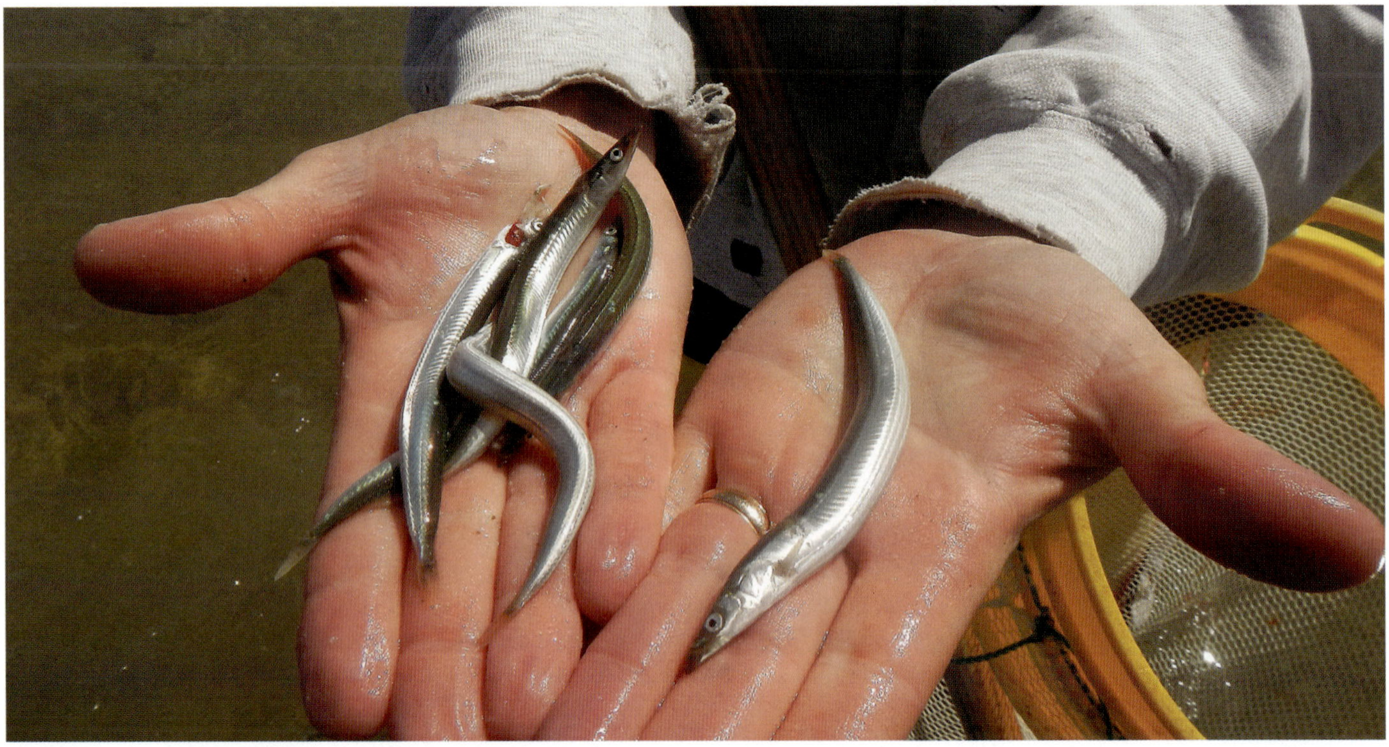

Sand eels have a thin profile that makes them hard for spin anglers to match, yet they are ideal bait for fly rodders because of their size. These sand eels from a Cape Cod Bay flat are large for early spring baits. Often sand eels are 3 to 4 inches long when they first move onto the flats. The key to matching sands eels is to build the fly with a thin profile, add some flash, and use colors like soft pinks and light greens.

a fly that looks and acts alive. And over the years I have at times been guilty of this.

When you are building flies, don't get carried away with making sure each one looks like a masterpiece to mount in a frame. Most flies do not need to be flawless, only fishable. Usually flies built to match baitfish do not need to be tied perfectly. The retrieve is what gives them life. I have caught some nice fish on flies that most anglers would not even use. The heads on some of my Slab Flies are often far from perfect, as are most of my epoxy flies. Actually, some of my epoxies look deformed, but they catch fish. Flies that flow through the water can be mediocre and still take fish. A pulsating retrieve is often effective and will make a fly bolt and roll, looking like a crippled baitfish. So using a fly that is somewhat off balance might even be an advantage.

Only a few patterns require perfection and specific detail, such as flies used for sight-fishing in clear, shallow waters where the fish takes the fly as it drops or takes it off the bottom. These flies need to look alive and remain balanced as they settle and sit upright on the bottom. This is especially true in locations with heavy fishing pressure where fish take a long, hard look before eating. These are the flies that demand more time and care during the building process.

I will discuss some major saltwater and freshwater baits in the next chapter. Knowing the baitfish and other food sources in your fishing area will help you determine which fly to use. Do you need to go out and collect these baits, drag them home, put them in your refrigerator, and try to copy them? No, but it can be fun. However, several books show all the important foods, in detail, and have excellent information about the habits of these baits: *A Fly-Fisher's Guide to Saltwater Naturals and Their Imitations* by George V. Roberts Jr., *Fly Fisherman's Guide to Saltwater Prey* by Aaron J. Adams, and my previous book *Guide to Saltwater Baits and Their Imitations*. Two other books that will help to identify baits along with gamefish are *Sport Fish of Fresh Water* and *Sport Fish of Florida*, both by Vic Dunaway.

First think about how the fish sees the fly. To decide what is most important about shape and profile, think about the fly type and how it will be fished. Does the fly look like a particular food source from all angles or at least the important angles? Remember, the view from the side and from below or behind is most important on baitfish patterns; often the top view is irrelevant.

This crab is trying to hide in the sand. Most sight-fishing conditions like this one require flies that look alive from above. The fly must still drop and settle upright, and the fish might see it then, but that top view will sell the fly and make it look alive. If the fly is lying on its side, a street-smart gamefish is seldom fooled. Flies used for sight-fishing must simulate a food source, but the most important characteristic is that the fly must settle properly and sit upright on the bottom.

But when using flies that match crabs or shrimp fished in clear, shallow water, the top view is usually the most important. The view from the tail, however, is important for fish that track flies from behind.

Using active materials in the fly's tail makes the fly more effective. The best way to judge the fly's shape is in a container of water. Hold the fly by the hook's eye, turn it over, and see how each view looks. Every special fly I make gets a water test. Any fishing location where you get few opportunities, especially on big fish, you want the fly to look real and alive.

Movement and Action

Perhaps the most overlooked feature is how the fly moves and acts in the water. I use mostly patterns with active materials that breathe in the water; they look alive even when they're not moving. Under many fishing situations I believe that a fly with active materials will outfish a stiff, lifelike fly. For certain fishing conditions, epoxy works well to create a more realistic fly. Yet I still try to include some active materials. A pattern that incorporates action and realism to create a fly that looks and acts alive will be a fish-getter. But I don't like sacrificing action to get a fly that looks alive in your hand yet looks dead in the water. Simple-to-tie patterns with the proper materials catch fish.

A fly with active materials is versatile in many water types. On a calm surface, flies with materials that keep moving after each pull of the retrieve look alive just resting on or near the surface. Fishing along the edge of lily pads for largemouth bass, casting to snook along mangroves, or fishing for sipping stripers at night requires a fly that keeps moving long after the forward motion stops.

Active materials in a fly also add action when fishing a flow. Even when the fly is swinging without being retrieved, it keeps swimming because of the moving water. It takes little effort to give excellent action to a fly that is built with breathable materials. Even the slightest puff of wind will bring some materials to life. Imagine how much action they will produce in moving water. This is also true of flies fished on the bottom

The mixture of materials in this Snake Fly produces constant action in the tail, much like a baitfish fleeing a gamefish. Many gamefish follow a fly before taking. All baitfish move their tails, swimming in an attempt to outrun or outmaneuver their attacker. This action can trigger a strike. The Snake Fly's active tail can often excite a gamefish into taking a fly even when not feeding.

This beautiful Alaskan arctic char in full fall colors took an adapted Snake Fly. The Snake Fly can be modified with a different tail or wing to produce any number of different looks, but the movement is key. I cannot remember how many variations I had of this pattern before I finally chose the final materials. All of the Snake Fly variations I use focus on the fly's movement or shape.

in shallow water. Active materials keep moving when they sit on the bottom, and even without current a slight wind chop gives the fly movement.

You can build flies with movement in several ways; one technique is to add heavy weight to the fly's head. Some anglers tie heavily weighted flies using lead eyes or coneheads, lead wire, heavy coats of epoxy, or a combination of these materials. Some of these flies are so heavy, nearly ½ ounce, that you could cast them with a spinning rod. Anglers retrieve these flies using sharp pulls, making the fly hop like a bucktail jig. This action is useful in some conditions because it simulates the hopping action of a jig, which is a deadly spin-fishing lure. Sometimes I fish flies that simulate jig action by using lightly weighted eyes, ⅛ to 3⁄16 ounce, and long, nonbuoyant materials. These patterns don't bounce as sharply as the heavier flies, but they still have enough bounce to excite fish. Longer material helps to stabilize a weighted fly in flight even if you shock the rod while casting. I also use flies with lightly weighted eyes and sparse materials when fishing shallow flats if I need a fly to sink quickly. To make a quick-sinking flats pattern, use a 3⁄16-ounce eye with a blend of less buoyant materials. This fly will track well when casting.

Lightly dressed, heavily weighted flies are hard to cast, can cause serious injury, and will damage a fly rod if the fly hits the rod while casting. Heavily weighted flies with short, sparse materials often get out of control during the cast. Any kick in the rod tip might cause the fly to track to one side and hit the angler. I have noticed that some anglers casting these heavy flies develop a twitch, flinching each time the fly whistles past their head. They try to tuck their head into their body to avoid being whacked by the fly. If an angler resembles a neurotic turtle when casting, keep your distance. Unless you are a smooth caster, avoid flies with heavy eyes unless they are dressed with enough material to keep them stable while casting.

Using active materials like marabou, ostrich herl, long saddle hackle, fur, or any of the active, synthetic fibers is the best way to incorporate action in a fly. Adding some flash so it blends with the active materials enhances the action while giving the fly a more lifelike look. These materials move naturally in water, giving the fly action with each pull, and the materials keep moving even when the fly stops. Heads with deer or elk body hair add a rippling flow that adds movement to the fly's wing and tail and makes flies more buoyant; with some mixtures of materials the fly will swim, nose up, like a stunned baitfish.

Most flies I use are neutral density, slightly buoyant, or nose down slightly. If you want a fly to nose down, use a lighter eye with a blend of materials that lets the fly's nose drop down slowly. A Sea Rat is an example of a fly with slightly nose down action that is easy to cast. I never use heavily weighted flies. Another advantage with neutral density and buoyant flies is their ability to suspend in the water column

Fly tier and excellent angler Dave Skok used one of his active material creations to take this nice striper. Many different fly-tying materials or combinations of materials will produce movement. Fly action is the key to a good baitfish pattern. You can make a fly move and look alive with the retrieve, but if you have both a good retrieve and materials that breathe well, the fly really comes alive.

like a natural baitfish. This is important in many fishing conditions when letting the fly drift while fishing with an intermediate fly line. Also, using the combination of a buoyant fly and a 9-foot leader with a fast-sinking line helps to keep the fly from dragging along the bottom when fishing a sandy beach. This setup is also helpful to prevent most snags when fishing over weed beds, mussel bars, or rocky areas.

Matching the movements of baitfish, squid, and juvenile gamefish is fairly straightforward. The fly needs to be balanced, swimming and moving like a small fish, and if the fly has materials that breathe, then most of the movement is controlled with the retrieve. A fly that acts crippled, appearing to struggle when swimming, is at times valuable, but this is how the fly design is combined with the proper retrieve to make the fly appear to struggle. A popper or surface fly often matches small bait feeding on or swimming on the surface. In freshwater lakes and ponds, a surface bug might match a frog, mouse, snake, or any number of large insects. And foods that hatch and move on the surface require a fly that looks similar in size and shape. Small baitfish, shrimp, worms, or crabs at times appear on the surface in large numbers, and getting the fly to float on or near the surface with little movement is important.

Often the gamefish will alert the angler to small, slow-moving foods; the fish feed in a controlled manner, sipping like trout taking dry flies, not feeding aggressively on the surface as they usually do—just the opposite is true with foods that live or move and hide along the bottom. They must settle, sit, or move along the bottom, looking alive and natural. Building a fly that lands softly, settles in a controlled manner, and sits upright on the bottom is important. A fly that lies on its side on the bottom looks fake to any educated bonefish and usually repels the fish to deep water. If the fly design is effective, then the angler only has to present the fly properly.

Knowing how materials act in water is important when building some patterns because the fly's size and shape will change when it gets wet. This is true of flies tied with some breathable materials. After making a fly, place it in water to be sure it is the right shape and profile. For testing the fly in water, a plastic shoebox works fine. Water testing is the only way to see how certain materials or a combination of materials will react in a fishing environment. Some materials bulk up; others slim down or remain the same. A blend of two materials may look hot on the vise, but in water that fly might look terrible.

Notice how unstable the top blue wing material is. A pattern like this would be difficult to use because the wing would wrap when casting or fishing the fly.

Here is the same fly with an epoxy body to prevent the material from wrapping. Using some active materials for a long wing or tail results in a fly that's difficult to fish. Some synthetics and furs need to be stiffened with epoxy or glue. Be sure to test any soft material before building a large number of flies.

After placing the fly in water, try holding it by the hook's eye and moving it to see how the materials interact. Never make more than a few flies, when developing a new pattern, without testing the first few flies in water. And if they look good in the tank, then try fishing them in open water using different retrieves to be sure the fly performs properly.

I developed a Sea Rat Squid that worked fine and looked ideal in the water, but after I compared it to the action of a Glow Squid in the water, I saw there was no contest. The Glow Squid looked better, and it pulsated with each pull of the retrieve imitating a squid's swimming motion. I like to keep improving and developing new patterns, but only when that new fly is better will it replace a known winner.

Testing all materials to see if they knot or tangle is a smart move. Take a section of material and try rolling it into a ball between your hands. If you can easily pull it apart and straighten the tangles with your fingers, the material will work. Nothing is worse than a fly that needs constant maintenance. Flies with shorter wings and tails have fewer problems, as do very sparse flies, but bigger, thicker patterns that tangle are not fun to fish with.

Placing a fly under the kitchen faucet is not a true test of how the fly will react in water. It might work with a few patterns, but when designing most new flies, testing in water will save you time and effort. Once you know how the combination of different materials works, then test in water only to check the size and shape. When building thin flies, using less material than you think is often the best method to tie the fly properly. Stiff, hard materials usually don't change in water, but they have less action and some have little movement. Materials like arctic fox or Finn raccoon fur are supple in the water and tend to wrap around the hook's bend or around the fly's body. If you are using longer sections of this fur for tails or wings, stiffen the base with epoxy or another glue. Some synthetics are also too soft for long wings or tails.

Balancing the proper action with performance can be a tough act—testing the fly in water is essential when using some blends of materials. This is especially true when you're building new patterns. It's a shame to make several dozen flies only to find out they are unfishable. Longer flies with active materials do not look right because the material hangs down behind the vise, but once the fly is in the water, it will come to life. Even if you prop

These two river herring, even though they are floating and almost motionless, still exude life and movement. Baitfish move, even when standing still. Even with no water flow, their fins and tail are constantly moving to maintain their position in the water. Materials that are active keep moving even when the fly is not traveling forward.

up the tail, some patterns still look different. One way to get a feel of how a fly will look in the water is to hang it by the head.

Remember ostrich herl and marabou will deflate when wet, so when you're building flies, plan on this. For larger flies, use more material. Marabou also adds some buoyancy to the fly. Both materials shrink as the fly moves and then puff up slightly when the fly stops, and they both keep moving, breathing as the fly sits in the water. Ostrich herl does not come in consistent sizes; some feathers are fatter and puffier. When choosing a bunch, start out smaller and then add a second bunch if needed. After making several flies, you will know how much material to use to get the proper dimensions of the fly.

Consider how using different materials can affect the fly's action. Using synthetics rather than natural materials or vice versa might alter how a fly swims, change the buoyancy, or make the fly too stiff. Eye types, hook types, and different flash materials can change the action of some patterns. It probably will not produce a poor fly but might not be exactly what you want. This type of experimenting is how new patterns are developed and can be fun, but remember to keep the materials, sizes, and weights the same to produce patterns for specific needs.

The best way to test and develop baitfish patterns is to film the fly's movement as it flows through the water. You can see how the fly looks in moving water and also try it in still water. The tension of the fly line, current, or wind moving the line affect how the fly looks. Just the settling of a sinking line, even in a slow current, gives a fly built with active material excellent action. Fly line types, leader lengths, leader types, and even knots might affect the action of certain patterns. Both fly line types and retrieve techniques can make a fly act differently. At times, choosing a good fly pattern is only part of the equation. The fly line, leader length, and how the fly is presented can be as important as the fly itself.

Living baits have movement as they flow in the water; they look alive. Without movement, some flies look like dead foods, not like living baitfish or crustaceans. Retrieving can make even a somewhat stiff fly look alive, and active material incorporated into the fly creates more movement. Tails with swimming action on epoxy flies improve fly movement and make the fly look alive. Many baitfish swim by using their tails to propel forward. Even baitfish that use their whole body to swim move their tails a lot. Some baits like sand eels, needlefish, eels, and worms appear to ripple as they flow through the water, and active materials are important parts of the makeup of patterns that match these foods.

Epoxy baitfish patterns or small baitfish flies have less action because they are short and stiff. They require a faster, steady, flowing retrieve to give them action.

Sometimes these flies are fished to look like a crippled baitfish falling from the school or fished as if the baitfish is hurt and trying to swim erratically. Imitating dead food sources is fine because gamefish at times do feed on dead baits, taking them from the bottom or as they drop below a school of baitfish. I have used this technique successfully on hard-to-take bonefish, but it also works on stripers or hardtails when they feed under or around schools of sand eels, anchovies, or peanut bunker.

Shorter patterns, epoxy flies, or patterns built with less flexible materials hold their body shape and change little in water. The advantage of rigid patterns is they retain their original shape in the water and require less testing. But the downside is a fly with much less action.

Eyes

I was never enthusiastic about eyes on flies until I started diving in clear water. My first exposure to diving was on the barrier reef off Belize in Central America. Two great friends, Pete and Ann Laszlo, were serious divers and wanted to explore what is the second largest barrier reef in the world. Being an avid water person, I took to this fun sport and found it gave me an interesting outlook on how a fish sees things differently than we do. An underwater background tends to change how objects look, though I didn't fully realize this until after looking at underwater photos. My first and lasting impression was how fish looked. Their eyes seemed to jump out. A school of small baitfish was a moving shape with thousands of glowing eyes. And as I spent more time underwater in different locations, the importance of eyes on a fly became more apparent.

Most of my fishing when I first started was in low light or in somewhat discolored water. Only when I started fishing Rhode Island, Cape Cod, and Southern shallow water locations did I realize the value of eyes and how the eyes of baitfish looked underwater. I started putting eyes on some flies. When developing my first squid flies, the eyes came to the forefront. Eyes on a squid stand out like a fancy hubcap on a sports car. Spotting squid underwater was easy because you almost always saw the eye before its whole body appeared. I'm sure that gamefish zero in on a squid's eye when picking a target. If you only use eyes on one pattern, put them on a squid fly. And that eye needs to be large and bright, often looking too large for the fly.

It's easy to add eyes to some patterns. There are flies that look better with eyes and some where eyes are mandatory. When you need weight on a fly, dumbbell eyes are easy to install, performing two functions: heft and looks. Painting on eyes is simple and works on epoxy patterns or patterns with thread heads like the Bonefish Fry. Glue-on eyes fit certain flies like the Glow Squid but can be tough to install, depending on the material and fly design.

I believe all baitfish patterns and most shrimp-crab patterns used for sight-fishing need eyes, not only weighted eyes to make the fly sink but eyes that give the fly a lifelike appearance. Flies used in clear, shallow water that must draw a fish from some distance and then fool that fish into taking need as much realism as possible. When a fish has time to look a fly over or sees that fly clearly, put your best foot forward—add eyes.

Over the years I have taken many fish using flies without eyes, such as the Snake Fly. Except for most sight-fishing, fish often attack from behind or below and never see the fly's head, unless the fly is matching a dead baitfish and falling to the bottom. Eyes on most poppers are cosmetic; the fish sees or hears the splash, locates the movement, and takes. However, if you're fishing the popper with an intermediate fly line or if a popper is designed to dive below the surface on each pull, then

See how the black eyes stand out in this school of baitfish. Eyes are important in some conditions but are not needed on all flies. Eyes are unnecessary when fishing in the dark or in discolored water, but they are important in clear water with bright sun. Some eyes have several purposes: they add weight and balance to the fly and attract fish.

This Southern baitfish, the pilchard, is a wide-bodied baitfish that is also a close match for a peanut bunker or small river herring. Note what a large eye it has for a small baitfish. Some baits have large eyes—a squid has perhaps the biggest eye of any food type—and often the eye looks larger in the water.

eyes might help to add a lifelike look. But I don't think that eyes matter when fishing at night, in low light, in rolling surf, in discolored water, or for most feeding situations for species like freshwater bass, stripers, bluefish, barracuda, or snook that often track the fly from behind before taking.

Using eyes on flies becomes important when sight-fishing or when fishing for offshore species that feed quickly by disrupting schools of baitfish. Whether tuna, albacore, or bonito are attacking in groups or schools, they usually take the bait or fly from many angles. They are swarm feeders, confusing the bait and then picking it apart. They see a target, and if it looks real, they take. An eye on your fly might make the difference because, even though they feed quickly, hardtails are masters at detecting a fake in clear water.

Most baitfish and squid have a white-silvery iris with a black pupil. Yet so many tiers use eyes that are yellow, red, or multicolored. I do! I love yellow, especially on a squid fly, or even a red eye. Yet to be accurate, most eyes should be silver with a black center—or should they? A lighter colored eye can be lost on a light-colored fly. The eye needs to contrast with the fly's color. It's why a darker, opaque eye stands out better on shrimp and crab patterns. Remember, the baitfish's eye appears larger and brighter than it actually is in the water. To judge your fly's eye color and to see if the eye has enough contrast, check it in the water.

Weighted eyes make a fly sink faster and can change the way it settles. Weight positioned in the rear allows the fly to drop with a straight posture; weight in the front makes it settle nose down. The best way to test the fly's balance and a good way to test the way it sinks is in water with a leader. Dropping the fly into a pail of water is not ideal because the leader and fly line influence the fly's descent and posture. At home, a good test is to use a plastic dish filled with water. Tie the fly on a section of leader, and drop the fly in the dish. But the best way is to actually fish with it.

I use weighted eyes for two reasons. One is when fishing shallow water where I want the fly to settle to the bottom and stay upright. This eye might be located at the tail of the fly and is not intended for appearance, but to make it sink in a controlled manner. I try to blend materials with just enough weight to let the fly fall at a slow rate. Less weight is better because the fly will land with less noise. With bigger crab flies, a heavier weight is often necessary, but with most bonefish patterns, I keep the weights light unless the fly is designed for fishing a deeper flat where landing noise has less effect.

The other reason is that dumbbell eyes add weight and realism. Weight stabilizes a pattern like a Sea Rat, making it settle slowly with the nose angled down slightly, giving the fly a crippled action. You get this same action when making a short, chunky Snake Fly. The heaviest weight I use is about ¼ ounce, and I only use that with a heavily dressed fly with natural materials. Too much weight on thinly dressed flies makes them unstable when casting. They catch fish, but they will break rods and might cause serious eye or face injuries because they make some patterns unstable in the air. I prefer baitfish flies that look alive in the water, not ones that drop to the bottom, dead.

See how the eye contrasts with some of the colors of the materials. One excellent rule is to use eyes that contrast with fly color. It's why using an eye with a yellow or red iris gives better contrast on some patterns where eyes with a white iris might not show up as well. To make melted mono eyes stand out on crustacean patterns, use bigger eyes that stand up above the body. The eyes on some shrimp and crabs when viewed in the water pop up above the body, but if you exaggerate this slightly in the pattern, it makes the eyes even more visible. If you plan to use eyes, don't hide them!

Sink Rate and Balance

For bonefish and other species that feed in shallow water, both sink rate and stability are keys to making the right pattern for fishing shallow flats, whether fish are taking a dropping fly or one that is sitting on the bottom. To build a fly that falls and sits properly takes some time and patience—especially when that pattern has a large upright wing. Adding features that make the fly perform properly can make a big difference. After tying a few flies, most fly tiers quickly learn shortcuts. And fooling that first tough fish makes the effort well worthwhile.

Locations that are fished hard offer few opportunities, and sometimes one shot at a single fish or small pod of fish is all the angler gets. Every presentation counts. Fish that live in shallow water, high-pressure locations exhibit certain behavior patterns, and they are often spooky. Fish approaching a dropping fly or a fly sitting on the bottom usually take. The fish sees the fly and moves to feed on a food source. If the fish slowly drifts away, you might have the wrong pattern or something is slightly amiss, but if the fish turns and bolts away, it often means the fly looks flawed.

In locations with heavy fishing pressure, a fly must be in balance. I don't care how fancy or perfectly tied the fly is, if it drops or lies on its side, it will entice few hard-to-take bonefish and big fish will make a beeline for deep water. Over the years I've developed several bonefish patterns. One successful fly is a baitfish pattern, the Bonefish Fry. Other bonefish patterns I build look like many standard bonefish flies: small, buggy flies with some active materials that match the bottom color. Lately, I have been focusing on getting the fly to settle and sit on the bottom properly.

Flies with large upright wings have difficulty remaining upright unless they are sitting in grass where the leader might keep them straight. And the hook must ride upright on flies used to fish along the bottom on a shallow flat to prevent snagging. Both a large upright wing and the hook riding upright can cause a fly to roll to one side. One way to prevent rolling is to add large, wide mono eyes to help stabilize the fly.

A crab body has a shape that usually keeps it sitting properly, and if weighted eyes let it dive to the bottom at an angle, it will look natural. Many small shrimp patterns need help to keep them looking real while they settle and once they reach the bottom. Another way to stabilize the fly is adding outriggers using materials like pieces of mono, Sili Legs, or boar bristles to keep the fly upright. Adding weight to the bottom of the hook will make it drop to the bottom without rolling if the wing and tail materials are tied uniformly. Form a double piece of lead wire, and tie it to the hook shaft. This creates a flat surface, and once you add body material, it softens the entry, making less noise when hitting the water's surface.

Some materials like hackle spun along the hook's shank also soften the fly's contact with the surface and stabilize the fly as it drops. Trim the fibers on the bottom so the fly sits on a flat surface of fibers. If the hackle is stiff enough and long enough, it might keep the fly upright on the bottom, but adding several other pieces of material will only make the fly more stable. Flies with heavy wings benefit from extra stabilizing material too. A flat, flared tail also helps to keep the fly looking real. Using deer or elk body hair near the head lets the fly sink slowly and helps keep it upright.

Sink rate depends on hook size and weight, eye size and type, type of material used in the fly, the fly's bulk, and how the

This fly does not have the proper balance to sit on the bottom. A fly that drops to the bottom on its side or lies there on its side does not look natural. To an uneducated fish, it might not matter, but to fish on high-pressure flats, it's like throwing a hornet's nest into a crowded room. Gamefish in locations that see many anglers require flies that are balanced, properly tied, and land with as little noise as possible.

The Wide-Eyed Shrimp dropping to the bottom. Note how stable it is.

The Wide-Eyed Shrimp sitting on the bottom. Note how the fly is always in balance. Balance is the key to a good fly for sight-casting in clear, shallow water. Bonefish in hard-fished locations are often difficult to fool. Even the slightest imperfection might spook a fish, if that imperfection causes the fly to look unbalanced as it settles or sits on the bottom. If the fly's color is a close match to the bottom and the size and shape are similar to local foods, then the fly should work. However, if the fly is unstable, then all the best-looking materials and fancy tying techniques are lost because the fly looks like a fake.

This fly has a different hook; the shape and style are like a nymph hook used in freshwater, yet it seems to settle properly like in the top photo and sit properly like in the bottom photo. There are many ways to build a fly that is balanced while settling and sitting on the bottom. Testing is important—a fly that is stable does not always fish well. Casting across a hard wind or current will cause even a properly balanced fly to sometimes tumble or drag along the bottom. Casting angle and retrieve are also important. Part of tying an effective pattern is to learn how to fish it properly. Check to see how the fly fishes long before you end up on a bonefish trip because you may waste precious fishing days learning how to work the fly properly.

material is positioned on the hook. It's not as technical as it sounds. To achieve a fast sink rate, use heavier eyes and beefy hooks and materials that are less buoyant. In deeper water, where faster sink rates are often necessary, you don't need to worry about the fly making noise as it lands, but you do need to get it to the bottom quickly. Keep the fly wet to get a better sink rate. Flies with dry materials can sit on the surface for several seconds before sinking.

On skinny flats use lightweight eyes, lightweight hooks, and materials that slow the fly's sink rate and soften the entry. I mostly wade when fishing for bonefish on flats that are often less than 2 feet deep. My flies are designed to land softly, sink slowly, remain upright while dropping, and stay upright once they reach the bottom. They often have spun hackle along a section of the body; soft, breathable materials; lightweight eyes or a keel with lead wire tied to the hook shank; and mono to stabilize the fly as it sits on the bottom. With small patterns, spun hackle might be enough to keep the fly upright, but test several before making dozens.

Color

One spring night in Martha's Vineyard at Edgartown Harbor, I watched in amazement as a fresh-caught squid put on an unbelievable light show. The still lively cephalopod was trying to match the color of the dock. The changes in color and the brightness happened so quickly that I don't remember how many colors flashed in front of me. The one thing that stood out was the glow—the flashes of color that this creature could produce to attempt to blend with its environment. I had seen baitfish light up when frightened, but nothing close to this. It took a few years for the lightbulb to light up in my head, but once it did I started thinking more about using bright colors in fly patterns. The Glow Squid was my first pattern to combine materials that created luminescence, a glow that made the fly flash as it moved. This pattern spawned a sand eel fly and then the Barracuda Fly, plus other patterns that incorporate this technique.

Color might be the least significant factor in fly design. Color is most important in clear water conditions when fish are selectively feeding. The colors of most baitfish are similar, and in different water conditions they might all look alike except for the shape. Crabs and shrimp are a different game, and matching color is more important. But matching the bottom color with the proper size is usually the best way to match them.

You might want to use different colors on some fly patterns for several reasons. One is contrast. Black, dark olive, purple, and dark brown give contrast at night or in low light, in rolling white water, and in discolored water. Try using one solid color or several different colors to make the fly stand out. Black is perhaps the most widely used contrast color for subsurface flies for both fresh and salt water. Sharp contrast of colors is sometimes useful, even though most baitfish are a blend from a darker top to a lighter bottom. Red over white, or red with a white tail are good combinations in Southern water, and work for stripers. Black over white is another ideal contrast and a good choice for night fishing. Orange, red, and pink are effective colors to imitate squid. Squid can rapidly change their body color to match the surroundings, and they brighten when excited or pursued by gamefish. This is when hot pink or orange incorporated under translucent materials like white and light pink make the fly come to life. Yellow and chartreuse are good choices in discolored waters and in low light. Both work as solid colors or blended with other colors. Yellow is a popular choice to match the big ocean sand eels; they have a tan to light brown shade when found along the beaches in rolling surf. When the water is filled with sand, yellow is a popular color for swimming plugs. Yellow is also a great color in morning light with herring patterns, giving off a glimmer that matches the reflections of these shiny-sided baits.

Discolored estuaries like the Kennebec River in Maine, sections of the Chesapeake Bay, many Southern estuaries, and most rainforest rivers that enter into open water—these locations all require contrasting colors like black or purple, and some flash makes the fly more visible too. Some rivers and freshwater outflows that flow into salt water look so discolored that you would not believe a fish could ever see the fly. Usually the water below the surface is much less discolored, and in some cases very clear. The discolored fresh water sits on top and does not mix well with seawater. Fish a sinking line to put the fly below the muddy fresh water and into the clear salt water. These conditions are somewhat like fishing in low light or a bright night because it's difficult for the sunlight to penetrate the muddy fresh water.

I believe one of the most valuable uses of color is to add a hot, bright color that makes the fly glow or change color as it moves. Use this trick when matching baitfish or squid in clear water in bright sunlight if fish are being picky. Baitfish are similar to gamefish: they brighten when excited or frightened. Offshore anglers use the term "light up" when a billfish is ready to take a bait or lure.

One material that works well is Success Fly Fluoro Fibre, which comes in a variety of colors that change in brightness as the fly moves, making the color appear to glow. This color change in a fly pattern can turn fish on. Use the softer colors of Fluoro Fibre on the top or the side of the fly to enhance the body, making a more lifelike fly. I blend hot pink or hot orange into flies to make the rest of the material change color, creating a hot pink or orange luminescence inside the fly. This material is also available in shades that offer a more subtle change in color. I like to incorporate the bright-hot colors internally to make a section of the fly appear to transform in color. I either tie the hot color in first and surround it with a translucent, light-colored material, or tie in a section of the hot material and then cover it with other material. Covering the hot-colored material dampens the brightness to a soft glow, changing the internal color of the fly. I discovered this when developing the Glow Squid. Using the materials in this manner makes the fly's color vary in several ways. As the fly's materials move, the color transforms, or as a fish tracks toward the fly and the angles change, the fly's color alters. Remember, all of this is often lost in rolling surf, in discolored water, and on dark nights. It might make a difference on a bright night in clear water, and certainly it's significant during the day in clear water.

An example of adding glow to a pattern is the Barracuda Fly. To add glow to any pattern, tie in Fluoro Fibre and cover it with any translucent material. The Fluoro Fibre produces a glow that lights up other materials. This technique works perfectly for both bulky and sparsely tied flies made with synthetic materials in lighter shades like white, tan, or yellow. Using hot orange or hot pink Fluoro Fibre produces a bright glow; lighter shades like green, tan, or chartreuse give a subtler glow. You may need to use more hot material in a thicker fly to make it brighter.

From this material I developed several different patterns and adaptations. During certain times and water conditions, a fly that glows will turn fish on. This is true anytime fish feed on squid, but in clear water any baitfish pattern can be improved by adding Fluoro Fibre. Barracuda in shallow water can be tough to fool, but adding Fluoro Fibre to a fly that looks like a small bonefish improves your chances. Offshore species are sight-feeders. A fly that flashes or changes color will stand out in the middle of feeding fish.

Blending color or using subtle shades of color is important when you need a precise pattern to match a food source. Often flies fished in clear water in daylight need to be more lifelike; fishing for species like educated bonefish in skinny water demands a more sophisticated approach. Most baitfish patterns should fade in color from a darker back to a lighter underside, because most baitfish are darker on top with a lighter underside. Tan, blue, green, olive, and black are several popular colors for fly backs. Blue, green, and olive are excellent colors for the backs of silversides, sand eels, herring, anchovies, bunker, and mullet. Most of these baitfish are shiny, so add some flash to both the underside and on the back. Usually the fly's underside is white, cream, or yellow-white (like the shade of a polar bear). Layering several colors or layering different shades of one color makes the fly more lifelike and suggests movement, but this requires more time. I might blend three colors, light to dark; that's enough to add realism without taking too much time.

Baitfish, like most fish, have a light-colored underside that gets darker toward the back or top. Layer sections of material, starting with a light color on the bottom of the wing or tail, and blend to darker colors on top. Mixing colors adds a lifelike appearance. When building a fly with a white belly and green back, adding a midsection of light pink, light olive, or tan with some flash creates the basic color of many baitfish. For a more precise pattern, blend two or three colors, always building from light below to dark above. Baitfish, actually most fish, don't have an abrupt color change—often the fish's sides are blends of colors with some flash. Even the undersides of baitfish are usually not pure white but more a cream to off-white mixed with other colors.

Use the same type of material in different colors, and tie in layers to create a multicolored tail. Like materials blend well together. Some materials do not blend with others. Most natural materials will fit together or at least will not take on two different characteristics. If you're blending synthetic materials with natural materials, put the natural inside the synthetic and use a slightly stiff synthetic that forms a jacket over the natural material. Putting a light shell of materials like Flash 'N Slinky or EP Minnow Fiber over long, thin saddle hackles produces great looks and ideal movement. Leave the feathers extending about an inch past the other material. This is the same technique used to make a glow fly (see Chapter 13), but keep the bright material inside the outer shell. Use this technique when you're

This Barracuda Fly shows how Fluoro Fibre can add glow to patterns that have semitransparent materials. Many years ago Paul Van Reenen, from South Africa, introduced me to this fascinating material. The fiber changes shades, creating a luminescence similar to what baitfish do when frightened. One technique is to use Hot Pink or Hot Orange Fluoro Fibre inside translucent materials so the inside of the fly appears to glow.

Blending several colors with a subtle flash makes the fly look lifelike. When blending color, try adding flash using the same color as the fly's wing or body. Pearl is an ideal neutral flash color that blends with many shades.

These river herring appear to glow from the sun's angle.

But under a different light, the fins appear to glow even more. Viewing food types that fish eat in different lighting conditions is a great way to understand how to build fly patterns. This is especially true in clear water locations where light can change the color of baitfish or make a shrimp appear to sparkle. Live baitfish, crabs, and shrimp can lose color when they are dead. Viewing live foods, or baits that are fresh, is the best way to learn how to copy that food. If possible, observe them under different lighting conditions.

using a softer synthetic with a synthetic that is firm—a firm shell over a softer core.

Trying to match the colors of different baitfish with one pattern using only one shade is impossible. Baitfish can change color to match their background, blending with the bottom color. I have seen two mackerel from the same school—one green and the other blue, yet both baitfish looked similar. Either color would match this food source well. A gamefish's color changes to match the surroundings too. Bonefish drifting from a creek with a dark-colored bottom onto a light flat look like green torpedoes. The angle of the sun, the brightness of the day, water colors, and water clarity affect baitfish color. Depending on the sun's angle, the fins and tail can give off a fluorescent hue.

One afternoon I took a number of photos. Scattered clouds continuously changed lighting conditions from bright to overcast. After looking at the photos, I noticed that some patterns actually looked like a different color fly. The fly was the same pattern, but it looked like it was tied with different colors. This is an excellent illustration of how color changes in different underwater lighting conditions. In some water types color changes might be even more noticeable. Matching the colors of different baits is an inexact science, and the bait's color may not change in the same way a fly's color changes. Trying to get this color variation effect using natural materials does not usually work—using a glowing color with semitransparent synthetic materials is much more effective.

These changes can be dramatic—on some baitfish their backs go from a bright green to light olive. The same baitfish from different estuaries can look totally different. The body shape is the same but water and bottom color can make that baitfish look different. This is why it's amusing to hear anglers boasting that they have a perfect match to certain baits. If you really want to match all baitfish under every condition, hire a pack mule to carry your flies. When I want to make precise flies for inshore fishing, I make patterns with subtle shades like light olive, tan, and lavender or a blend of those colors. These are the colors that most baits become in clear water over light- to medium-colored bottoms. And it is these conditions that usually require more precise flies. For offshore fishing or clear water, sometimes a richer color might work, but you never go wrong fishing subtle shades.

Another approach is using bright colors and colors that create a glow, an internal brightness, inside a light-colored

A dark-colored fly is the best choice in rolling surf along a beach or when fishing in white water along rocky structure. Black, dark green, or dark purple flies work well in white water because they stand out. A light-colored fly might not show up in rolling surf unless you fish it below the white water, but even there the darker pattern would still stand out enough for the fish to see the fly. Flies fished in low light, rolling surf, discolored water, or with a fast retrieve attract fish with movement. The fly's action provokes the strike. In these conditions gamefish must react quickly and seldom look the fly over—they strike fast and hard.

As I researched and experimented with different materials and then started to shoot underwater photos of different flies, I became overwhelmed by how different materials changed a fly's action and character, and how the colors in certain fly patterns changed in some lighting conditions. Even the difference in the fly's color between full sunlight and cloud cover was surprising. The change in light changes the background, making the fly's tone different.

Trout can be color selective in some conditions. Brown trout in hard-fished locations can distinguish different shades of olive. However, they are usually this selective only for dry flies or nymphs. When anglers are fishing streamers, trout seem to be far less selective, perhaps because they often need to strike quickly at a moving target. Fish have more time to examine dry flies and nymphs than they do with a fast-moving baitfish pattern.

translucent material. This emulates the effect that nature produces in some fish and squid that causes color change or creates a flash of color when the fish is frightened. Perhaps this reaction allows smaller fish to avoid capture. This same reaction also occurs when gamefish become aroused before taking a fly. On different occasions I have seen a gamefish glow before it took the fly.

To keep color simple, here are some thoughts. Use darker colored patterns over dark bottoms or when fishing on dark nights and in discolored water or in rolling surf. Lighter colors are best fished over light bottoms on bright nights and in clear water during the daytime. I remember fishing one night with the legendary angler Cooper Gilkes on Lobsterville Beach, Martha's Vineyard. There was a bright moon and Coop was fishing white, while I used black. The sky was partly cloudy, and when the moon was bright, Coop took fish; when the night turned dark, I took fish. This is not always true, so keep trying different colors when fish are feeding but not cooperating. Tough-to-catch fish might require many changes, both in fly type and color to find the best pattern. When fishing in clear, shallow water on Southern flats, match the bottom color. Most foods that live on flats need to match the surroundings or they would not survive.

White is a valuable color because many juvenile baitfish are light in color, the undersides of many of the major baitfish are white or light tan, and some species of shrimp are light in color. Also, all white is a popular color in many locations down South even when no food source is all white. To me small baitfish do not look white—they appear light tan—but perhaps they look mostly white to gamefish. I'm sure that this is true in trout streams, where white baitfish patterns catch fish even though there are no white-colored baitfish. Perhaps what we see is different than what a fish sees. As anglers, we need to look at color differently.

The combination of two colors like red and white or orange and yellow baffles me and shows that fish see color differently. Both of these color combinations are not found in any baitfish, so anglers must keep experimenting to see what colors might work in different conditions. This might tell us something about what fish see compared to what we see, and why black and white are not really colors because they reflect or absorb other colors. The fact that both white and black reflect or absorb color

This Alaskan Dolly Varden was one of several different species that I took in Alaska on my first trip. All of these fish took the Snake Fly aggressively. I found that just this one fly pattern in several different colors was effective for every species that I fished for. Having one good go-to pattern makes fishing easier.

might tell us that underwater these colors may not appear the same to some gamefish as we see them.

You can choose from a number of all-black fly patterns, and black is popular with spin and casting plugs and rubber baits for both fresh and salt water. Yet few food types are solid black; I cannot come up with one important food source in salt water that is all black. In fresh water, sculpin, a small food fish found in many rivers and streams, are very dark to almost all black, but they can change color to blend with the bottom. Black is perhaps the best nighttime color, and it is also ideal for discolored water and in rolling surf because it stands out well. Yet I have taken fish on all-black flies in shallow, clear water during the daytime. Black or other dark colors certainly give the best contrast when fished on or near the surface on a dark night. When you look at all different types of fishing from black bass, to striped bass, to snook and tarpon, to trout and salmon, black is a popular color, whether it is used as a solid color or blended with other colors. One year I fished flies of only two colors, all black and all white. I had great success in many different fishing situations. There were cases when I wished I could fish a fly with a different color, but that was perhaps 30 percent of the time. And that 30 percent was fishing on clear, shallow flats in bright sun and fishing in clear water for hardtails.

One question I have pondered is whether fish see some colors better in discolored water or does that color give a more positive reading when fish use their sonar system, or their lateral lines, to feed? If a fish does not sense or pick up one color versus another, perhaps different fly-tying materials produce favorable vibrations that trigger a strike. Research shows that the fin movement of a baitfish alerts a gamefish to its presence—the gamefish can actually track that baitfish's location. Feeding, using their sonar system, fish pick up vibrations using their lateral lines located along both their sides. One line runs from the tail's base to the edge of the gill plate, another runs above the eye.

Lefty Kreh showed me a trick that illustrated a fish's capabilities to pick up sound. While drifting on a flat in the Florida Keys, Lefty lured a shark into casting distance by splashing the tip of a fly rod lightly in the water. Even though the sound was almost nonexistent to us, that shark homed into the splashing sound like radar. Do different materials produce vibrations and sounds that we are not aware of? Rattles attract fish at times. So much to learn with so little time to fish.

Except for fluorescent colors, most colors become flat or lose their tone when submerged into deeper water or in murky water. Water affects light; thus it changes color. Most anglers fly-fish in water of 20 feet or less. The only color that is drastically affected by the water depth is red, which turns to a moss green at about 10 feet. I learned this when spearing a fish while snorkeling in the tropics. I hit a nice grouper in about 30 feet of water, and a stream of green poured from the fish. It only turned red when I got up near the surface. Green and blue remain unchanged beyond what a fly angler could reach. In discolored water, most color is lost, turning the fly to a dark silhouette.

In locations where color matters, build flies that fit the need. But for general fishing, don't get caught up in the hype that only specially dressed flies of a certain color will catch fish. I strongly believe that in half of the situations we fish, if you put a white, olive, tan, yellow, or black fly with action in the right place and work it properly, it will catch fish. Two fine books have information on color and the effect water depth has on color, plus other tips about the sounds a fish hears: *The Scientific Angler* by Paul Johnson and *Through the Fish's Eye* by Mark Sosin and John Clark.

CHAPTER 2

Important Baits and Food Types

Here are four small wide-sided baits from a Florida beach. Sometimes bait found along a beach can be affected by sunlight or might dry out, so it can be hard to get an identification. The three on top, I believe, are scaled sardine, called pilchard. The small one on the bottom has a different eye but I can't identify it. Along this beach these baits could be easily matched with any flat-sided fly that is built to look like a juvenile menhaden, herring, or any number of small, flat-sided baitfish. It's why one fly pattern can match many bait types—because many food types are quite similar.

Food types differ from one location to another. From Canada to the mid-Atlantic, baitfish are the major food source for gamefish. But south of Hatteras, North Carolina, shrimp and crabs, at certain times of the year, become the major diet of many gamefish, especially inside estuaries. As we travel farther south, crustaceans become a more significant food source of certain gamefish. Several baitfish are dominant along the Eastern Seaboard and the Gulf, but many locations have heavy concentrations of several baitfish that might last for a few weeks to several months and can change each year. In locations where gamefish rely on certain food types and that bait becomes scarce or not available, gamefish will forage for other foods.

Many patterns used for saltwater gamefish also work in fresh water and vice versa because many baitfish are similar or in some cases, like the gizzard shad, the same bait. Wherever you fish, most foods types in the major categories are somewhat uniform. There are numerous types of anchovies, but one or two patterns will cover the species adequately. Silversides, smelt, sardines, and anchovies have similar body shapes and colors. And at 4 to 5 inches long, a scaled sardine, menhaden, alewife, threadfin herring, and gizzard shad are similar in both shape and appearance. Many schooling baitfish have only a subtle color difference. Perhaps we see the most significant color difference when baitfish move from a light bottom to a dark bottom and change color to blend in with the surroundings. Schooling baitfish have shiny sides to protect them from predators. This helps them to blend together, never giving gamefish a specific target. Only when separated from the school do they stand out.

Take time to look at food types when finding dead bait along a beach or when schools of bait are holding by a jetty or when worms, shrimp, or crabs are floating out of a small creek. By looking at all the different foods that gamefish eat, you can build flies that mimic those baits. You can adapt patterns to copy many foods by changing the length, width, bulk, or type of material, or the hook type or size. You only need to be creative.

Patterns that are designed properly can catch fish in many locations and in different water types thousands of miles apart because the fly looks right and has the right action that suggests a food source. Anglers that fish in different locations or fish in both fresh and salt water need to think about how a fly pattern might be effective for many species that feed on similar food sources.

The look and movement of a fly triggers a feeding response in gamefish that produces strikes. I believe fish often take a fly even when not actively feeding because the fly's appearance or

The anchovy is a popular food source for more gamefish than any other baitfish I know. This small baitfish is important from New England right into the Caribbean; actually there are more than 100 different species around the world. I have caught over two dozen gamefish when they were feeding on these small baits.

Sand eels this thick along an ocean beach often mean excellent fishing. If you do not find fish when you see the eels, keep fishing the location every morning—fish will find a food source like this. When sand eels are this thick, they will draw fish often at first light when they begin to emerge from the sand bottom. Fishing, at times, can be difficult when bait is thick. One advantage when fish feed on small bait is that the fish need to feed for a much longer time to fill their gullets. The same is true when fish are feeding on spawning worms, crabs, shrimp, and other tiny baits.

action sparks a feeding instinct. A fly that looks crippled, like a struggling baitfish, triggers a response in a fish much like a cat seeing a mouse run across a living room floor. Effective patterns take fish in many surroundings, under different conditions, even when fish are not actively feeding.

The Bahamas and the Caribbean don't have large schooling baitfish, but they do have many small, 2- to 4-inch long baitfish that are a food source for gamefish. Other important food types for fly fishing are small shrimp, crabs, needlefish, scaled sardine, and Spanish sardine. I could not even begin to list the many different crabs and shrimp that live in these waters.

I learned early on in my fishing career that without a food source, finding fish in most locations was difficult. In Long Island Sound, a run of sand eels produces hot fishing in the spring and early summer, and if they stay longer, fishing stays hot. Locations like river and creek mouths that have spawning river herring attract bigger fish when the bait moves back into open water. Finding these places takes some careful research. River herring also produce a bumper crop of young herring for gamefish in many freshwater ponds and lakes. Look for baitfish such as menhaden or runs of mullet to turn on the fish at large points like Cape Point off Hatteras, North Carolina. Cape Point can be a wasteland until these baits turn the place upside down. This is also true when runs of peanut bunker from Cape Cod to Montauk and south are present. And the mullet runs along the east coast of Florida create excellent beach fishing. Anchovies, called rain bait, are the catalysts that produce hot fishing for hardtails from New England down to the Carolinas. Scaled sardines and Spanish sardines bring excellent fishing to many locations in the tropics and make even spooky bonefish feed like bluefish.

Many species of baitfish occur in both fresh and salt water. Some species live in both waters, and others, like river herring, spawn in the early season in fresh water before returning to the sea. Many baits have several names, and two different baitfish might have the same name. Many food sources are similar in both fresh and salt water, and fly patterns used in both waters can be interchangeable.

The Ever-Changing Food Supply

Foods that gamefish eat change throughout the year. Baitfish go through cycles from spring to fall. Baitfish spawn throughout the season, most starting in late winter to early spring, and in Southern locations the spawning begins early. River herring migrate up the coast, spawning in freshwater ponds and lakes. Silversides spawn near or inside estuaries. Sea herring and menhaden spawn in open water, and the larvae move inshore, developing into juvenile baitfish by late summer to fall. Each baitfish is different, and the gamefish's foods constantly change from adult to young baits that grow quickly. Some baitfish like silversides live only a year, two years at most, but sand eels, another small baitfish, might live over ten years. Most baitfish grow quickly, especially those with short lives, and most follow a pattern. Exceptions like menhaden appear later in the year and can provide a large food source all summer and into fall, and an influx of other foods might alter this pattern. The big adult baitfish appear early in the year or in midseason, tiny juveniles develop through midsummer, and they keep growing into fall. Menhaden are bigger than silversides, and juvenile bunker might be bigger than adult silversides by fall, but the pattern remains. Big flies early in the year, small flies in the summer, and midsize flies in the fall.

Crustaceans like large shrimp follow a pattern similar to some baitfish. White shrimp spawn from March to April, with the young moving into estuaries and developing quickly, reaching 6 inches by late fall; brown shrimp spawn in fall, with larvae moving inshore in mid to late winter, developing to 3 to 4 inches before moving into open water. Some shrimp remain in estuaries, but most move to open water. Blue crabs are also similar, developing in estuaries from late spring to summer up north and late winter down South; some Southern locations have several spawning events, with small crabs from March into April. They grow quickly, so the fishing is only good for a short window in some locations. You can also fish during hatches of small foods like the cinder worm, shore shrimp, and small brown crabs.

Building Flies to Match Food Types

Thin flies for thin baitfish: Sand eels needlefish, ballyhoo, worms, and eels are foods that have a long, thin profile and, because of their shape, have great movement in the water. In this category, sand eels are one of the most important baits in New England. Sand eels, a thick-schooling, thin-bodied, shiny bait, are 2 to 5 inches long and show up in early to late May, sometimes lasting through October. The best runs usually are

In clear conditions when bonefish are moving slowly and inspecting each piece of food, they are hard to fool. These situations require a fly that looks and acts like the real thing, and the proper presentation is also vital. If fish are spooky, try casting well ahead of the fish, and move the fly as the fish approaches.

Worms and eels are thin foods that wiggle their bodies to move through the water. This movement, shown by this sea worm on a sandy beach along the coast of Maine, resembles a snake crawling across the ground.

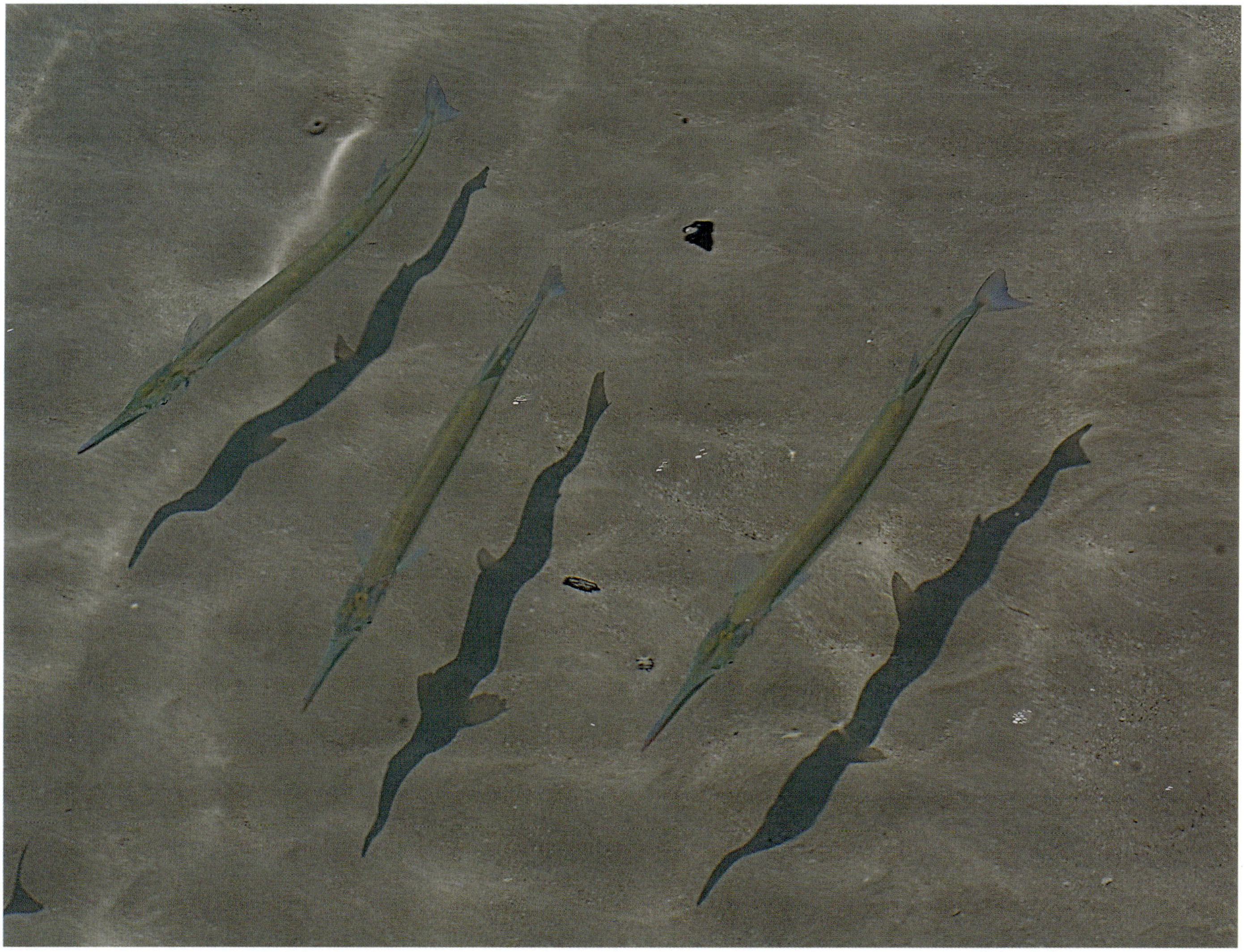

Needlefish and ballyhoo are larger, thin baitfish that range from New England to the Gulf of Mexico and throughout the Caribbean. These needlefish are about 12 inches long. Their color will change to blend with the bottom. They are fast swimmers that jump, sometimes greyhounding when chased by gamefish.

Spearing, often called shiners, are a small baitfish 3 to 5 inches long. Smelt are close in color and shape but can be several inches longer. Both baitfish are ideal bait, a perfect size to match with a fly. They're often found in and around estuaries from the Gulf of St. Lawrence to Florida. In the fall, at times, they will school up along jetties at the mouths of estuaries.

from spring to early summer. During prime years when schools of bait are thick, gamefish concentrate along shorelines and in shallow areas. Often, you can find football fields of feeding fish. Though tiny early in the spring, sand eels are a baitfish that can produce excellent fly fishing in the Northeast for several months and sometimes all summer.

Midbodied flies for midbodied baitfish: Silversides, anchovies, mullet, whitefish, mackerel, squid, sardines, and smelt are thicker than the thin-bodied baitfish. Silversides, called glass minnows in the South, and anchovies are major midbodied small baits. There are seven species of silversides from New England to the tropics. These 3- to 5-inch-long, midbodied baitfish with a stripe along their sides spawn in spring and are ideal baitfish for fly rodders to copy. Often shiners—another common name for silversides—are found along shorelines and in and around estuaries when they splash on the surface. This can be exciting fishing, and topwater flies and popping are deadly.

Anchovies are most important in late summer into fall; these 2- to 5-inch-long baitfish are the food that draws and keeps the offshore hardtails close to shore. They ball up in thick schools around the mouths of estuaries, creating good surface-feeding action. They are midbodied with a silver stripe along their side. In New England, the bay anchovy range from 1½ to 2½ inches long. Farther south, the striped and silver anchovy are larger, and fish seem to feed more aggressively on these bigger baits.

Mullet range in size from finger mullet, 3 to 6 inches long, to adults that can grow to several pounds. Mullet are a major food source from New Jersey south into the Gulf. Mullet are perhaps one of the most important baitfish from New Jersey into the Gulf. Finger mullet 3 to 6 inches long are an ideal bait to match with a fly. Along the Gulf and parts of Florida, small mullet are an ideal food source all year long, and into the mid-Atlantic the season runs from early spring into winter. Mullet develop in estuaries and then move into open water and along beaches; their fall run along the east coast of Florida is exceptional.

Two species of whitefish in streams and lakes throughout North America look similar to mullet. In New England smelt are often confused with spearing in salt water because they are similar. Smelt are a significant freshwater baitfish in many Northern lakes. Saltwater smelt, a coldwater baitfish, occur on both coasts. In the Gulf, Florida, and down into the Caribbean, Spanish sardines are an important baitfish. In the Bahamas when these 3- to 4-inch-long baitfish move inshore, they attract cuda, snapper, grouper, and turn on bonefish in some locations.

This adult mullet was found along a beach on the west coast of Florida. Juvenile mullet have thinner bodies. Most juvenile mullet are in the 4- to 10-inch range. They have a round shape and taper slightly at both ends. Mullet range from New England south to Florida—they become a major, important baitfish from Cape Hatteras, North Carolina, to Florida. The mullet run in the fall along the east coast of Florida can produce hot fishing.

Squid are fast growing, important to striper fishing in the Northeast, and abundant in many Southern locations. Squid is a regional bait that can bring good fishing to specific locations. From one year to another, these baits can create excellent fishing in the Northeast in spring into early summer. DAVE SKOK

Baitfish like the sea herring in the photo or menhaden are large foods when they reach full size. Menhaden are the largest baitfish along the eastern Atlantic, but sea herring are also big baits and tough to match with a fly you can cast when they become adults. These baits are flat-sided throughout their existence. The juvenile baits in the 3- to 7-inch range are easy to match with a fly, but once they reach over 10 inches, the flies become more difficult to cast.

Wide-bodied flies for wide-bodied baitfish: Alewives, pilchards, herring, shads, and butterfish are major food sources from New England to the Gulf. Menhaden, both Atlantic and Gulf, are a major wide-bodied baitfish on the Eastern Seaboard into the Gulf of Mexico. Menhaden usually appear early in the summer to midsummer and into late fall. This is also true for most mid-Atlantic and Southern locations. When there are large numbers of this bait, especially peanut size, fishing can be excellent. Overharvesting has seriously affected this baitfish. The adults are large, 12 to 16 inches long, and not the important bait for fly rodders that peanut bunker are because they are big and difficult to match. When thick schools of 3- to 6-inch, long, shiny-sided peanuts appear in mid to late fall, fishing can be exceptional. Small to midsize menhaden are a key bait in the Gulf and along the entire Atlantic coast.

Wide-sided baitfish are an important food source in many locations in both fresh and salt water. Spring spawning runs of herring and alewives provide excellent fishing in many locations. Scaled sardines, like the Spanish sardines, are a major food source for gamefish in Florida, the Bahamas, and into the Caribbean.

Blueback herring and alewives are both important baits from New England to the Carolinas with blueback herring ranging to Florida. Both species spawn in fresh water from January in Southern locations to early May in Northern areas. These big, wide-bodied baits are 6 to 10 inches long. Alewives are the first to appear, with the herring about a month later. When they flow back to open water, they become a significant food source for gamefish. The juveniles develop in fresh water, providing a valuable food source for freshwater ponds, lakes, rivers, and streams.

Crustaceans: Shrimp and crab flies become major players from the mid-Atlantic down to the Gulf. Blue, lady, mole, green, fiddler, and sand flea crabs are found in many locations from New England to the Gulf. The blue crab is abundant throughout most of the Eastern Seaboard down to Mexico.

Several important species of shrimp—white, brown and seabob—are 3 to 6 inches long and require larger size flies. Grass shrimp and shore shrimp are smaller, 1 to 2 inches long. Crabs and shrimp are important food sources, at times, in the Northeast, but not like they are once you get into the mid-Atlantic and farther south. From the Carolinas down to the Gulf Coast, these foods are not only abundant, they are ideal for fly

River herring join menhaden and sea herring as another big, wide-bodied baitfish. Adult river herring are smaller, and matching a herring of this size is not too difficult when using lightweight materials that don't absorb water. When trying to match a larger, flat-sided baitfish, build the largest fly you can cast using sparse synthetic materials. Remember, you need to be able to cast and present the fly well.

Juvenile bluefish called snappers can produce hot popper fishing in late summer. Often in and around estuaries and along sheltered beaches, the small bluefish feed on small baits. In turn, stripers and larger bluefish feed on them. This bait can produce hot fishing for about a month in mid to late summer.

The lady crab, or similar species, is an important food from New England into Florida and south. Found along shorelines and up inside estuaries, lady crabs are mobile. In Southern waters, several other species are close in color and size and reside in similar waters. The crab's size makes it easier to match than the larger blue crab. Flies for lady crabs and their relatives are castable even when the crabs are full size.

Here are two river sculpins. Notice their shape looks like a tadpole: the head is large and the body tapers to a tail. Even in clear streams, these fish are dark in color.

rodders to match. Shrimp and crabs make up perhaps 90 percent or more of the diet of bonefish and permit on Southern shallow-water flats. The rich flats of the Florida Keys, the Bahamas, and the Caribbean have varieties of crustaceans that are too numerous to mention. And even on Northern flats, crabs become an important food source in the summer when schooling baits are less active.

Special foods: Cinder worms, sandworms, mud minnows, crayfish, chubs, and juvenile gamefish are foods of less importance. Many of these foods might be hot for a short time, or like the cinder worm and palolo worm, are mostly present during certain moon phases. Cinder worms hatch in limited places for short periods of time, as palolo worms do in the Florida Keys in May and June. Although these foods produce excellent fishing, they are not like sand eels in New England, mullet in the Gulf, or shrimp in most of the South. Like many food sources, these baits are significant only for limited times and for certain types of fishing.

These hatches occur usually on full or new moon during periods of large tides. Both hatches are hard to predict, although the cinder worm is more dependable. The palolo worm is tough to predict and much less frequent, occurring during low tides around full moon. Both hatches are affected by bad weather and fronts, but you won't forget the swarming worms after you see a hatch.

In the Northeast, young bluefish, called snappers, begin appearing in mid to late summer, growing quickly into September. Stripers and bluefish feed on snapper blues in late summer. The way the snappers feed, splashing on the surface, creates an ideal feeding environment that often draws gamefish to feed.

Larger trout feed heavily on baitfish, and young trout become food for grown-ups. A favorite food source of barracuda is small to midsize bonefish. Also other small gamefish, like snook and redfish, are food for different adult gamefish. Young-of-the-year gamefish usually develop quickly—often this food source is short-lived, but the fishing is exciting. Some baits like Mud Minnows and chubs might be overlooked because they lack the luster of other foods or they appear and vanish before most anglers are aware of their presence. When the special foods turn on, you can find great fishing.

CHAPTER 3

Fly-Building Supplies

Building a fish-getting fly requires the right tools, the right materials, and proper tying techniques. Even to tie a fly that seems as simple as this bonefish pattern requires all the essentials.

You need to follow several rules when building a fly. The hook should be barbless, sharp, and of sufficient size and strength to get the job done. For special patterns, the hook's design needs to fit the fly's design. Build the fly so the gap of the hook is not clogged with heavy material that would affect the hook set. Most useful fly patterns need to have action or look like a food source and be easy to cast. And the fly pattern must move through the water with a natural flow or settle to the bottom and sit there in a lifelike manner. All the fancy materials, all the expensive hooks, and all the best fly-tying equipment are meaningless if these considerations are not met.

Don't get caught up in the hype that you always need to have the exact type of eye, flash, hook, or tying thread listed in the pattern. Some patterns do require certain materials to get the best results, but for many fly types, you can use alternatives. For years I tied flies with materials that in some cases I didn't know the names of. Only when I started writing about flies did I realize the need to keep track of what I was using. Luckily, most anglers are much more organized.

Most flies work fine using a different eye design as long as the eye is close to the original in weight and size. Materials like flash need to be similar in weight and stiffness to achieve the same action. In a pinch most hook types will work to produce a good general fishing fly. In most cases hook types are interchangeable—they might not be perfect, but they still work.

You can use many furs in short lengths where patterns call for feathers like marabou or Bird Fur, which is actually a feather. Sometimes you can produce a better fly by substituting a material. When I travel and don't have the right material, I find that necessity is often the mother of invention.

Not all the materials I list are mentioned in the fly recipes. I might list a building material that I don't use but feel some tiers might consider using. Some of these materials would work in patterns that I show in the book, but I prefer other materials. And there are materials that I no longer use, but which would still work fine. So many flash types are interchangeable and would work for many patterns. Some of the materials mentioned are mostly food for thought.

One interesting aspect of writing a book was learning about and trying all the new tools and equipment that are on the market. I have never been a fanatic fly tier or needed the newest equipment or latest materials. Most of my fly-tying gear is over 30 years old. These tools work fine, perhaps requiring a little more patience and time, but the end results are flies that catch fish. However, offering advice about equipment to other anglers demands giving the best recommendations to make the experience easier and more fun. I was stupid and struggled with

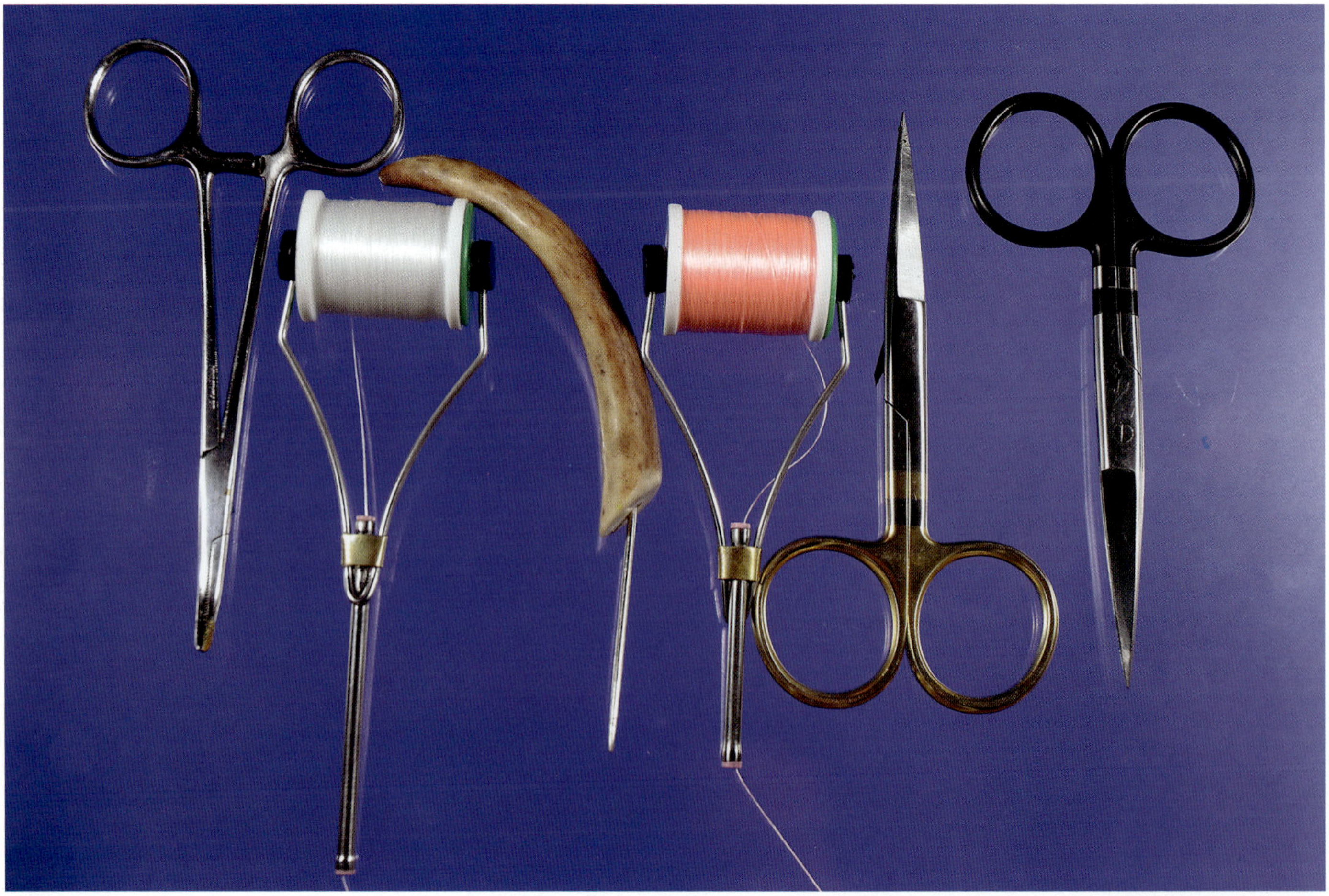

Here are some basic fly-tying tools. From left to right—a pair of forceps, two tying bobbins with a deer antler bodkin between them, and two scissors. The right fly-tying tools are not that expensive and are worth buying.

My favorite fly-tying vise on the left is a homemade pair of vise grips welded to a steel rod. The Regal Vise on the right is a fine vise that can handle large hooks, but no vise can grab and hold a hook like a small pair of vise grips.

old equipment for years, but you should not. One email and a phone call to Steve Fournier who runs Dr. Slick (a company that sells high-quality fishing and fly-tying equipment) set me on the road to the twenty-first century. I can't thank him enough for his help, information, and recommendations on fly-tying tools—just learning about different types of scissors made my fly-tying much easier.

Tying Vise

The best saltwater tying vise I have ever used is a pair of small vise grips welded to a steel rod. If you have a fly-tying vise with a 5⁄16- or 3⁄8-inch shaft that slides into a foot, the device that holds the vise to your table, all you need to do is match the shaft size with a steel rod and have a shop weld the vise grips to the rod. Make the rod about 12 inches long. The vise grips with little or no adjustment can grab any hook without it moving, and this vise even works with freshwater hooks in larger sizes down to size 10. And vise grips are ideal for crushing down hook barbs.

Joe McCarthy of Milford, Connecticut, made this vise for me nearly 45 years ago, and it is still ticking. Other fly-tying vises have different qualities, such as rotation. Many excellent vises are on the market, but the main concern when tying with bigger hooks is holding power. Most quality vises will work, but nothing grips hooks like a pair of vise grips. It's the best vise for tiers who use larger hooks. To show the tying techniques more clearly, I used a Regal Vise for the step-by-step photos, and the foot of this vise is the foot for my vise grips.

Tying Bobbin

I generally prefer a longer bobbin (4 inches works fine) for bigger flies and for flies with spun deer hair heads. Spinning deer or elk body hair requires more reach and a big wrapping swing to create the flair as the hair stands up on the hook shank. Bobbins with ceramic or titanium oxide inserts allow the thread to flow better and smoother as you rotate the bobbin, meaning you have less chance of breaking the thread, which can happen when spinning hair or when tying in hard materials or large bunches of material.

Scissors

For years I plodded along with one type of scissors, wondering why they kept getting dull so fast. I used different types of fly line to fish changing water types, so why didn't I use different scissors types to cut different types of material? Cutting some synthetics can be hard on scissors designed to cut natural materials. Cutting most synthetic materials is easier with tungsten carbide or scissors designed for cutting synthetics. And they also work for cutting other materials. Hair scissors are ideal for trimming deer hair heads but will eventually lose sharpness if you use them to cut some synthetics. I now have several pairs of scissors for tying different patterns and prefer scissors with lengths of 4 to 5 inches.

For tiers who make large numbers of small crab and shrimp flies, a pair of razor scissors makes the task easier. Certain shapes of scissors can make some trimming easier, and some tiers prefer curved scissors to straight ones. I prefer straight for almost all my tying, but choose the tool that works for you. Tiers have many other interesting tools and devices they can use, but I like to keep it simple.

Natural Materials

Most natural materials are easy to identify. There are different types of hair, feathers, and fur, such as bucktail, saddle hackle, ostrich herl, and rabbit fur. Synthetic materials are another beast. There might be three different names for the same material or the names sound the same but are spelled differently. The other problem is that so many different synthetics look similar in the package. The only way to judge the material is to feel it. Synthetics that are too soft have excellent action but tend to knot on flies with longer wings or tails. I find that stiffer materials are easier to work with. If you have been making flies for a long time, you might have materials that are hard to identify. Most will be useful, unless through carelessness they have become matted and will not straighten.

Natural materials fall into several different categories—hair, fur, and feathers. They give warmth and protection to animals and birds. Being the products of living creatures, hair, fur, and feathers are tapered because that shape allows for better protection and more warmth. Feathers are tapered to help birds to control flight. Each single feather is not only tapered, but the fibers of each feather are also tapered. Hair and fur have the same properties. Look at each hair of a deer's tail; the base is much thicker, tapering down to a tiny point. Even as fine as some furs are, they all taper, and some furs have somewhat stiffer fibers with a lighter fur mixed in. This perfect blending of some furs would be next to impossible to duplicate by hand mixing. Yet with only the snip of a pair of scissors, you can cut a section of material to use for a fly's wing or tail that produces both a good-looking and naturally moving fly.

Three deer tails of different colors. For most patterns I like deer tail that is not too soft at the base. When building flies with long wings like the Mole Nose Bunker, firmer bucktail will help hold the tail in place. The Slab Fly is another pattern where long, firm hair fibers are best to hold the fly's shape. For any popping bug, stiff hair holds up the tail and keeps the bug tracking straight to produce a better splash. For smaller flies with shorter wings or tails, softer, thinner hair fibers work better.

The key to movement in natural materials is their taper. And that taper also produces a living shape to match many foods. All baitfish have a similar shape, tapering from a larger head and body to a smaller tail. Also most furs and feathers move more once they hit water. This is especially true with finer materials. Another major advantage of natural materials is that a little steam is all you need to refurbish any fly. A big plus for unorganized people like me.

Bucktail: Deer tail is an important material for a number of patterns. It's easy to work with, fits many applications, and is easy to dye. It is buoyant, holds the right profile, and the longer fibers provide flowing action like the slow kick of the tails of some baitfish. The best tails come from wild animals, not farm-raised deer—if you know someone who hunts, ask him to save the tails and belly fur from his next harvest.

There is an easy way to get more action from long bucktail without adding too much bulk. Cut a section of bucktail and grab the section near the tip of the tapered fibers with your thumb and first finger. With the other hand, gently remove the shorter fibers of bucktail from the bunch. This leaves the longer fibers for the fly's tail or wing. The closer to the tip that you grab the fibers, the longer and sparser the tail will be. I use this technique for making long, thin-tailed flies like sand eel patterns or for the tail section of a Snake Fly when I blend several colors and want length without bulk. If you want the tail to be even, remove the few very long fibers. (Some patterns look better with an even tail, but if you leave the long fibers, they make the tail move better.)

Here is one trick to use when tying on larger sections of bucktail, which can slip if it's not tied over a hook shaft coated with thread or not tied tight enough. When tying in larger bunches of deer tail, use enough pressure and put a drop of superglue over the wrapped thread that holds the bucktail. This will prevent that beautiful wing or tail from slipping off the hook shaft.

1. Cut a section of long bucktail hair off of a tail.

2. Grab the section of bucktail hair with the thumb and forefinger from the tapered, thin end. This will be the section of longer hair.

3. With the thumb and forefinger of the other hand, grab the base of the bucktail hair. This will be the section of shorter hairs.

4. Then pull out the loose section. These are the shorter hairs that should be saved for smaller flies.

Marabou comes either strung or in small packages. For most tiers packaged marabou is easier to work with. When building flies like the Snake Fly or Sea Rat, the best marabou fibers are ones that have no webbing. The right feather is just a bunch of fibers that look like a round plume of feathers. If the marabou feather does have some webbing, it will work for larger flies, but for the wing or tail on any small fly like the Worm Hatch Fly, I prefer to use feathers without webbing. Feathers with webbing look flat, not round. If the marabou feather is large enough, grab a bunch of fibers and trim them off, using just a clump of fibers for the wing or tail.

The orange and tan are elk body hair, and the chartreuse and pink are deer body hair—both work fine, but the elk is a softer hair. For spinning small heads on flies like the Snake Fly or Trout Rat, choose softer, thinner body hair. If the hair is too stiff, it will form a head that is too big. Softer body hair flares better. For larger flies like the Long Saddle Snake Fly or a big Sea Rat, choose long-fibered, slightly thicker hair. I avoid stiff, large-fibered body hair because it is much harder to work with.

Marabou: The best feathers are ones that have a light stem with little or no web. A large web will work on bigger flies but will not form a tail or collar well on smaller patterns. The large feathers often have stiff stems that you can use, but you must trim the webs off the feathers and tie them on as a bunch. This might take a little longer, but you get the same results as if you tied on a whole, smaller feather. However, the one drawback is that if the pattern requires a longer feather, then using only the web will not work. I use cutoff sections of webs when blending several colors for a small tail or wing for bonefish flies, for example.

Mottled marabou is a mixture of brown to tan, white, some gray, and black wound on a bar. This blend is ideal for trout and freshwater bass flies and also for shrimp patterns. And it makes a nice wing on Snake and Rat Flies.

Body hair: The best deer and elk body hair for spun heads should have soft, straight, flexible fibers. The stiffer, larger diameter hair is fine for bigger, buoyant heads, but it's difficult to form small heads with stiff hair. If the hair is crinkled, it will not spin as well, but it will work for large, chunky heads. I try to keep on hand both thin, soft body hair for building small-headed, neutral density flies and thicker hair for topwater flies or flies that will nose-up between strips. Elk hair seems to be the softest of the body hairs, but it can vary depending on processing and what section of the skin the piece of hair comes from. If the skin feels soft and the hair fibers are flexible, it will be workable.

Saddle hackle: Long, thin saddle hackle works best for sparse patterns, and the thicker, wider saddle are ideal for beefy patterns. I prefer whole capeskins because they have a variety of lengths. Some necks have feathers that are different shades where the color didn't blend properly, and often these necks are sold as seconds. Many times I make the tail of a fly with six to eight feathers, each one a different length to add action. If you plan to tie a number of patterns that require one size and color, packaged or strung saddle is better. Saddle hackle is ideal for a thin sand eel fly tail. Several thin feathers produce a fine, thin profile with good action that blends well with flash. Saddle feathers are ideal for making palmered bodies for slow-sinking, shallow-water patterns and forming wings and bodies on bonefish flies and shells on crabs. Furnace hackle has a much thicker stem color and is often darker. Badger hackle has a thinner stem with lighter outside color. Both feathers give the appearance of a centerline along the fly's side.

The orange and chartreuse here are bundles of feathers, and the green and black barred feathers are a full cape. Use thinner saddle hackle for all flies with long tails, like the Long Saddle Snake Fly, Sea Rat, or Rat Needlefish. Also for any patterns tied to match sand eels, worms, or eels, the thin saddles work best. Thin saddle hackle also gives better action—for a thicker fly body, use more feathers. For palmering a hackle on bonefish patterns like the Wide-Eyed Shrimp, most hackles will work fine.

These are ideal quality feathers—note how they are all tapered. A full-size ostrich herl feather should be shaped like a tall Christmas tree. The fibers cut from this feather will form a tail on a fly that has different length fibers—this creates better action. The Snake Fly is so effective because it has great action.

The yellow-green neck on the right is Bird Fur. It's an excellent material for the Sand Eel Snake Fly or any other thin pattern in which tail movement is important. Bird Fur is not actually fur, but a feathered neck with an assortment of different feathers that can range from marabou to very thin saddle. The material on the left is Mottled Marabou that is marabou feathers wound on a bar. This bar is ideal marabou that is excellent quality for short-tailed flies or wings. The color is perfect for the Trout Rat, but it also will work for shrimp and crab patterns.

The shorter fur, the fox, is on the left, and the raccoon is the longer fur on the right. I use both of these furs for the Wide-Eyed Shrimp, the Blue Lady, or the Rat Chovy, plus many other small patterns. The fur is easy to work with, and it comes in a number of different colors. Tail or hook wrapping is its one fault, but you can avoid that if you use it properly.

Ostrich herl: This feather is mostly soft and flexible, but look for the smaller feathers with tapered tips for making small-bodied flies. Generally, I prefer the plume feathers that are less than 8 inches long and are not uniform length, but if making a long fly (more than 8 inches), then I prefer long, thin feathers. I like to mix feather lengths. I also like plume feathers that are slightly tapered. This allows me to make the tail section of a fly by grabbing a section of fibers along the ostrich herl and cutting them off the main stem. Each fiber is a different length. Ostrich herl gives excellent action even in short lengths, making it ideal for freshwater patterns. It is the mainstay of the Snake Fly, giving the tail that swimming action. Add a few strands of flash to make the tail glitter or some Fluoro Fibre to make it glow.

Bird Fur: Bird Fur is a new material that I'm still testing; it is feathers that are similar to a mixture of ostrich herl and marabou. From different sections of a neck, the feathers vary from a soft, webbed feather to a longer, soft feather. The longer sections are ideal for sand eel flies and shorter sections work for the tails and wings on bonefish flies. I like the longer feathers that resemble saddle hackle for making a thin wing or tail, but you do not get a large number of any one feather. I feel that it has potential, but I need to spend more time working with it. Seasoned fly makers should give this material a try.

Arctic fox Zonker and Finn raccoon Zonker: These two furs fall into the synthetic confusion zone because they are natural materials, but they are labeled with different names. Now Finn raccoon is also labeled as "temple fox" or "temple dog." Both are soft furs that can be blended, giving bulk with great action. And both work fine for wings on small Snake Flies and Sea Rats and for bonefish flies or any epoxy fly. If you want less bulk, remove some of the soft fur from the hair. Some of these furs are supple, particularly Finn raccoon, which is much longer than arctic fox fur. If using a longer wing or tail, you might need to stiffen a section of the material with glue to prevent tail or hook wrap. These two furs are ideal for short to midsize tails and wings on many fly patterns.

Rabbit Fur is perhaps one of the most popular bonefish fly materials. Use only the fur or strips of fur for longer applications. Rabbit fur produces great action on small wings or tails. Rabbit is also ideal for shorter, chunky trout flies or 2½- to 3-inch Southern shrimp flies. The character of this fur allows the fly to settle more slowly than other, stiffer materials. It produces great claws on the Blue Lady.

Synthetic Materials

Synthetic materials can be confusing because some of them look alike and have similar names. Many different types of synthetic materials might work for one application when building a tail or wing. Materials that are limper and offer more action can tangle after catching a fish and require a comb to straighten the fibers. These materials work better for small to midsize patterns. One major advantage with synthetics is they do not absorb water and will produce a larger fly with a thicker body but less weight and bulk. This makes a bigger fly that is easier to cast than a fly made with natural materials. Synthetic materials are durable, but the downside is that some materials need more care and are harder to bring back to life if they are stored improperly. You have to store your flies carefully to avoid damaging all your hard work.

Bozo Hair and Big Fish Fiber: These are good materials for building bigger patterns or flies requiring longer tails. At one time I used them for patterns requiring a wide body like the Mole Nose Bunker, but in recent years I prefer using Metz Flash 'N Slinky and Steve Farrar's Flash Blend. They seem to give better action with less bulk.

Metz Flash 'N Slinky and Steve Farrar's Flash Blend are blends similar to the softer Kinky Fibre material mixed with flash. Both materials make easy work of forming a midsize to chunky tail or wing, or an ideal outer shell for blending with other materials. What's neat is that the flash is built in to these materials, giving both color and flash in one material. I use Steve Farrar's Flash Blend in natural, wild olive, and shrimp. The problem with both materials is having too many colors to choose from. You could become crazed with all the choices.

Enrico Puglisi offers a number of different materials that work with many flies. The EP Fiber 3D makes a long, thin tail or a midbodied fly, and the EP Fiber SE makes a thicker body with less material. The EP Sparkle Brush, Shrimp Dub Brush, and other brush materials are ideal for forming the front section of a squid pattern or making a crab fly. Enrico is truly a genius at developing many great materials and tying techniques to complement his materials.

Fluoro Fibre: This material is a cross between a flash and glow. Paul Reenen of South Africa introduced me to this material along with Kinky Fibre and other materials. Used inside translucent materials like Kinky Fibre, Fluoro Fibre, especially the hot orange or pink, produces a glow. Adding a few fibers to the wing or tail of any fly makes the fly glow. The material actually changes tone as it moves. It is also a good tail or wing material with great action. I think I started using this material in the late 1980s or early 1990s; it was Fluoro Fibre that made the Glow Squid possible.

EP Brush is an ideal material to form the head of a Glow Squid because it makes the fly look translucent. For the body of the Blue Lady, it can be shaped and then covered with a clear caulk to form an undershell. It adds bulk without weight, and you have many colors to choose from.

These are four effective synthetic wing and tail materials. From left to right: Enrico EP Fiber 3D, Farrar's Flash Blend, Kinky Fibre, and Flash 'N Slinky. Both Farrar's Flash Blend and Flash 'N Slinky are my kind of material because you don't have to mix flash with translucent material. These work well for Mole Nose Bunker, Mullet and Whitefish Snake Fly, or the Glow Squid. All four materials work fine for these flies, but I'm just lazy.

Fluoro Fibre material adds the glow to both the Glow Squid and the Barracuda Fly. It is also an excellent wing material for flies like the Bonefish Fry or for the tail of a Glow Sand Eel. This material is ideal for making small patterns or blended with other materials to make the entire fly. It will add luminescence to any pattern, even when using more natural colors like pink and light olive.

Kinky Fibre: Also known as Slinky Fiber, this material forms thick, bulky-bodied flies easily with less material, making even larger flies easier to cast. It's easy to work with, but if you store it improperly, you need to use heat to straighten the fibers to make it fishable.

Here's a tip to prevent flies with soft, light tail material like Fluoro Fibre or raccoon fur from fouling at the hook's bend: Tie in the tail material right at the hook's bend, wrapping the thread several times under the tail material. To stiffen wings or tails to prevent the soft material from wrapping, use a fast-drying glue such as superglue or five-minute epoxy on the first 1/4 to 3/8 inch of the tail's base. You could also put epoxy on the body to prevent tail wrap.

Flash: The shiny side of baitfish is what helps these creatures to blend together. A school of baitfish swims closely together to protect themselves from gamefish because no single fish makes a distinct target; they are just a flowing mass that parts as the gamefish attacks. Flash adds glimmer to a fly and can bring it to life. But flash can change in different lighting and is overused in some flies. I try to match the color of the flash to the fly's colors. Two universal flash colors are pearl and lavender, but shades like polar, shrimp, light blue, and light olive also blend with many colors. If the material is translucent, place the flash inside, or mix it into the material to produce a more subtle flash. I use several different flash materials that blend with many different flies. If a material is blended with flash, this allows one snip of the scissors to cut a wing or tail that saves time because it doesn't force you to cut both types of material, then blend them together. Holo Chromosome Flash, Holo Fusion, and Polar Flash blend with other materials and are ideal for bigger flies because they blend in and do not overpower the other materials. Krystal Flash, Angel Hair, Comes Alive, and Wing N' Flash work well with smaller flies because they add enough sparkle to the fly without overwhelming it.

In off-colored water or low light, bright silver or gold can help a fly stand out. This is also true with strong colors like red, green, or yellow. One way to find the right amount of flash is to start with a few strands, check the fly in water, and keep adding if necessary. Probably you will find that the first attempt is right, or even too much. Perhaps more than any other family of materials, flash can overwhelm a fly tier. I stick mostly with four to five shades that I feel give me the best-looking fly and then use a special color for a special application. One flash material I will never be without is Krystal Flash in pearl.

Place small sections of flash material between the layers of the wing or tail material or place the flash on either side of the wing or tail. If the fly has both a wing and tail, place the flash between the two. Place the flash in between the layers if the fly design uses several layers of material to form a wing or tail. Use

The material in the middle is pearl Krystal Flash, my favorite. The other two materials are Holo Flash and Chromosome Flash, and there are many more excellent flash materials. Many of these materials are interchangeable, and they work well for adding flash to most patterns. Remember, don't overuse flash—a small amount goes a long way. Both Farrar's Flash Blend and Flash 'N Slinky have a nice blend of flash mixed into the material.

a flash color that is close to the color of the material used to make the fly, or try adding a contrasting color for a different effect. Pearl flash blends with many colors and adds a darker shade when tied on top of white, cream, or tan. Tie the flash on the top or along the outside when using opaque materials. With translucent materials, mix the flash into the fibers. With synthetic materials, extend some of the flash a short distance beyond the tail to add action to the back section of the fly. When using natural materials like saddle hackle or ostrich herl, keep the flash inside the tail.

Hook Types

The main concerns when choosing the best hook are having the proper length and size for building a specific pattern, and having a hook strong enough for the species of fish you are planning to catch. If you are tying a fly with a new style of hook, be sure to test it first to check if the hook works with the fly's style—usually most standard-shaped hooks can be used on a number of patterns. No matter what hook type you use, make sure it's barbless. This makes releasing fish easier and increases survival rates, and if you hook yourself, your release will also go more smoothly and be less painful. I started fishing barbless in the early 1970s, and after hooking tarpon fairly consistently I have completely stopped fishing with barbed hooks—even when plug fishing.

I never recommend using a tandem hook system. The chance of deep-hooking a fish increases and removing hooks is much more difficult—it's not a fish-friendly fishing system. Also, I use stainless steel or noncorrosive hooks when making all flies so they can be used in both fresh and salt water. The Mustad 34007 has been a workhorse for me. With this hook I have taken a number of large fish, including tarpon and bluefin tuna. The 34007 requires sharpening and more maintenance than more expensive, sharp-out-of-the-box hooks like Tiemco or Gamakatsu, but it still catches fish. In recent years I have used both the Mustad C70S D and the Mustad C68S SS for smaller flies that require smaller, stronger hooks. The Eagle Claw 254SS is a good short, strong hook. For big flies the Gamakatsu SP11-3L3H is lightweight and strong. For a long-shank hook, the Mustad 34011 is popular. I still use an old standby, the Eagle Claw 66SS. It is strong for a long-shanked hook, but some materials can wrap around the tail. It works fine for the Pop-Hair Bug.

For building weedless flies, I like the Gamakatsu B10S Stinger Hook. It is ideal for adding a mono weedguard. You need to add a slight bend about ½ inch before the eye. With the right materials, it will ride inverted, but even if it rides point down, with a weedguard it works effectively in weeds. Also it is a fine hook right out of the box for bonefish and crab patterns.

The other weedless hook is a straight eye Gamakatsu Shiner Hook. The shape helps it ride with the point up on some fly designs, but this does not always work. I'm still testing to find a better system to make the fly perform properly, so these hooks are a *work in progress* for me. I will continue to experiment, but the initial performance looks favorable.

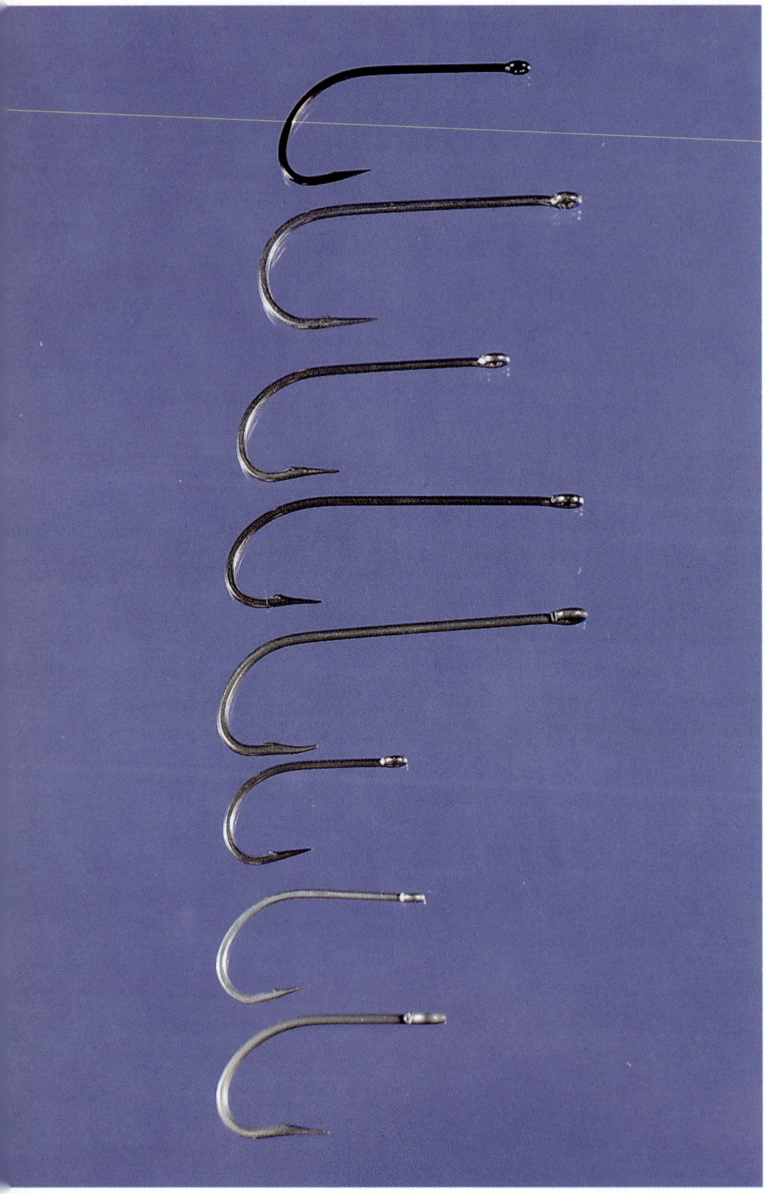

The choice of excellent nonrusting hooks available for the modern fly tier is endless. When I started making flies, there wasn't a good stainless steel hook on the market—we are so lucky today that in most cases we have multiple choices for any fly we choose to make. Choose a hook type and size to fit the fly's size and strength requirements, and also consider hook weight and gap size for better hook sets. I have mentioned different hook types for building my fly patterns. But this is only a suggestion—if you have a special requirement for a certain fly, select the hook that is best for the job.

Top to bottom: Gamakatus B10S Stinger Hook, Gamakatsu SP11 3L3H, Mustad 34007, Mustad 34011, Eagle Claw 66SS, Mustad C68S SS, Gamakatsu SC 15, Eagle Claw 254SS.

If you constantly fish for tarpon, big tuna, and other big, hard-pulling fish, evaluate your needs to choose the best hook for your fishing. The Gamakatsu CS 15 is a popular tarpon hook in larger sizes and is also ideal for smaller flies. Its shape is similar to the Stinger Hook, and in fact you could substitute it for the Stinger in the Winged Weedless Rat pattern.

Over the years I have used a number of different hooks. Some are no longer in production, but they still work. If you have old hooks that are in good shape, use them. It's a mistake to go out and buy new hooks because someone tells you only a certain type of hook will work for a particular fly. Except for special flies, most quality hooks work for general patterns.

Popper Bodies

Popper bodies come in different forms, from preshaped foam to cork to foam cylinders to foam blocks. Foam cylinders and preformed popper bodies are reasonably priced and require little work to produce a popper head. Some bodies, like foam cylinders, require one cut, and if you want you can hollow one end and you are ready to build a Pop-Hair-Bug. The predrilled bodies are even simpler: they have a hollow, cupped end, and the predrilled body lets you slip it right onto the hook shaft.

For most tiers preformed bodies are a smart choice. They are easy to work with and come in a variety of types, shapes, and sizes, and most anglers can alter the length or shape to build any popper. An excellent selection of popper building material can be found at Bear's Den Fly Shop in Taunton, Massachusetts; Complete Angler in Darien, Connecticut; or Eldredge Bros. in Cape Neddick, Maine.

For fly builders who want to cut their own popper bodies, foam blocks are available. Closed-cell foam used to build boats or surfboard foam is excellent. The best foam is ATC Core-Cell Foam, a hard, closed-cell foam that does not absorb water and is incredibly strong, buoyant, and fairly easy to work with. I got some after visiting Hell's Bay Boat Works and Action Craft. For poppers, nothing is better, but these foams are often hard to find and require much more time and effort than preformed popper bodies.

Bright colors are usually better—they are easier to see in choppy water or in low light. Color is often not an issue for the fish because most of the bug is above the surface, especially when you use a fast action. Fish strike at the silhouette, or target that is splashing on the surface, not homing in on a specific food source. Surface poppers create excitement and noise, and they often attract fish from many feet away.

If fish are following and being cautious, then using more lifelike colors might be more effective. Build a few bugs with layered color from a light bottom to a darker top. A good color combination for anglers who like to spend time painting is a lifelike bottom and sides and a bright orange top.

Preformed foam popper bodies come in many shapes and sizes. I use both a tapered and a straight body with a cupped front. The face should be about the size of a nickel, with some a little larger. Most of the poppers I use for salt water are 5 to 6 inches long from the front of the popper body to the end of the tail. When you are fishing fresh water, 3- to 4-inch poppers are ideal for fishing around weed beds or along shorelines.

A popper that floats straight and well above the surface will produce more splash. Note that the tail is fairly long compared to the body. This makes the bug track better. If you want a popper that dances from side to side, use a short tail or no tail at all.

Legs

Both Sili Legs and Crazy Legs work for shrimp and crab patterns to improve the looks and action and to help the fly sit on the bottom properly. Some tiers make patterns that use mostly these soft rubber legs to build flies. They create legs and claws on flats patterns, and many tiers use them. I am not a big fan of these legs, but I am working with them on several patterns I'm currently developing.

Eyes

Dumbbell eyes, either lead or pewter, add weight and realism to flies. The Sea Rat and Slab Fly series of flies use this type of eye—the weight stabilizes the fly. Small patterns, however, cannot use such a heavy eye, and gluing on an eye is difficult. Painting or drawing on eyes with a permanent marking pen is the best answer. Putting a drop of epoxy over the eye makes it come to life. I like large, plastic 3D eyes for squid patterns and big herring flies. Choose an eye color that contrasts with the fly's color so the eyes stand out. A red eye on a pink fly is often lost. Even if the eyes are stick-on, I prefer to glue them on with Goop. Monofilament melted eyes are ideal for small shrimp and crab patterns. Not only are they fine, lightweight eyes, but by altering the size and spread, they make claws on crabs or legs to stabilize a fly on the bottom.

Cements

One-minute, five-minute, and thirty-minute epoxy add a lifelike look to patterns designed for this material and add a durable finish on small flies like sand eel patterns. Epoxy is also the best glue to cement popper bodies to the hook shaft. For a big saltwater popper, use epoxy. When building a number of flies at one time, you can also use a small batch of epoxy as head cement for maximum durability. Superglue is easy to use for a head cement and to secure dumbbell eyes or thick amounts of materials to the hook shaft. You can also use superglue for stiffening the wings or tails to prevent soft materials from wrapping around the hook. Goop is ideal for gluing eyes on any pattern or to stiffen a section of material. It is a good glue to use for cementing foam popper bodies onto a

Stick-on eyes come in several sizes and are easy to use. Dumbbell eyes can be found in many sizes, weights, and colors. Make sure to match the size with your imitation. Squid have large eyes in relation to their size, while mullet have small eyes compared to their size. Other than squid that require an oversize eye, most baits should have eyes that stand out but do not overwhelm the fly. Keep weighted eyes light to make sure you can cast the fly if the design is sparse.

At the top is a clear caulking silicone I use for forming the bottom shell on the Lady Crab. In the middle is a glue called Goop that has thick consistency and is very strong. On the bottom is five-minute epoxy, used for building epoxy bodies. To the left is Super Glue, an ideal bonding agent for coating the tying thread after the fly is finished.

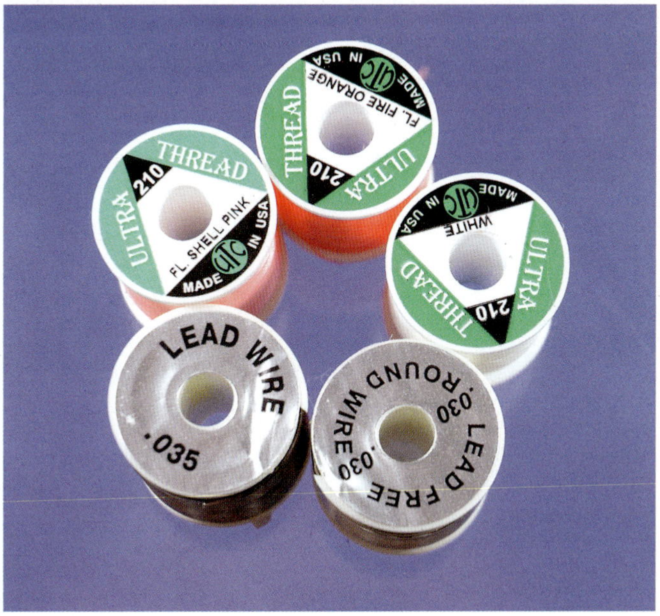

Here are three different colors of tying thread and two different wraps for adding weight. I prefer a stronger thread for most patterns so that I can apply the pressure I need to secure the materials without the thread breaking. For years I used the old square lead wrap, which has been replaced with round lead wire for adding weight to the fly. The lead wire comes in different sizes, and there is also a lead-free round wire. For the several flies I tie that require wire, I chose size .035. One spool builds many flies, and the wire is easy to use.

hook shaft. I started using this material in the plumbing trade; it's ideal for bonding plastic threads to metal threads. If it can withstand high water pressure, it will easily perform any gluing requirements for fly tying. Silicone is also good for stiffening the base of a tail or body and is easy to use. When using any of these products, read the labels carefully, and use them only in areas with enough ventilation.

Tying Threads

Most thread materials are fine for general fly tying. Two instances when a certain thread is important is when tying larger dumbbell eyes with a chrome finish to the hook shaft and when tying on large clumps of material. For these two functions, a flat thread is best—a hard, round thread is too smooth, and the eyes often slip. A round thread will spin body hair slightly better, but my choice is a flat thread with enough strength that it won't break under tying pressure. This is especially true when building big patterns. For tying small flies like bonefish patterns that require many parts, a lighter, round thread allows for more room.

Selecting Materials for Travel

Choosing a list of fly-tying materials for traveling is also a smart way to develop a box of important patterns that catch many different species in different locations. One effective way to select your most important flies, the go-to flies, is to think about packing fly-making materials for a trip where you plan to fish from shore. Let's say you need to put together a fly-tying kit to fish a new location without knowing the bait types. There might be half a dozen species of fish in a location, but you don't know which is hot. You have limited space, so you can include only the most valuable materials in the important colors. I have done this several times—at first you stuff bags full of materials but quickly run out of room a third of the way through the process. With limited space, only consider the best and most important fly types. Unless a specific food type is dominant and a special fly type and color is important, you can fish most locations with several types and colors of flies.

Anglers planning a bonefish trip to a destination with light-colored flats might think they need only materials to make small, light-colored patterns, but this is shortsighted. Bad weather or other conditions could require bigger baitfish patterns to fish for snapper, grouper, or barracuda. Having alternate plans can save a trip. A one-gallon plastic baggy holds enough material to make a number of different flies, from small crabs and shrimp to 6-inch-long baitfish. This bag adds little weight and takes almost no space in the luggage.

Several key colors will go a long way to building a decent fly arsenal. Light tan and off white are the basics for many bonefish patterns on light-colored flats. And these colors are important when blending different shades for baitfish patterns. Light olive, yellow, light green, and chartreuse are ideal for layering color in baitfish flies. Include some black, purple, brown, and orange if water conditions are off color or you plan to fish in low light. Material like marabou, ostrich herl, saddle hackle, and rabbit and fox fur add great action while taking up little space. Several chunks of deer body hair for spun heads and several small sections of deer tail, several types of fake fur, and several packages of Fluoro Fibre in pink, green, and hot orange will build dozens of patterns. Also bring several types of synthetic material in white, tan, light olive, yellow, and pink. If I could bring only one flash color and type, it would be pearl Krystal Flash.

Hook sizes 4 to 3/0 give a wide range of fly types and sizes—if I could carry only two hook sizes, they would be 2 and 2/0. To pack a small bag of materials for building just bonefish flies, include rabbit fur, marabou, fox and raccoon fur, fine deer body hair, and a small package of fine saddle hackles. Best colors are tan and cream with pearl Krystal Flash and hook sizes 6, 4, and 2. Throw in some small dumbbell eyes, and make up several dozen mono melted eyes. If you have special patterns that you like, add the materials to build these flies. The materials to build three to four dozen bonefish flies will fit anywhere and add no weight. Even materials to make bigger flies take little space and add practically no weight. If you choose materials wisely, you can make a number of useful flies while traveling and make a fun fishing experience better.

CHAPTER 4

Snake Fly

The key with the Snake Fly is its movement, breathing even when it's not being retrieved. In the water a Snake Fly becomes somewhat deflated, slightly smaller. The mixture of materials in the wing and tail slims down, but the head keeps its shape.

The Snake Fly is my go-to pattern. It has caught over twenty-five species of fish from Alaska to the tropics. When I need a fly that looks alive in many water types for fish from stripers to snook to brown trout to smallmouth bass, the Snake Fly gets it done. Also this pattern is relatively easy and fast to tie. I make a number of variations of Snakes from 2 inches to about 9 inches long.

You can alter the pattern—using different tail materials, wing types, and head sizes—to design a fly for many fishing conditions. If you need a buoyant fly, make the head bigger and leave it bushy. For a sparse fly, make the head small and trim it close. A tail of long saddles makes a lengthy, slim fly, or you can eliminate the tail and use a short marabou, ostrich herl, or fox fur wing to match small baitfish, worms, or shrimp. This is the ideal Southern pattern for redfish, sea trout, or snook.

The secret to this fly's action is the flared hairs in the head. A properly designed head of spun deer body hair vibrates and moves through the water, adding more action to the already active materials. When trimming the head of a Snake Fly, cut the bottom flat and short, and then taper the sides and top, forming a cone-shaped head with a flat bottom. Leave some long fibers toward the back of the head to enhance the action of the fly. When building the head, spin the back section with the tapered hair pointing back toward the fly's tail. Depending on the head size, these tapered fibers should extend back about ½ inch for a small fly to about 1½ inches for bigger flies. To make the head even more buoyant, spin on the deer hair, pack it, and then tie in another bunch of hair to make the head dense. With the exception of a surface slider (a fly that floats just on the surface), most of my Snake Flies have standard heads that are buoyant enough and are less time-consuming to tie.

My basic Snake Fly was built with an ostrich herl tail, a marabou wing, and a spun deer hair head. The combination of ostrich and marabou on the back of the fly with spun deer hair makes the fly move and breathe even when not being retrieved. Built correctly, the flies with larger heads should slightly nose up between pulls, and even while flowing across a current the fly has a swimming action—the tail never stops wiggling. The nosing up action is not as important if you are fishing a fast-sinking line and a short leader. If I'm using feathers, I like to vary the length of the saddle hackles when building longer flies. A good trick is to take a bunch of six to eight feathers between your

Although this pattern was built for saltwater fishing, it is also a fine pattern for many sweetwater species. A fly with active materials is versatile in many water types. On a calm surface, flies with materials that keep moving after each pull of the retrieve look alive even when resting on or near the surface. Fishing along the edge of lily pads for largemouth bass or casting to snook along mangroves or fishing for sipping stripers at night requires a fly that keeps moving long after the forward motion stops.

Spinning Deer Hair

I like to use spun elk and deer body hair for flies. The Snake Fly, then the Slab Fly, and the Sea Rat all have spun heads or collars. Over half the patterns in this book have spun body hair. Body hair performs many functions: The hair fibers produce waves, or movement in the water that adds action to the wing and tail materials. The hair fibers also make the head stable when using a weighted eye, and the buoyancy produces an ideal surface slider when using a densely tied head with no eye. With the right combination of materials, body hair will keep a fly suspended along the bottom or over a weed patch, preventing it from nosing in. It also adds a look that I like, suggesting the front portion of a baitfish or the head of a worm or eel. And spinning body hair on a hook, even in a tight location as with several of the Rat patterns is not that difficult once you get the hang of it.

Because you need to know how to spin hair for a number of the flies in the book, I will show you the technique in a little more detail here.

1. Cut a section of deer or elk body hair, and lay it onto the hook's shaft so the fibers are parallel to the hook shaft, with the tapered sections of the hair pointing back to the fly's tail. Make 1½ turns in the middle of the hair with the tying thread.

2. Continue wrapping the thread, adding pressure as you wrap to make the hair stand up. This should make the hair start to flare. Continue to wrap until the hair stands up. It usually takes three or four turns of thread to make the hair flare properly.

3. The finished flared head should look like this. With some heads I begin tying the hair closer to the butt section of the hair to make the tapered sections of hair longer.

4. For a thicker, denser head, spin on two sections of hair and pack them together by sliding the second bunch of hair into the first bunch. Leave space on the hook shank in front of the first section of hair to add a second or even a third section of hair if you want a large head. Add the extra section of hair and push it up against the first section. Be sure to pack the additional sections of hair to form a tight head.

5. Once the head is complete, the hair should flare, forming a circle around the hook with a flat front and hair sticking out the back of the circle. ■

One of several big rainbows I caught that could not resist a Snake Fly. This fish refused several other offerings until I tied on a Snake Fly. Just watching the fish's reaction convinced me that this was a valuable fly pattern. When a big trout becomes aroused and bolts upstream to crush a fly, you know it was the action that excited that fish into taking. A good blend of different materials creates a special action that can often make a fish strike.

thumb and forefinger and tie them to form a tail. This is a fast way to form the tail and will vary the way the feathers lay on the hook, giving the fly more action and more bulk. For thin patterns sometimes only two thin saddle hackles are enough to form the tail with some flash or several ostrich herl fibers. Long, thin flies work best when matching baits like sand eel and worms.

If I could fish only one pattern for the next five years, it would be a Snake Fly. Perhaps the only drawback would be fishing for bonefish, but with enough effort I might be able to design a Bonefish Snake. It would be a hard sell, although with some work it could fool bonefish. But for all other fishing the standard design of this fly makes it so effective.

I knew after seeing how Eric Leiser's Angus Fly breathed and seemed to exude life in the water with even the slightest movement that I had to build a simple-to-tie pattern with the same action. I don't remember how I came up with the pattern other than trial and error. I do recall my interest in both marabou and ostrich herl because they produced excellent action with little fly movement. The spun body hair head gave the fly shape, but I never envisioned it would add such excellent action. It took a few tries to develop the sequence of materials until the fly came to life.

This pattern is not difficult to tie and produces movement that never stops. I soon learned that the fly was adaptable, working in many fishing locations for both freshwater and saltwater fish. Everywhere I fished this pattern, I caught fish. And the more I use the Snake Fly, the more I learn about fishing it. I build them in a number of color combinations and I use other wing and tail materials, but the standard fly with an ostrich herl tail, marabou wing, and a spun body hair head is still a winner.

The Snake Fly is a great pattern in many fishing locations, but the first time I tried fly fishing a beach with heavy rolling surf, it was obvious that the flow was much different than any other water I had ever encountered. It was not just casting and retrieving—this water required finesse. Fishing Nantucket surf was my baptism by fire. I learned that basically you are fishing a constantly changing flow of water that varies both in speed and direction. And the flow can reverse direction, pushing the line right back up the beach. During that first week of fishing off Madaket Beach, I learned techniques like dead drifting, feeding line, and how to work the line and fly to swing with the flow, letting the power of the surf work the fly.

Fishing an outflowing wave off a beach takes timing. Cast as the wave flows down the slope of the beach and into the trough. The best technique is to pick the last wave of a set. Most waves develop timing called sets, with groups of three to seven per set. Pick the last wave and cast as the wave moves down the beach. If necessary, feed extra line until there is less pull on the line. Hold on until the force diminishes, and then begin retrieving using long, sharp pulls. Also try adding long pulls as the wave flows down the beach. Do not take in line, but give the fly action as it moves down the flow and into the holding water, the pocket, along the beach. The trick is to keep in touch with the fly as it moves through the trough. Keep trying different casting angles and vary the casting length until you get the right flow down the beach. Remember, nothing is set in stone because wave angle, size, and speed will vary—keep working the water until you develop a system.

If you try to fight the flow, you will lose. Heavy rolling surf is a section of water with no set rules—each wave, each location, requires thought and planning. The best advice I can give to beginning anglers is to do what I did the first few days: watch how the water moves and how each wave breaks and recedes. Watch for patterns that recur and then try to fish that movement. The whole trick is timing, getting the fly to flow down the beach with the wave while maintaining line control. It took time and patience, which was hard for an angler who thought he knew it all. The patience paid off with several nice-size fish and my first striper over 30 pounds from the surf. And I discovered that the Snake Fly's flowing action is perfect for fishing one of the toughest fly-fishing environments I know. Fishing big rolling surf with a fly rod is a humbling experience; move slowly, keep the casts short if the surf is broken, and most of all, be safe.

Flies for this fishing should be 5 to 7 inches long and dark if the water discolored. Even when the water is clear, in big surf a dark fly will stand out better in the white water. In smaller surf if a certain bait type is along the beach, try to match that food type in size and color. The fly was also effective in Alaska for salmon, char, and Dolly Varden. In water with little or no movement, a medium to fast retrieve works best. Depending on the water types and conditions, an intermediate or fast-sinking fly line is the best way to fish this fly. In a decent flow with 4 to 6 feet of water, I prefer an intermediate line, but unless the flow is slow, the fast sinker works best in water over 6 feet. In a fast flow, I'm going with the fast-sinking line.

The Snake Fly is also an ideal surface slider fished with a floating line. This fly works, from fishing along shorelines and lily pads for largemouth bass, or trying to entice snook around dock pilings, or along soft rolling beaches to enticing stripers sipping small baitfish on the surface. No matter how slowly the fly moves, it continues to have action. Even sitting on the surface, the fly never stops breathing. No other fly I have used has ever come close to taking the number of different species of gamefish that the Snake Fly has.

Build Snake Flies from 3 inches to 7 inches long with the body size and shape to match the food source you plan to copy. A thin fly will match a sand eel; a chunky fly would be for mullet. I tie them in any color or combination of colors. I build them with different materials for the tail and wing, but the head is always spun deer or elk hair. Vary the head size to match the bait or fishing conditions. If you want a more buoyant fly, make the head thicker. When adding flash over the tail or wing, choose any of the different flash materials. If you want to add a glow, mix some hot Fluoro Fibre into the wing.

STANDARD SNAKE FLY

Hook:	#1/0 Mustad 34007
Tail:	Chartreuse ostrich herl with optional Holo Fusion flash
Wing:	Marabou plume feathers with optional flash
Head:	Spun deer or elk body hair
Eye:	Dumbbell (optional)

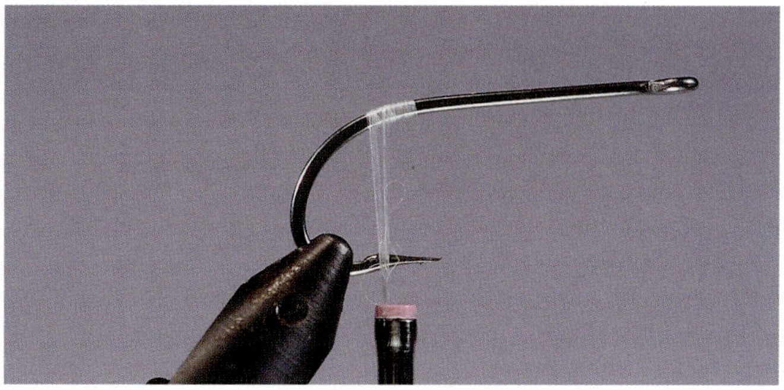

1. Choose a hook to fit the fly size, anywhere from 2 to 2/0 standard length stainless hooks. If the head is thick and bulky, use a larger hook for a better hook set. Start with the tying thread at the hook's bend.

2. Tie in a bunch of chartreuse ostrich herl 4 inches long for the tail. This is a midbodied fly matching a spearing—use enough ostrich herl to produce a tail of about $\frac{3}{4}$ inch wide. In the water this will reduce to a profile of about $\frac{1}{2}$ inch.

3. Tie a small section of Holo Fusion, about a dozen fibers, over the tail. The fibers should extend to the end of the tail.

4. Tie a single chartreuse marabou feather over the tail material for the wing. It should extend about halfway to the end of the ostrich herl, matching the tail in bulk. I like using several shades of the same color to vary the body color. In this case the wing is lighter in color than the tail.
For flies with thicker bodies, use two large feathers tied one over the other. When you are tying longer flies, the wing will not extend as far because marabou feathers are not that long.

5. Form the head with chartreuse deer or elk body hair. Make sure you tie in the hair with the tapered ends facing the fly's tail. Spin the hair on the hook shank by forming a bunch of hair around the shank and wrapping over the bunch three times with the tying thread, and while applying pressure, making another wrap. Try different numbers of wraps depending on the material's bulk and stiffness until it spins on easily. The hair should spin and flare around the hook shaft, forming the fly's head. Tie off the head and coat the thread with superglue.

If you're spinning body hair for the first time, use softer, thinner material and try spinning several heads on a bare hook before building a working fly. This is a technique that requires a little practice, but once you learn it, spinning body hair heads is fairly straightforward. Slightly stiffer, larger fibers are best for big heads. Most standard Snake Flies work best with one bunch of body hair fibers matching the head size to the body size.

Remember that stiffer fibers are more difficult to work with. For some of my smaller flies, I like small, soft fibers, but if I'm tying a bigger head, I tie in several bunches of body hair. The back portion of the head, the tapered fibers, forms a hood over the base of the wing. When you are using longer body hair, the flared hairs will lay back over the wing.

6. Trim the head by cutting the bottom flat and tapering the top and sides to form a cone-shaped head, leaving the longer fibers that lay back over the wing of the fly. These flared body hair fibers that form the head send waves back to the wing and tail materials as the fly moves through the water.

To add an eye, spin on one bunch of hair, tie in the eye, and then spin on the second bunch. An eye will make the fly either neutral density or slightly nose heavy.

7. Close up, side view of trimmed head. Note that the head is tapered and the back of the head has tapered body hair that extends back to give the fly more action.

8. Front view of a properly trimmed head. The top of the head is round and the bottom is trimmed flat to leave the hook point open for better hooking quality.

Four different color versions of a standard Snake Fly. This pattern permits many color combinations using either a mixture of different colors or any number of solid colors.

CHAPTER 5

Sand Eel Snake Fly

An underwater photo of a Snake Fly Sand Eel. Sand eels are thin baitfish. The profile of this fly needs to be almost pencil shaped, with a body that moves but does not flare. The tail should move some, but the fly must remain thin.

I developed this fly when first fishing stripers in shallow water during the day. Stripers can be picky in clear water of 4 feet or less—when they get into 2 feet, they can become downright difficult. I tie this fly as a thin Snake Fly for fishing some locations but also have trimmed down flies for certain conditions. The first fly was actually a standard Snake Fly that I trimmed down when fishing a grass flat in Pleasant Bay, Cape Cod. Stripers were nosing sand eels out of the grass bed in about 2 feet of water. By trimming the fly down, I made it less buoyant and I could fish it above the grass using a floating line.

Once I started building these flies, I modified the heads, coating them with superglue on some flies so they would sink at different rates. Then I can fish the fly with a floating line on shallow flats or use the fly with an intermediate line when fishing the edges of flats that might be 4 to 6 feet deep. Putting on glue is no science; use trial and error to get the proper sink rate.

I planned to have enough flies when fishing different flats to have the right fly with the proper sink rate when I needed it. Only a few locations required the perfect fly, which would remain at the same level with a slow retrieve. Building a dozen flies would produce four that are ideal, sometimes more, but the other flies were still fine fishing tools. Again I stress using water for testing flies to get the proper action and sink rate when building special flies.

This fly also can be used when fish are feeding around schools of sand eels and on open flats. Where a precise presentation is unnecessary, building this fly requires much less care and testing. As a basic sand eel pattern, it is effective, but in tough-to-fish conditions when a certain sink rate is important, this pattern shines.

When sight-fishing shallow grass flats, use a floating line with an 8- to 9-foot leader. Unless the conditions are ideal, spotting fish and determining if they have taken the fly is difficult. You will have to hook fish mostly by feel, and at times it's guesswork. Most often, the only way to spot fish is by the tip of a tail, a fin, or any surface activity. If you believe that fish are on

Cape Cod Bay and Pleasant Bay are two ideal locations to find stripers in shallow water. The many flats around the Cape offer excellent access and two types of water. On Nantucket Sound tides average about 3 to 4 feet, but along Cape Cod Bay the tides range 8 to 12 feet. There were many different flats to fish, and during the prime years, the fishing was exciting.

the flat, try making short casts and fishing the fly blind. This is a good technique to use with a wind chop that hides the landing noise. On a calm day, watch for any movement, and get the fly to the spot. If you feel any slight bump or see water movement near the fly while retrieving, make a long strip. This is tough sight-fishing because there's no visible shadow and the fish blend with the grass.

For most sight-fishing conditions on sand flats in 2 to 3 feet of water, use a floating line with a 9-foot leader. Getting the fly in front of the fish quickly is important. The pickiness of the fish will determine the best retrieve. If the fish are hot, keep the fly moving. They will sometimes swim to the fly and take—that's the ideal outcome. If the fish are difficult, let the fly drift or move it once to get their attention. If fish are in groups or schools, usually a steady retrieve is best. Stripers get picky when they are overfished in shallow water, and they can drive anglers nuts.

Along deeper edges in the 3- to 5-foot range, seeing the take is more difficult. Use an intermediate line with an 8- to 9-foot leader, and try to lead the fish enough to intercept the fly. If there is current and the fly is not close enough to the bottom, they will swim right under the fly and never see it. Usually fish that first move onto a flat will take a fly well up in the water column, but once they have spent several days feeding in the shallows, they mostly look for food along the bottom. The primary food on most flats in New England is sand eels, which often hide in the bottom. Even when the baitfish are schooled up, stripers often pick the dead and crippled baits along the bottom. Fishing under or on the edge of the thick schools of baitfish is the best chance for hookups. Casting into the middle of thick schools of baitfish often doesn't work—too much competition.

If the fish are nosing along the bottom, choose flies that settle faster. I always have several flies that sink quickly for conditions that require more depth. Even on shallow flats, fish often take a fly right off the bottom. Stripers that move onto flats on the first part of incoming tide are looking for dead baitfish. These fish are often more aggressive. One trick to try is placing the fly 8 to 10 feet in front of the fish, let is settle to the bottom, and give it one twitch as the fish nears the fly.

You can make this fly with a variety of different materials, but they must form a tail and body that has a thin profile. Both ostrich herl and marabou add too much thickness to this style of fly. If the sand eels are larger, they might work, but I want a fly that has a thin profile to match the early spring sand eels.

SAND EEL SNAKE FLY

Hook:	#4 Mustad C68S SS
Tail:	Blend Holo Chromosome with a Bird Fur feather
Wing:	Small bunch of arctic fox fur
Head:	Light olive or tan fine deer or elk body hair

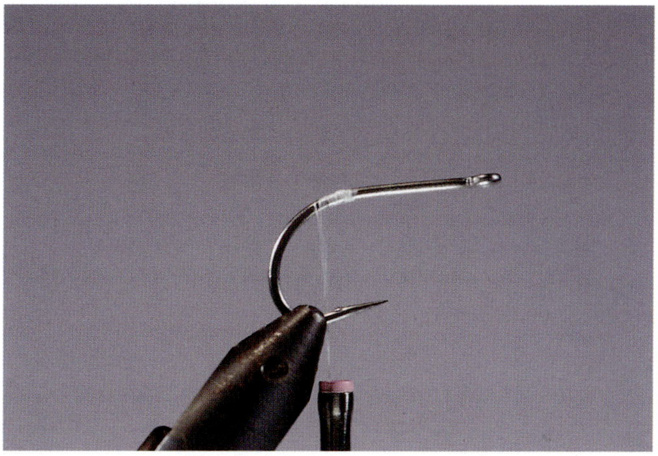

1. Use a size 4 Mustad C68S SS and tie in the thread at the hook's bend. This hook style, a rounder shape, requires the tail to be a little farther away from the hook's bend. You can also use a standard length stainless hook up to size 1.

2. For the tail use a thin, yellow Bird Fur feather (or thin saddle hackle) about 3 inches long, tied onto the hook shaft just back from the hook's bend.

3. Over the Bird Fur, tie on a thin section of Holo Chromosome the same length as the tail. Another possibility for the tail is olive Fluoro Fibre and Holo Chromosome on bottom with purple Fluoro Fibre on top.

4. For the wing tie a small clump of arctic fox fur just ahead of the tail, extending about one half of the way back to the tail—keeping the fly sparse.

5. Next, spin a small section of fine body hair—keep the head small. Tie off the head and coat the thread with superglue. Early season sand eels are often 3 to 4 inches long and very skinny. Keep the fly's length 3½ to 4½ inches long.

6. Trim the head so it is not very buoyant. Also coat some of the flies with a light glue or head cement to make the fly sink slowly. Depending on the fishing location, I want flies with different sink rates from slow to slightly buoyant. This pattern can also be a mixture of other colors. But the main focus is keeping the fly thin.

CHAPTER 6

Worm Hatch Snake Fly

An important feature of this fly is that it rides on the surface, leaving a wake, like the worms it matches. Even though the fly is small, make the head about half the hook shank in length. This produces a fly that stays on the surface. The size is important—the worms are small (2 to 4 inches), so keep the fly less than 4 inches in length. In locations with daytime hatches, the color is important—at night it is less significant. The marabou gives it the tail wiggle that makes it look alive.

This fly was easy to design. Fishing a worm hatch can be an experience. The spawning of the *Nereis* worm, called cinder worm, is an event that takes place in different locations throughout New England in and around estuaries. This hatch also occurs on flats in Florida where it's called the palolo worm. These hatches are fickle and take place only when conditions are right, usually on a warm night with calm conditions and stable weather. Stormy weather disrupts hatches.

Fishing a hatch one night, I needed a small topwater fly with decent action. I cut the ostrich herl tail off a Snake Fly and presto: I had a fly that matched the small cinder worms swimming on the surface. I had used Muddler Minnows in the past but was not carrying one that night. Out of ineptitude a pattern was born. I altered a small Snake Fly, my original pattern, by building a fly with a marabou tail and a head of spun deer body hair.

One effective fishing technique is keeping the pattern on the surface to produce a surface wake. If fishing the surface does not work, try letting the fly swing just below the surface. From day to day and hatch to hatch, the fish might feed differently, but keep trying different levels until something works.

In heavy hatches fish often sip along the surface rather than singling out a target. This fishing can be frustrating because fish are busting all over but you get few hookups. When the fish are selecting a target, then getting the fly in front of a fish is important, but if the fish are cruising, try casting to intercept the fish. The best scenario is when the fish take up feeding stations, holding like trout in a stream. Here you can work on a fish that is feeding by seeking out each piece of food, not randomly eating. The key is to drift the fly right to the fish. Get upstream from the fish and keep letting the fly swing to the feeding location.

Since you are often fishing at night, you'll have to feel for a soft take. Use a floating line and shorter leader. I like about a 5-foot leader. This takes some of the guesswork out of fly placement and gives more control. In the dark, fish will not see the line, and usually worm hatches take place in locations with discolored water, further disguising your line.

Another useful technique is casting straight downstream to a feeding fish, holding the rod high and dropping the fly back to the fish. The worms are mobile, so a true drift is not important. Keep watching or listening for the take. In some locations there might be enough light to see the take. In early morning light, this can be fun fishing; on a dark night, you need to detect the take by feel and sound.

On some nights when there are too many worms, try fishing a larger fly below the surface using an intermediate fly line. Fish the fly fairly fast with a stop-and-go retrieve. It's not as fun as fishing on the surface, but it's still worth a try. This is often

This is an orange Worm Hatch Snake Fly without the peacock herl nose. Note how this fly also sits right on the surface.

In some back bay ponds in New England, hatches occur during the day. This Rhode Island pond had spawning worms in shallow water. In some cases you can sight-cast to cruising fish. I always carry a few worm flies for events like this.

the case with a heavy hatch. But even if you don't catch fish, look forward to the next night. The night after a heavy hatch will have fewer worms and sometimes three times the number of fish. The nights following a heavy hatch can be hot fishing.

Worm hatch fishing requires patience and some luck to hit the hatch on a hot night. In some locations, plan to lose a lot of sleep. Serious worm hatch anglers often take on the appearance of a raccoon with dark puffy bags under their eyes, trying desperately to get through the day to fish another night.

WORM HATCH SNAKE FLY

Hook:	#2-4 Mustad 34007
Tail:	Orange marabou
Head:	Orange spun elk body hair
Nose:	Peacock herl (optional)

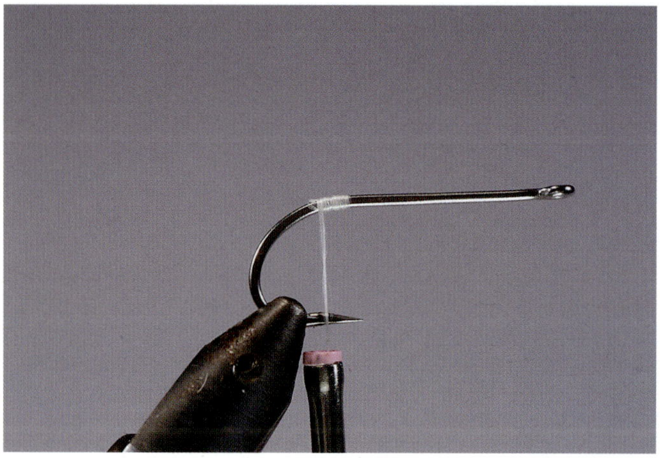

1. Tie in the thread at the hook's bend.

2. Tie on small, orange marabou feathers for the tail. (Red or black are also fine.) The tail should be about 2 inches long and about ½ inch wide.

3. Spin fine-fibered orange elk or deer body hair to form a head. Make the body about ¾ inch long, stopping short of the hook's eye to leave ⅛ inch for the nose. Use a second bunch if necessary to build a larger head. Depending on the quality of the material, sometimes one bunch is enough.

4. Tie in a section of peacock herl just in front of the head to make a nose.

5. Wrap on the peacock herl, tie it off, finish wrapping off the head, and coat the thread with superglue. Adding a nose is probably not necessary, but it looks like the real thing.

6. Trim the head close to form a wormlike body and head. Leave some longer body hair fibers over the tail. Most worms are less than 3 inches long.

CHAPTER 7

Long Saddle Snake Fly

The long saddle hackles make this fly ideal for matching longer baits. They give the fly great action, and for its size, the fly casts well, even in longer lengths. Eels are a favorite food for stripers, as are sand worms. Both these baits swim actively at night. A good choice for color is orange, black, or dark blue and green.

Sometimes, a long, flowing-action fly is the best choice. The American eel is favorite striper bait and an excellent food source to copy. Along outer beaches thin plugs 7 to 8 inches long are popular with spin anglers copying needlefish or larger ocean sand eels. These baits are long, with a flowing action that matches the snakelike swimming movement of the eels.

Many gamefish feed on many types of long, thin baits. The key to mimicking them is creating the right tail movement plus a flowing body. This pattern lends itself to many options from a thin fly to a long body about an inch thick. To match baits up to 7 inches long, I use a standard Snake Fly, but over that length the Long Saddle Snake Fly is a better choice. Depending on local food types, this fly works well in many colors from all black to a mixture of light olive and pink on top with a light underside. I like to make some in bright colors like orange, hot yellow, or chartreuse.

Most fly sizes for this pattern range from 8 inches to nearly a foot long. Flies 10 inches and over require larger rods and good casting skills, unless the fly is very thin. Sinking lines are better suited for casting any large pattern because they give more line speed with less rod speed and cut through the air much better. When casting any big fly, using slower rod speed is a better technique with any line, in fact. One problem with casting bigger flies with a sinking line is that the line generates greater line speed. This is fine when casting smaller flies, but with big patterns a fast-moving loop tends to open too quickly. When the loop opens, the cast stops. A loop with too much speed will open before carrying out all the running line. With sinking lines and big flies, slower loop speed often gives better casting distance and puts less pressure on the body. A slow-moving loop drags the big fly through the air while carrying out more running line. A slower loop opens slower so it tends to pull more running line out the rod tip before turning over.

The original Snake Fly's length was restricted because even long ostrich herl could not compete in length with a long saddle hackle like the ones used on this fly. Some saddle hackles are over a foot long, and feathers from the right neck can produce long flies with great action. I prefer using thin feathers, and if the fly needs to be thicker, I use more. Thin feathers produce more action if they are tied at different angles, not married together. I do not have a favorite color, but for matching an eel, a mixture of black and blue with a cream to yellow bottom is close. I have caught fish along beaches with flies that were all yellow, orange, and blended colors, but I think it's the fly's action that makes it deadly rather than the color.

Along beaches I usually fish this fly with an intermediate line and a 4- to 5-foot leader, using a medium to fast retrieve. The only time I use a longer leader is during the day in clear water. Work the holes and drop-offs, letting the fly move with the flow, using a steady retrieve. In small surf keep moving down the beach, covering pockets along the beach, and if possible fish the outer bars. In locations with smaller holes, you can often reach the outer edge. Fish the fly right through the hole, bringing it from the edge of the outer bar to the shore-

Here is a nice striper that I took on a Long Saddle Snake Fly while fishing the rips off Nantucket with Capt. Bob Luce. When fishing big water like this rip, larger flies are often necessary. In late summer into the fall, ocean sand eels move into offshore rips. The baits are longer and thicker compared to inshore sand eels, some above 8 inches in length. The Long Saddle Snake Fly is an ideal match for these baits in both length and action.

This nice pike ate a fly with long, barred orange and pink saddle hackles. The best way to fish for pike in most locations is to cover as much water as possible and keep casting. This is why many anglers fish bigger rods like 9 weights to make longer casts with bigger flies.
DAVE SKOK

line. With enough wave action, the flow in the hole along the shoreline is a good holding spot. Cast at different angles to the flow, working the fly with long, sharp pulls. In bigger surf use short casts and time the waves flowing off the beach so the fly keeps flowing into the roll outside the first wave. Fish the flowing water with this fly as I described in the section on beach fishing with a standard Snake Fly (page 60). In low light or at night, try a slower retrieve with soft pulls, letting the fly dead-drift between pulls.

Fast sinking lines and short leaders are the best combination in bigger, deeper flowing water. In offshore rips, cast quartering downcurrent, working the fly with long pulls so it swings across the flow. Also try casting straight across the current or even up, working the different angles to the flow. If you need to get more depth, let the line and fly sink before retrieving. In a drifting boat, begin the drift above the rip line, cast a little upcurrent, and let the line and fly sink for at least the count of 10 before starting the retrieve. Use a fast retrieve with long, hard pulls. Getting the fly to swim down and across the flow and then turn up makes it look like a fleeing baitfish. That action can even excite fish that are holding on the bottom.

Pike fishing has become more popular in recent years. Several friends that fish for pike thought that the design of this fly, with its long flowing tail, would take these great gamefish. Dave Skok, Boston-based fly-tying extraordinaire and great friend, is a serious pike angler. His favorite color combination is chartreuse and orange with gold flash, 8 to 10 inches long, tied on a long-shanked hook. Dave is looking for bigger pike, but if you are looking to catch a variety of fish including small and largemouth bass, then go to a 6-inch fly.

For pike fishing most anglers use a floating line with a 6- to 8-foot leader and a 12- to 18-inch bite guard to fend off the teeth. Pike like to hold along shorelines, weed beds, and in holes. The fishing near home in Connecticut is mostly river fishing. However, lake and pond fishing requires moving the boat. When drifting a river, you must keep casting to cover more water. Lake and pond fishing is usually a slower pace. Keep casting into shore and using long pulls to move the fly out from the bank. The local locations where I fish have mostly discolored water, so you can't spot fish. I can imagine fishing a clear location where you could spot the fish and see it rush the fly. But even seeing the wake behind the fly is a rush.

Other color possibilities are to mix in some flash to match the fly's color and try making some glow flies by adding hot pink or hot orange Fluoro Fibre between the tail and wing if you are using lighter colored materials. Tie in the Fluoro Fibre first so it lies under the wing. Make the wing bushy with two large marabou feathers. The heads should be larger if using a 2/0 to 3/0 hook because of the greater hook weight. If you want a larger head for larger flies, spin on three sections of body hair and pack it tight. If you are making a fly to match a needlefish, though, the wing and head need to be sparse. Trim the spun hair tight to form a head that is sleek with few hairs sticking above the wing.

LONG SADDLE SNAKE FLY

Hook:	#3/0-1/0 standard stainless steel
Tail:	Long furnace saddle hackles and optional Polar Flash
Wing:	Two large, dark olive marabou feathers
Head:	Dark olive deer or elk body hair
Eye:	Dumbbell (optional)

Note: There are many possible colors for the tail: all black, all yellow, and light olive, or try mixing colors like pink, orange, and yellow. I like some flies to have barred-colored hackles.

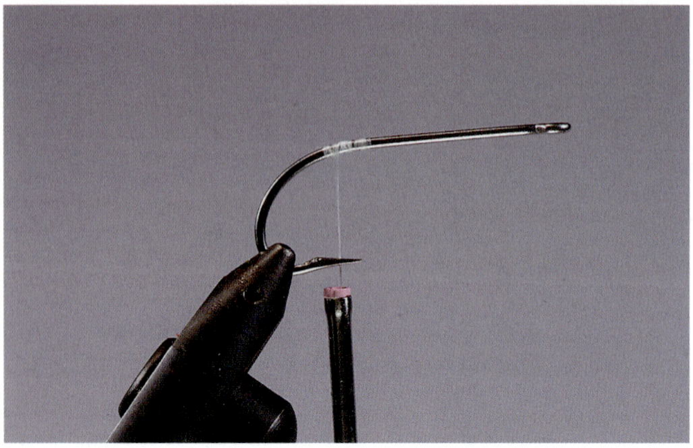

1. Tie in the thread at the hook's bend.

2. Tie the furnace hackles at the bend of the hook, extending back about 5 inches. Furnace hackles are black in the center with light yellow edges and look similar to badger hackle. Tying any long feather, I often pinch six to eight saddle feathers of varying length between my thumb and forefinger and tie the bunch of feathers on the hook shaft. If cutting the feathers from a neck, spin the bunch between your fingers so they are not all lying in one direction. This will position the feathers at different angles to the hook shaft. Use this technique any time you tie on four or more saddle hackles. It's a fast, easy way to tie in a tail, and the feathers will usually lie on the hook in a cluster, giving the tail more action. If you want flash, add it on top of the saddle hackles.

3. Put in the two dark olive marabou feathers next, tying them together on top of the wing. This should give a wing of about 3 inches. Leave enough room if you plan to use two sections of body hair for a larger head.

4. Spin in a section of dark olive body hair. Place it between the base of the wing and the hook's eye, remembering to keep the tapered hairs facing toward the tail of the fly. Be sure that the head is thick.

5. Spin in the second bunch of body hair, if needed, in front of the first bunch to finish the head. If you have good quality body hair, one bunch usually gives the right size head. If you are adding an eye, tie it in front of the first bunch of spun body hair, and then spin in the second bunch of body hair and push the hair so it packs against the eye. Tie off the head and coat the thread with superglue. Some tiers might find it easier to tie in the eye first and then spin the body hair to either side of the eye. Both techniques work—just pick the system that works for you. I seldom use eyes on Snake Flies, though.

6. Trim the head and the fly is finished. If you are using an eye, be sure to trim around it so it is visible.

Here are a few different color variations of Long Saddle Flies.

CHAPTER 8

Mullet and Whitefish Snake Fly

The Mullet and Whitefish Snake Fly has both the shape and color I was looking for: a round shape with a blend of colors like the light greenish blue and pink that mullet and whitefish have. Using a core of light pink hackle feathers and natural Holo Fusion flash with a shell of Flash 'N Slinky made the fly look alive. Both the inner flash and shell are a light green-blue, producing a mixture of color that matches other baitfish. A bonus is that the blend of materials not only gave the right shape but also enough action.

Mullet are a major baitfish from New Jersey south, and the fall run of mullet along the Atlantic Coast, especially the east coast of Florida, makes for excellent fishing. Whitefish are found in many freshwater lakes, streams, and rivers, and juvenile whitefish provide a food source for many freshwater gamefish. Anglers who target big trout with streamers are often matching small baits like whitefish.

Flies matching whitefish give anglers an excellent opportunity to take nice-size trout. Once trout grow to a certain size, they often look for larger meals such as small baitfish or juvenile gamefish. In some waters even 14- to 18-inch trout will attack a large fly that looks like a small fish. Spin anglers use 4- to 5-inch swimming plugs that match the young of these shiny gamefish to catch big trout in Western rivers, and trout often take the fly aggressively there. By using bigger flies, I can do the same.

With all this in mind, I wanted a fly that would look like both a finger mullet and a small whitefish. Both fish look similar, with the same body shape and color, and a number of other small fish resemble them. With one fly and several different lengths, you could produce a good match for many different food sources in both fresh and salt water. A standard Snake Fly would work, but I wanted something more realistic, particularly for fish like trout and snook that can be picky in hard-fished locations. Mullet live in many different places, and most bays and inland waters are loaded with them. They range in size from finger mullet 3 to 6 inches long to adults over 3 pounds. The small ones are a favorite food for many gamefish.

Along the east coast of Florida during the mullet run, fish often feed just outside the first wave. Work the fly with a floating or intermediate fly line in the flow off the beach. Snook roam the first wave, and sometimes you can sight-cast to them. Cast the fly to intercept the fish so the fly swings and turns near the fish. A baitfish that appears to be fleeing from a gamefish will often draw a quick strike.

When you're fishing in backwater locations, retrieve the fly with different speeds, covering as much water as possible. When sight-casting, present the fly so it moves across the fish's path or away from the fish. Remember, baitfish do not swim toward gamefish. If sight-fishing along a beach, use an 8- to 9-foot leader, and for snook you need at least a 40-pound section of fluorocarbon leader 12 to 18 inches long as a rub guard. In bigger surf if the flow off the beach is strong, use a use a fast-sinking line with a 4- to 5-foot leader.

Although this fly was originally designed for salt water, it has become my favorite trout streamer. Here is a brown, one of five big trout that Chauncey Goodrich and I caught on this fly one afternoon from a small stream in western Wyoming. We both fished other patterns, but the Mullet and Whitefish Snake Fly was by far the best fish-getter.

Along calm beaches and up inside bays and coves, you can fish this fly along weed beds, over the edges of bars, and along mangroves, where Southern gamefish hold. Try a steady retrieve, but also use a stop-and-go retrieve so the fly bolts and then pauses along the edge of structure. Cast across the flow so the fly swings and then turns upcurrent. Along a calm beach, sight-fishing can catch fish. Walk along the beach, keeping about 20 feet from the water's edge. Look for fish that are cruising in the trough along the beach. Often fish follow a pattern, traveling in one direction. But keep watching both up and down the beach in case fish are moving in both directions. Getting the fly in front of the fish is important, and these fish are often looking down. I like an intermediate line with a 9-foot leader and fish the fly with short pulls. Try two different approaches to see which one works. If a fish turns and swims toward the fly, either stop the retrieve and let it drift or try making several quick pulls as if the food is trying to escape. Fish the flow along any edge or a flow that dumps into deeper water. Dead-drifting the fly using long pulls without retrieving is an effective way to fish. Use this pattern to cover water, as you would with a standard Snake Fly.

In trout streams and rivers, cast across the flow and swing the fly downcurrent using a darting action. This is a good way to fish at the head of a pool with a decent run. Try fishing at different angles to the flow, getting the fly to swing near rocks and along ledges. Fishing the fly straight down the flow using a fast retrieve is also effective, even in small streams. Another fun technique is casting upcurrent and then mending the line down the flow. This allows the fly to swim straight downstream and then swing and bolt up the flow. Cover as much water as possible because sometimes trout will not move far to take a fly. In bigger, deeper water, sinking lines are best, but in small water, floaters are also effective. The trout version of this fly in lengths of 3 to 5 inches could also match spearing or smelt.

The fly's shape creates a rounder, fuller body. Mullet and whitefish are round, chunky baitfish, ranging from 3 to 5 inches for finger mullet to 10 inches for bigger baitfish. The hackle forms a center with the Holo Fusion and the shell of Flash 'N Slinky creates a rounded body that matches the shape of both baitfish. This style of body works well with other blends of materials, making a full-bodied fly you can cast.

You can also use synthetics in the center, mixing in materials like Metz, Holo Fusion, EP Fiber, or Ultimate Fiber with Flash 'N Slinky as an outer shell. Be sure to taper the tail to match the shape of the baitfish. The saddle hackles form a basic taper, and often you don't need to trim the outer shell.

MULLET AND WHITEFISH SNAKE FLY

Hook:	#2/0-4 Mustad 34007
Tail:	Four light pink saddle hackles and natural-colored Holo Fusion
Wing:	Natural Flash 'N Slinky
Head:	White and gray
Eye:	Dumbbell (optional)

Note: Add a lightweight dumbbell eye between the bunches of hair if an eye is desired. I seldom use eyes on any Snake Fly because the eye changes the action.

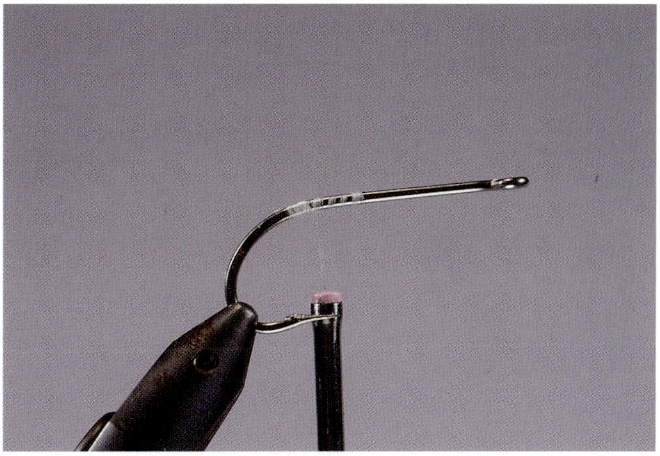

1. Tie in the thread at the hook's bend.

2. Tie in four light pink saddle hackles about 3½ inches long at the hook's bend, keeping them fairly uniform. (Use more for larger flies.) This is one time I try to match saddle hackle because the feathers need to stay in a tight bunch to prevent them from separating the outer shell. I have had fine fishing using light pink saddle hackle for trout.

3. Tie in a thin section of Holo Fusion on top of the saddle hackles about the same length as the saddle hackle.

4. Next, take a section of natural Flash 'N Slinky, and form it around the tail about the same length as the other material to create a shell over the Holo Fusion and saddle hackles. Use only a light coat of material. The Flash 'N Slinky might blend with the hackle feathers, but most will remain outside the feathers. You can also use natural Steve Farrar's Flash Blend.

5. For the head, spin white elk or deer body hair onto the hook shaft just in front of the wing. Be sure that the tapered hairs are facing backward.

6. Spin on the second bunch of gray body hair in front of the white body hair—most flies built for salt water need two bunches of body hair. Trout flies work fine with one bunch, but in this case I use a two-color head for the trout fly to show how the bigger fly for salt water would look. All white is a good choice, but also try gray and white. Tan is another effective color. This pattern is a whitefish imitation for trout. The fly is about 4½ inches long with a 3½-inch tail.

7. Trim the head to form a bullet shape with a flat bottom.

CHAPTER 9

Slab Fly

Many years ago I needed a pattern to match bigger, wide-sided baits, so I designed the Slab Fly, a fairly simple tie with a wide tail and a head that is flat on the sides and thin from the top view. This shape can produce a slight wobbling action if the head is large enough and the hook is not too heavy. However most Slab Flies remain upright during a slow retrieve. Using long, hard pulls with a brief pause in between is the best retrieve. But the key to this fly is the shape that matches flat-sided baitfish.

I got my biggest striper from the surf with the Slab Fly. The fish inhaled the fly while holding behind a gravel bar in Pleasant Bay on Cape Cod; it was 48½ pounds and over 52 inches long.

The October morning was still dark when I started fishing the shoreline below the weather station on Morris Island in Chatham. It was the last hour of a falling tide, but the water in the Bay would continue to flow out for several more hours. I had found fish holding in that location the morning before. I expected a fish on each cast but began to wonder if the fish had moved with the tide when I didn't get any takes. Just then a fish took the fly. Expecting a big fish, I was so keyed up that I landed a striper of about 20 pounds without the fish even reaching the backing.

In the gathering light, I noticed a rip line and hoped that it would hold fish. Casting above the rip, I kept swinging the fly over the bar and into the drop-off. On one cast I let the fly swing a little longer, and the line tightened. Unlike the first fish, this fish bolted off, smoking line, and I needed to almost run to keep pace as it headed down the flow. I knew I had room to fight the fish, but as it kept powering down the flow, a moored boat to the south came into view, and I needed to make a stand. Well below the bar there was a back eddy; that saved me. Using sideways pressure, I worked the fish into the eddy. The weight came off the fish because it moved into slower-flowing water, and I could gain back most of my lost line. Once I got the fish near shore, it made another run, but it had spent most of its strength on the first run. Working the fish back in again, I used only moderate pressure. I knew the fish was mine to lose, as long as I didn't make a mistake. It made several more short bolting runs, but each time I used soft hands to steer the fish back to shore. As the fish turned into the shoreline, one quick pull put the fish on its side in 6 inches of water. I quickly grabbed it and dragged it onto the beach. Only then did I realize the fish's size, a lifetime fish, and there was the Slab Fly firmly hooked in its jaw.

At the time the Slab Fly was my largest pattern, designed to copy a large, flat-sided baitfish. There were large numbers of menhaden in the bay that week, although the fly I fished was much smaller than the adult baitfish. Even so, that morning it fished big and fooled the best striper of my life. The new tying materials of the last fifteen years have helped to generate bigger, easier-to-cast patterns, and better rod designs and improved fly lines have made casting larger flies easier.

This was my first big-fly creation that tried to simulate baits like herring, alewives, and menhaden. Casting a fly that is even half the size of some adult baitfish is difficult. The only way to sell big fish on a fly that is in some cases not even close to the size of food they are feeding on is adding action to the pattern. It was only after I built the fly that I discovered it had a slight wobbling action. If you tie the Slab Fly properly, it tends to roll slightly because the deer hair head is flat and wants to turn on its side. I designed the head that way, though, to match members of the herring family. The rolling action was an unexpected bonus.

What makes the Slab Fly great is its ability to catch big fish when they're feeding on big baitfish like menhaden, even though the fly is not even close in size to these baits. I have taken some big fish in different waters with this fly—none as big as this striper, but I still marvel at the Slab Fly's ability to catch big fish.

Surf Fishing

Never wade too deep when surf fishing. Waves can roll up the beach on one side and come down behind you out of nowhere. And never turn your back on the surf—it will bite you every time.

One piece of equipment that makes all fly fishing easier is a stripping basket. Fishing in rolling surf would be next to impossible without a stripping basket; the trip to Nantucket reinforced the value of fishing with one. It allows for better line control and keeps the line from tangling. Also a basket prevents line from being washed away or wrapped around your legs or feet. I started using baskets even when fishing in fresh water in the 1960s, way before they were fashionable. Now fishing without a basket, even in easy conditions, would be a substantial handicap for me.

In heavy surf, a fast-sinking line works best because it does not get pushed around as much. The thinner diameter line and heavier weight keeps the line tracking better. An intermediate line is my choice for small to midsize surf when fish are holding in the drop-off in 1- to 3-foot surf. Both snook and stripers like to cruise right off the beach in small surf, and sight-fishing is possible. Here the combination of an intermediate line, a longer leader, and a Snake Fly is a sure winner. When I'm covering water, blind casting the surf, I like a shorter leader unless the water is clear with ample light. Even when you're not sight-casting, if you can see the fish, they will see the fly line with a short leader. One combination that works well for fishing over oyster bars, grass beds, or broken bottoms is a buoyant fly with a longer leader. I build some Snake Flies with bigger heads. After each pull, they will nose up with a 9-foot leader. This setup with an intermediate fly line is ideal for fishing deeper flats in the 4- to 8-foot range.

Rolling surf is one of many locations where the Snake Fly is effective. The Snake Fly is ideal for any moving water, salt or fresh. Cast at different angles to the flow and vary the retrieves from slow to fast. Mix up the retrieve length using both short and long pulls. One smart technique when fishing outflows from shore is casting to different angles of the current, letting the fly swing across the flow without retrieving. Try this technique at night if fish are holding in the flow waiting for food to spill out of the estuaries. Many trout streams and rivers have similar flows, and the same techniques also apply to other species. Many different species like stripers and snook often feed this way. As the fly flows across current, keep adding pulls but do not take in any line. And let the fly drift at times, adding no movement. The Snake Fly's makeup, its ability to breathe and move without a retrieve, gives the fly a lifelike action like a baitfish or shrimp drifting with the current. ■

This fly is built to fish with a sinking fly line and swing across the current. As the line begins to straighten, use long hard pulls to make the fly swing, turn, and dart upward, looking like an escaping baitfish. Also try different speeds and different lengths of pulls to give the fly a darting action. The fly's natural buoyancy will cause it to nose up and bounce, looking crippled. I have used it mostly as a striper pattern, but I'm sure it would work on any fish feeding on flat-sided baits.

When fishing a rip above a drop-off, get the fly to swing into the pocket, work it so the fly flows through a section, and then add hard pulls to bring the fly toward the surface. I also use this technique when fishing fast offshore rips, but it is ideal when fishing from shore. Depending on the depth of the drop-off and the flow's speed, I use either an intermediate or a fast-sinking fly line with a leader of about 4 to 5 feet, unless I'm fishing clear water and bright sun. When fishing water under 5 feet with a modest flow, use an intermediate line. Stand uptide of the bar, and cast at about a 45-degree angle to the rip. Start with a shorter cast, and then keep making longer casts to fish all the water carefully. Try some casts along the bar, and even try casting above the bar. Get the fly to swing and then dart toward the surface like a feeding baitfish. The design of the Slab Fly is ideal for this action because it should kick and bolt on the swing and rise up in the water column.

The Slab Fly is a useful tool for fishing along jetties. Fish the edge of the rocks, working the fly close to the structure. Often there is a current, so let the fly swing with the flow. Keep the casts short unless bars are out from the jetty; in that case, cast to the bar's edges and fish the pockets that form between the bars. Often these locations hold fish. However, the structure along the jetty is the best holding water. Fish often cruise the rocks, looking to pick off baitfish holding in the structure. Short casts are effective and give the best line and fly control. Some days along a jetty, I never cast over 30 feet. Fish the flow along the jetty, and cast quartering down the flow and retrieving with short pulls. As the fly swings near the structure, let it hang there for several seconds. Strikes near a jetty are often slow and feel like a weight on the end of the line. Never pick the fly quickly from the water. Lift slowly and make another cast. Fish jetties with bad footing from several easy-to-reach locations, and let the fish come to you. I work a spot for several hours as long as there is a flow. Where the jetty meets the beach is a hot spot on low incoming tides. One trick to remember when hooking a big fish from a big jetty is that when the fish first starts to run, get to the beach quickly and start moving up the beach away from the jetty. Every big fish I have landed from a jetty ran away from the structure. Only after they finish their first run do they head back. If you get enough distance from the rocks, they never make it back.

I make this fly in several different sizes and many different color combinations. The first flies were about 6 inches long with a body of mostly white bucktail with a pink bucktail back and peacock herl on the top and a white spun deer hair head. That's the one that appears in most pattern books. You can tie smaller flies with either a marabou wing or a wing of ostrich herl and a spun body hair head.

Tying On Dumbbell Eyes

1. With tying thread cover the hook shank and attach the eyes using several wraps of thread over the bar between the eyes.

2. With your forefinger straighten the eye so it crosses the hook shank at a 90-degree angle and add enough wraps to hold the eye firmly.

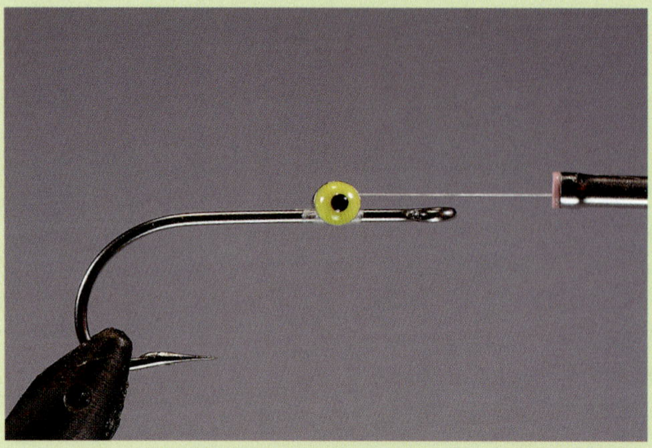

3. Start wrapping the eye with thread at different angles, crisscrossing the wraps.

4. Continue wrapping thread over both the eye's bar and the hook shaft, locking the eye in tight.

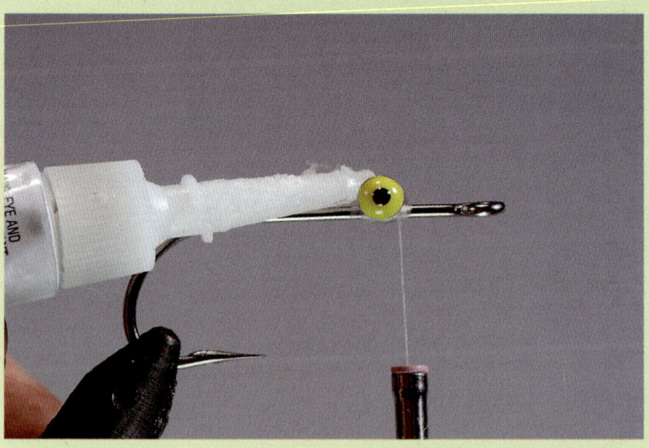

5. Apply superglue to the base of the eye for added strength. ■

This striper took a Slab Fly along a jetty with only 20 feet of fly line out the tip. Though I always fish this fly on a sinking line because it keeps the fly tracking so well, I plan to experiment, fishing it with a floating fly line. With a floating line, sometimes the fly swims on its side, perhaps looking like stunned bait swimming on the surface.

SLAB FLY

Hook:	#4/0 SP11-3L3H Gamakatsu
Tail/Wing:	Long, white and pink bucktail and peacock herl
Eye:	Pewter barbell eyes
Head/Shoulder:	White deer or elk body hair

Note: The eye should be tied on the top of the hook shank between the hook's bend and the hook's eye.

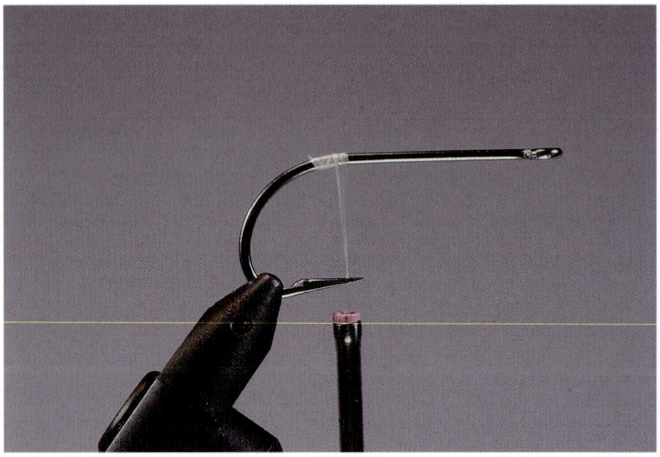

1. This is a large fly, so use a 4/0 SP11-3L3H Gamakatsu hook, and tie in the thread at the hook's bend. For flies 3 to 4 inches long, use a 1/0 hook.

2. Tie in the first part of the tail with a section of long, white bucktail at the hook's bend. The tail should be about 4½ to 5 inches long, about as long as the bucktail fibers. Use thinned bucktail (see page 43). Tie in the hair so it is encompasses the hook shank, tying with enough pressure to hold the hair. The long, thin bucktail helps create a fly with better action. For small flies, use marabou or synthetics for the tail and wing. I like a heavy marabou tail tied with two feathers using the same head as the larger fly but smaller to fit the hook size.

3. Tie in a second smaller bunch of thinned white bucktail on top of the first section, again using enough pressure on the thread. The first bunch gives the second bunch a better holding location to lock onto the hook's shaft.

4. I put a drop of superglue on any large section of bucktail to lock it to the hook. In this case I'm locking both bunches of bucktail to the hook shaft.

5. Then layer thinned pink bucktail over the white bucktail tying it right in front the first two sections of white bucktail. Run the thread over the first two sections of bucktail, locking the pink bucktail on top of the two bunches of white and tying the base of the bucktail onto the small section of the hook shaft. The glue should still be tacky, locking the bucktail and giving an even better bond to the hook shaft.

6. Tie in about a dozen peacock herl strands over the bucktail. The bucktail and peacock herl make a tail and wing combination. For smaller patterns use marabou or ostrich herl, or try natural Flash 'N Slinky or Steve Farrar's Flash Blend. Run the tying thread over the hook shaft in the eye's location to give the eye a base.

7. Add another drop of glue to the tail. Most materials do not require gluing, but bucktail is tough to bind when in larger bunches. The base of the hair is large and almost spongy, so it slips off the shaft even if the shaft is coated with thread.

8. With tying thread, wrap the pewter barbell eye to the hook about a third of the way from the hook's eye, halfway between the hook's eye and the base of the tail.

9. To form the back section of the head, spin in one section of white elk or deer body hair between the tail and the eye. The tapered ends of the hair should point toward the tail.

10. Spin in the second section of white body hair in front of the eye, forming a large head. If you need a third section of hair, add it to the front.

11. Trim the head hair to form a flat-sided, wide-profiled head with the tapered hairs on the back section of the head forming a collar over the tail and wing. The head does not need to be perfectly smooth. The main concern is that the head is flat on the sides. And be sure that the eye is clear of hair fibers.

12. Side view of head. The flat head along with the fly's wide tail produces a pattern with a wide shape that looks like a herring or bunker.

13. Note the flat-sided head in this front view. This gives the fly a large profile with less bulk.

The top Slab Fly is a smaller version with a marabou tail, the bottom is a standard Slab Fly with bucktail for the tail. When fish are feeding on small menhaden, also called peanut bunker, shorter patterns are the right choice. This smaller version will also have more tail action because marabou is much more active than bucktail.

CHAPTER 10

Badger Sand Eel

The Badger Sand Eel is simple to make. Using thin badger saddle hackle on the fly, shown here in a pond on Cape Cod, gives it the thin profile that matches inshore sand eels. Saddle feathers have great movement even with a slow retrieve, and matched with the right flash, they make the fly appear to move even when it's motionless.

This fly is a direct descendent of a Lefty's Deceiver. I wanted a sand eel imitation that was thin, not buoyant, and easy to tie. Sometimes, the only way to catch fish in thick schools of sand eels is to get the fly under the schools of bait. Fishing in sand eels can be frustrating, with fish busting all over but few takes. During times with too much bait, gamefish often binge-feed rather than strike a target.

One way to take fish is to work the fly under the schools of bait, targeting the fish that are picking the dead and crippled bait near the bottom. Try working the edges using an intermediate fly line, and move the fly close to the bottom, adding short hops to make it look like it's wounded. Also try casting into the breaking fish, letting the fly and line sink and the fly swim and flutter like a dead or crippled sand eel. Start counting once the line hits the water to try to determine the right depth so the fly drops below the school of bait and flows below the competition.

This fishing takes patience. It is against most anglers' nature to fish a fly slowly near the bottom when fish are crashing the surface, but this is often the only way to catch fish. Along with an intermediate line, use an 8- to 9-foot leader. If you have enough light, make a close cast, watching how long it takes for the line and fly to reach the bottom. Count the seconds and be sure to take more time so the fly reaches below the school. If there is any current, make the cast straight down or quartering down the flow. This will keep the leader straight and help detect strikes. When working a slow retrieve, or a stop-and-go retrieve, make a long pull if you feel any resistance. The takes might be subtle because the fish are not feeding on a moving target.

Also try letting the fly and line sink, and then use foot long pulls like a stunned baitfish trying to regain its equilibrium. Try casting away from the thick schools of bait, and retrieve to keep the fly moving. In this way you are targeting fish before they reach the thick bait. Sometimes these fish take a single target before they begin binge feeding. A fast retrieve excites these new arrivals. Fish that have too much food can be picky and are often not aggressive feeders. Bigger fish tend to be lazy, feeding on the dead baits, and this gives you a better chance to hook a nice fish.

Sight-fishing is perhaps the most rewarding way to take fish. When you place the right pattern in the path of a fish in clear, shallow water and it locks onto the fly, watching the take is exciting. Big bonefish like this one are difficult to take in shallow water. The key is getting the fly in front of the fish without spooking it. In some cases moving the fly too much or using too much speed on the retrieve can spook fish. And whether it's a nice bonefish like this one or a big striper, fly selection can be critical. I do not know if this pattern will take bonefish, but it is effective on stripers.

This pattern works well for sight-casting. Follow the information about sight-fishing the Sand Eel Snake Fly (see pages 66–67). Both flies match thin foods like the sand eel and other small baitfish. Tied with three or four thin hackle feathers, this fly is an ideal match when stripers are picking small sand eels in clear, shallow water.

This fly is easy to tie. Tie it in any combination of colors and alter the body size to make it fit your needs. For general fishing, work the fly at different speeds. Get the fly to bolt through the water, and then let it settle slightly, using longer pauses between strips. Use this technique with a sinking line in 4 to 6 feet of water with a flow or in flat water in low light. When fished with a floating line and a steady retrieve, it flows near the surface. When you're sight-casting with a floating line, this fly will sink faster than the Sand Eel Snake Fly. When you're not fishing thick schools of bait, this pattern, like the Snake Fly, is ideal for prospecting.

BADGER SAND EEL

Hook:	#2 Mustad 34007
Tail:	Two to four thin badger saddle hackles and strands of Holo Chromosome
Body:	Pearl Krystal Flash
Wing:	Polar bear
Eye:	Plastic stick-on eyes or painted eyes (optional)

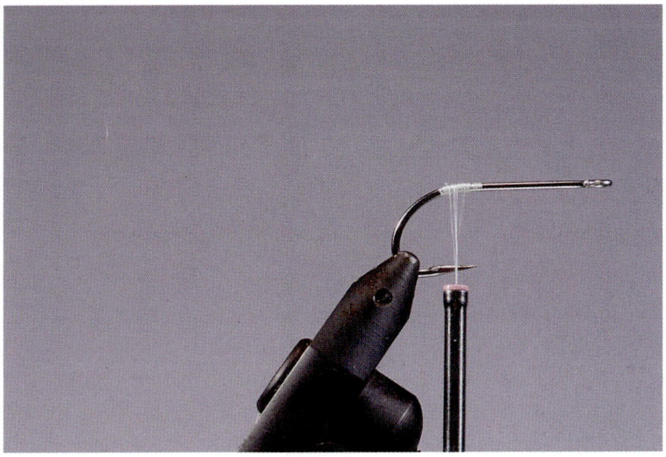

1. Tie in the thread at the hook's bend. This is a size 2 Mustad 34007, but you can use standard stainless steel hooks up to size 1/0.

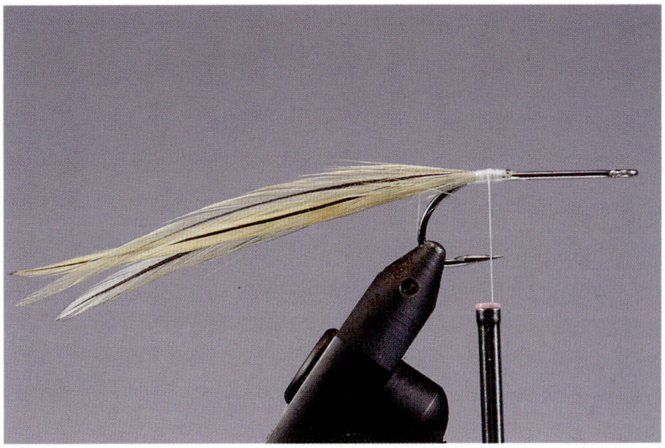

2. Tie the badger saddle hackles at the hook's bend, selecting only enough feathers to keep the tail thin. Make the tail $2\frac{1}{2}$ to $3\frac{1}{2}$ inches long, which will produce a finished fly of about $3\frac{1}{2}$ to $4\frac{1}{2}$ inches long.

3. On top of the saddle hackle, tie in enough strands of Holo Chromosome flash to maintain a thin profile.

4. Tie a small bunch of pearl Krystal Flash in front of the wing base and wrap the thread to the hook's eye.

5. Wrap the bare hook shank with pearl Krystal Flash, stopping about ¼ inch from the hook's eye.

6. Tie in the polar bear hair for the bottom wings near the hook's eye, extending just past the hook's bend.

7. Tie in the polar bear for the top wing, keeping it low. Both wings should be thin with a low profile. For the wing, you can use light tan, pink, or light green Fluoro Fibre, polar bear, or fine bucktail. The wings can also be trimmed marabou or a light marabou plume. I'm still lucky enough to have a supply of polar bear hair, which makes a tight wing. The fibers do not flare like bucktail does, keeping the fly's profile thinner. Fake polar bear is a fine substitute and is easy to find.

8. Basically, this is a very thin Deceiver. You can glue on small eyes with Goop or use a permanent marking pen, placing the eye on the tying thread next to the hook's eye. Most of my Sand Eel Flies do not have eyes. The key to this pattern is a thin profile.

CHAPTER 11

Mole Nose Bunker

The Mole Nose Bunker is basically a Lefty's Deceiver modified with a larger, wider tail and a spun body hair nose to make the fly swim slightly nose up. Larger flies, 11 to 12 inches, are possible but casting becomes more difficult and often requires an 11- or 12-weight outfit. You can cast a 9-inch version of this fly even with a 9-weight outfit, but an 8- to 9-inch fly with a 10- to 11-weight is a better choice. I changed the original design of the tail section of this pattern using the Mullet and Whitefish Snake Fly technique after having success with that fly. This fly is effective because its size and shape mimics herring and menhaden, it casts well, and it has excellent body movement.

I wanted a pattern bigger than the 6- to 7-inch Slab Fly to match large herring and Atlantic menhaden. Trying to build a bigger Slab Fly made the head too large, affecting the hooking qualities of the fly—too much material around the hook bend makes hooking fish difficult. Also the Slab Fly's length is restricted because bucktail is only so long, and even decent bucktail 5 inches long is hard to find. I could have used other materials for the tail, but it was easier to build a new pattern.

With the Mole Nose Bunker, I could make the head bigger, and the bucktail wings will collapse when the fish strikes, making a better hook set. The Slab Fly's design would not allow for a larger pattern, but the Mole Nose Bunker has no such restriction. Both the tail and the wings that form the head can be longer to create a longer fly with a flowing action that is easier to cast. The top and bottom wings plus the nose of the Mole Nose Bunker make the fly somewhat buoyant. Depending on the amount of bucktail and the size of the nose, the fly's head will wobble either nose up or nose down, looking like a stunned baitfish. A slow retrieve accents this action. But remember, adding more buoyant material to the fly also makes it harder to cast. Using longer tail materials gives good action and allows you to build a fly of over 10 inches long you can still cast. I make most flies in the 8- to 9-inch range, which are easier to cast; bulky flies over 10 inches long might be tougher to cast.

I fish the fly with either an intermediate or a fast-sinking fly line. The fast-sinking line is much better for casting distance or casting into the wind. If you need to get the fly down quickly, heavy sinking lines are more effective. When fish are holding along the bottom in big rips, a fast-sinking line is the best tool. With this pattern, you will not get the penetration that is possible with longer, thinner, less buoyant patterns.

The Mole Nose Bunker is a shallow to middepth fly effective for fishing rips to 15 feet deep. It also works well along beaches with small surf, and along shorelines with rock and pockets. When fishing along beaches and shorelines with small wave action, cast the fly at different angles to the shoreline to cover the water. Mix up the retrieve speed by using mostly long pulls to make the fly bolt and then pausing so it looks like a crippled baitfish. For most of this fishing, use an intermediate line; the only time I use fast-sinking lines is when thick schools of bait are along a shoreline with deeper pockets where I need

When river herring move back into open water, big gamefish look for these large baits. This is the time to fish big herring patterns. After spawning in the spring, the adults begin to flow out of their freshwater location back to the sea. This occurs from early spring to summer depending on the location–the early returns are in Southern waters. Their average size, about 8 to 10 inches, makes them a favorite food of big stripers in the Northeast.

Casting Big Flies

Casting bigger flies requires a different approach and different techniques. Big flies and popping bugs add drag to the fly line and slow down the cast. Most anglers try to compensate by adding more rod speed during the cast stroke, but more line speed with a bigger fly makes the loop open faster and usually shortens the cast. Instead, slow the casting stroke down and open the loop slightly, letting the cast flow out with less speed. Follow this technique particularly when casting a fast-sinking line, which will often shoot out quickly, causing the loop to open prematurely, with the leader and front section of the fly line landing in a pile. The longer the loop takes to open, the farther the cast will travel and the better it will turn over. Also, lengthen the casting stroke and hold the line on the rod tip, the front section of the rod, longer during most of the casting stroke. Begin the forward casting stroke behind your head, and push it forward so your casting arm extends well out in front of your shoulder. During the forward casting stroke, rotate your body so you use your whole body to throw the cast.

One other trick is to slowly close the wrist during the forward casting stroke. Turn your wrist over, but be sure not to break it, which opens the loop. This helps to keep the line on the front section of the rod tip longer. Most casters close the wrist right at the end, which is OK for most casting situations, but when throwing bigger flies, heavy rods, and heavy lines, it slows everything down. Holding the line on the rod tip for a longer period gives more loop control and a smoother cast.

A slower casting stroke requires less strength and is less tiring. When I was a 30-year-old construction worker, I could cast a big rod all day and not think about proper technique, but now I need every advantage. Watching the rod tip and backcast during the casting stroke helps you use your body. You should transfer your weight from your back foot to your forward foot during the forward cast. The backcast should be the reverse of the forward cast, rotating your body around backward and throwing the loop behind. I don't extend my arm straight back like some casters do, but by using a full body rotation, I get the same effect with more control.

I have always preached how important it is to use your whole body when making a fly cast. But one day while fishing with a guide in Florida, I found an excellent example that taught me something. I was standing on a small casting platform in the bow of a boat. My casting was off. I was rusty, but the bigger problem was I couldn't use my body because with my feet close together I could not rotate. I never realized how much my casting stroke relied on body rotation until I could not do it. Fly casting, like any other sport, requires you to use your entire body. Forearm and wrist casting is fine for short casts with small flies, but you better be strong and have perfect timing if you're casting that way with big flies and 12-weight rods. The key to casting big rods and big flies is to slow down the casting stroke, use full body rotation, and keep the fly line on the rod tip as long as possible.

You also need the proper equipment to cast big flies. Fast-sinking lines and the sinking-tip lines are the best choice for this application. I like the fly line's head to be about 28 to 30 feet long with a longer back taper and an intermediate running line. A longer back taper allows you to extend more line outside the rod tip, which means the cast will take longer to turn over, producing more distance. Choose an intermediate line with a short front taper and a weight-forward head of about 30 feet long.

Many of the high-tech rods are too fast—too stiff for most casters handling rods 10 weight and above. One way to dampen a fast rod is to increase the line weight. For years I have advised anglers to overline a rod to make it cast better. To the chagrin of several rod manufacturers, I often overlined the rods I fished with. Most rods will cast one line size, or even two sizes, above their recommended line weight. Overlining will change a tip-casting rod to a midflex. This gives the caster more feel, improves timing, and makes the rod slower and less tiring. Unless you're fishing in water that is clear with bright sun when casting big, wind-resistant flies, use leader lengths of 4 to 5 feet. ■

to get down. In those situations, getting under the bait might be the only way to take fish.

This fly is ideal for fishing inside estuaries when river herring are first leaving their freshwater spring spawning areas. Many locations are tiny creeks that spill into the backwater of small bays. Often these bays and small river systems are not deep, 10 feet or less. Intermediate fly lines are ideal for most shallow water. When these baits first drop back into open water, they are easy targets for big stripers. Fish the estuaries where rips form around the bogs or flows that run into open water. Also look for channels with good flows, and fish the edges of the bars.

These are ideal locations for fishing from a boat. Anchor up and work a spot, casting along a bar that drops into deeper water. Cast either quartering upcurrent or across the flow, fishing the fly on a swing, using long pulls. On a falling tide, gamefish will start feeding inside the estuary and keep moving with the flow as the water drops. They often continue to look for food until reaching the mouth as the water slacks. In some places there might be on-and-off fishing for several hours.

These big baits also spill into larger bays and rivers. One famous run is the Herring Run that flows into the west side of the Cape Cod Canal several miles west of the Sagamore Bridge. Many of these locations have a variety of different water types. When you're fishing along the Cape Cod Canal and other similar waters with a steep drop-off and fast current, a fast-sinking fly line is the best tool. Cast at different angles to the flow, let the line sink, and use a fast, hard retrieve to make the fly settle, swing, and then bolt to the surface.

For shore fishing locations like rips from a point or along a drop-off, cast at different angles to the flow and vary the retrieve. Here, dead drifting, adding long pulls while letting the fly swing with the flow, is an effective technique. Focus on getting the fly to swing with the flow and looking like a struggling baitfish. Use an intermediate line in areas with shallow bars and holes of 4 to 7 feet. Many larger back bays have shallow areas where these baits hold for several days to a week before moving into open water.

This pattern is useful along any outer beach with runs of herring or Atlantic menhaden. Menhaden, also called bunker, are large baits. Adults can reach over 3 pounds and up to 16 inches long, with most adults 12 to 14 inches long with a deep body. From shore, find a point with a rip or a strong enough flow between an outer bar and the shore, and keep fishing it until the flow slows. Cast at different angles to the flow, trying different retrieves from fast to slow, and mix it up using pulls of different lengths. If a swell is running, fish the fly to flow down the beach and swing into the trough off the beach. Follow the surf-fishing instructions on page 60. Even in open water with little flow, I like using long, hard pulls with a pause in between so that the fly darts slightly, looking like an injured bunker. Sick or wounded menhaden appear to be disoriented, swimming nose up or sometimes in circles.

When you find gamefish attacking schools of bunker, try fishing near the bait, letting the line and fly sink, and then work the fly so it looks like a baitfish struggling to rejoin the school. Gamefish often pick out a crippled fish for easy feeding. This is when a fast-sinking line is best for getting the below the school of bait. Big stripers often feed under schooling baitfish, waiting for easy picking as the sick baits drop below the school. When big bluefish are hitting schools of big baits, stripers are often below cleaning up the pieces. This is one reason chunk baits fished on the bottom catch fish. If you see striper action below a school of big baits, your fly should attract attention.

MOLE NOSE BUNKER

Hook:	#4/0 Gamakatsu SP11-3L3H
Tail:	Long, white saddle hackle, Holo Fusion, hot orange Fluoro Fibre, and natural Steve Farrar's Flash Blend
Body:	Orange Crystal Chenille
Wing/Head:	Pearl Krystal Flash and bucktail
Nose:	Spun deer or elk body hair
Eye:	Glue-on, 3-D, soft plastic eyes (large)

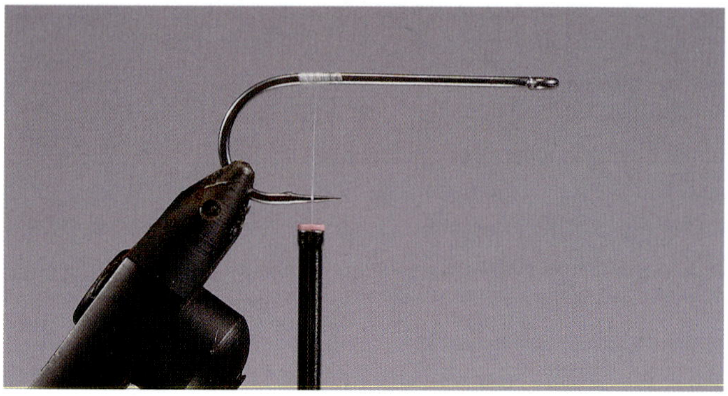

1. Tie in the thread at the hook's bend.

2. Tie in three or four white saddle hackles about 5 inches long at the hook's bend.

3. Tie a section of Holo Fusion on top of the saddle hackles, making it about the same length as the hackle feathers. Make the tail 7 to 8 inches long, which produces a finished fly that is around 9 inches long.

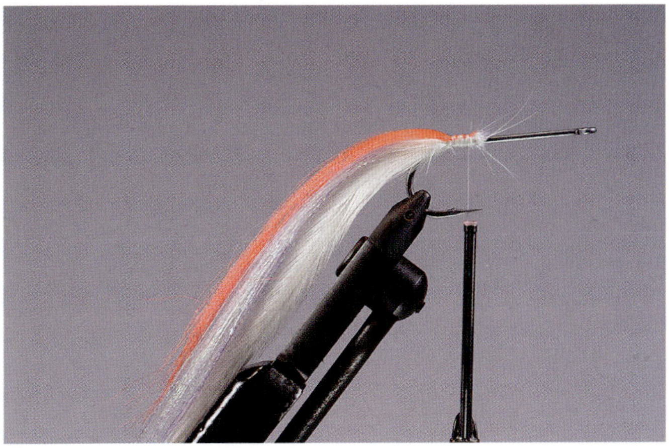

4. Next, tie in hot orange Fluoro Fibre on top of the existing wing. You can also use a more subtle color like light green or pink. To save time, you can tie the Holo Fusion and Fluoro Fibre onto the hook shaft together.

5. Tie a large enough section of natural Steve Farrar's Flash Blend (or a blend of Flash 'N Slinky) to form an outer shell over and around the existing tail materials. The outer shell needs to cover the inner tail materials. Be sure to form a nice coat over the saddles, Fluoro Fibre, and Holo Fusion. If you need to do this outer shell in several steps, tie in the bottom first and then the top. The inner materials should be visible through the outer shell. The outer shell should extend about half an inch past the inner tail.

6. At the base of the tail, tie in orange Crystal Chenille (or Crinkle Flash pink or orange) to form the body.

7. Wrap the Crystal Chenille around the shaft, stopping about a third of the way from the hook's eye. Remember to leave enough room to tie in both the bucktail wings and spun body hair nose.

8. Before adding the top and bottom wing, tie in some pearl Krystal Flash to both the top and bottom of the fly so it extends back about 1½ inches beyond the hook's bend. This flash creates a back wing behind the bucktail. Use double the length of flash you need. Tie it on top first, just in front of the Crystal Chenille.

9. Tie off the Krystal Flash and fold the remaining material back on the bottom of the hook shaft to form both back wings. If you want a brighter fly with more glow, use Fluoro Fibre or brighter colored flash.

10. Add the bottom wing first. This forms the fly's front section, the head or wing. The bucktail should extend about 2 to 3 inches beyond the hook's bend.

11. Tie in the top wing using the same amount and length of bucktail as the bottom wing. If you want a more buoyant fly, make the wing thicker. It's smart to add some glue to the base of the wings.

12. Add a drop of superglue to the wings to lock them in place.

13. To form the nose, spin a section of elk or deer body hair in front of the wings. The base of the nose should be about ¼ to ⅜ inch, and the tapered ends should extend back about 1 inch. Better to have more nose than less if you want more buoyancy.

14. Trim the front section of the nose to form the mole look.

15. Glue on the eyes with Goop at the base of the top and bottom wings. The bottom of the eye should pinch the hook shaft. The two eyes should form a bond to each other, pinching the wings and hook shaft. The eyes bring the fly to life, making it look like a big, wide-sided baitfish. If the hook shaft is exposed anywhere, coat that spot with chenille to give a solid bond for the eye. Most big flies have enough room to place the eyes. On smaller flies, just behind the hook's eye is often an ideal location; right on the head, or back from the fly's head.

When you're using Goop or other thick glues to stick on an eye, try using a big needle or bodkin to place the eye on the fly. Lay the eye on a flat surface with the eye looking down and the back of the eye up. Using the needle point, pick up a small glob of glue, and with the glue on the needle point pick up the eye and place it on the fly. Once you have the eye located where you want it, place a finger on the eye, slide out the needle, and press the eye onto the fly.

16. The finished fly. This fly has a wide profile, and the blend of materials produces a good flowing action, yet it is still very castable for a large pattern.

CHAPTER 12

Glow Squid

Squid are the only fast swimming bait that usually travels backward. They can move in either direction, but their unique design allows them to move backward quickly when fleeing. But it is the glowing color of this fly that makes it effective. Squid light up when excited. The blends of different shades of color on this Glow Squid taken in a back bay on Cape Cod make this fly come alive in the water. Another nice feature of this fly is its light weight—for a big fly, it is not a chore to cast.

Squid are special baits because they are not baitfish but sea creatures with tentacles, large beaks, and giant eyes. They can swim backward and forward, quickly change directions, change colors in a flash, and shoot a cloud of ink to cover their path as they flee. When fish feed on squid, they are often aggressive and usually feed near the surface. Both points make squid ideal bait for fly rodders chasing big stripers and other gamefish.

Making a squid fly that glowed seemed logical to me because that's what squid do. When changing colors or when frightened, they become bright, lighting up. This was not difficult to mimic with the proper materials. Once I discovered Fluoro Fibre from South Africa, the rest was easy. Using a translucent material like Kinky Fibre (today you'll find many decent substitutes) with hot orange or pink Fluoro Fibre inside the translucent wing produced a fly that glowed and changed color as it moved. The fly works best in clear water during the day when the glow blooms. The only significant change from the original Glow Squid pattern is using EP Shrimp Dub Brush for the fly's body. This wrap is ideal, simple to use, and available in many colors and sizes. Also the new tail materials are endless and give the fly better action than Kinky Fibre. And for a larger fly, you can cast it well even with a 9 weight.

Squid inhabit much of the open water in the world and provide food for offshore species. And squid are often close to shore in shallow water, where gamefish find them. I have not used squid patterns enough in different fishing situations, but I plan to change that in the coming years. I have failed to see the opportunities that a squid fly could offer in Southern locations. Many times while snorkeling in the tropics, I have seen squid in small groups and pods, usually along structure. Squid are catalysts on the rips from Cape Cod south to Rhode Island and farther south to New Jersey, turning on both stripers and bluefish. When there is a good run of squid, fishing is often hot, and the fish usually feed on top. In deeper rips when stripers are holding near the surface, it's a sure bet that squid are present. They become active at night, moving into shorelines and harbors in the spring to feed. Squid patterns are always worth a try when fishing shorelines at night in locations that hold them.

In shallow, flowing water, fish with an intermediate fly line, swinging the fly across the current. Use sharp pulls and keep the fly moving. I like a fast retrieve because squid swim quickly, often bolting to escape predators. They will at times glide or hold in the current and then shoot forward like a speedy dart.

Along a beach at night, look for concentrations of small baitfish near the shore. Fishing a squid fly around schools of baitfish will simulate a feeding squid. In this way, you offer gamefish a larger food source, and often they will single out the larger meal. Fish the fly with long pulls, and let it sit after several pulls. A steady retrieve works, but I like to mix up the movement at night, adding an irregular flow to the fly. Squid often bolt and then hold in one place before turning and heading in the opposite direction. If there is a flow along the shoreline, cast at an angle and use a stop-and-go retrieve. Squid feed by catching small baitfish with their many arms and using their beak to eat the bait.

In deeper rips, fish a fast-sinking fly line across the current to let the fly drift and sink with the flow. As the line begins to move across the flow, use a fast retrieve with long, sharp pulls. This will get the fly to swing, turn, and dart toward the surface like a fleeing squid. If the fish are close to the surface, cast quartering downcurrent and give the fly a steady, pull-and-stop action. In many cases you won't need to reach deeper water, but casting a fast-sinking line at even a slight angle to the flow gives the fly enough depth to fish properly. In this case a fast-sinking line is a quicker, more useful tool. When drifting big, fast rips in a boat, you need to get the fly to fish properly and into the sweet spot quickly. In clear water you will often see the fish coming. Fair warning: wait for the take; don't react to what you think is the fish taking the fly. Be sure to feel the line tighten before setting the hook.

When fish are blitzing on squid, they often feed recklessly, taking anything that moves. In these conditions, special fishing tactics are not necessary. Casting into the feeding fish often means a quick hookup. But don't let this easy fishing fool you; the right fly and proper techniques are important in most situations when squid are the prime bait.

GLOW SQUID

Hook:	#3/0-1/0 Mustad 34007
Tail:	Hot pink Fluoro Fibre, white Metz Flash 'N Slinky
Body:	White EP Shrimp Dub Brush
Eye:	Glue-on, 3-D, soft plastic eyes

Note: You can substitute EP Anadromous Brush for the body.

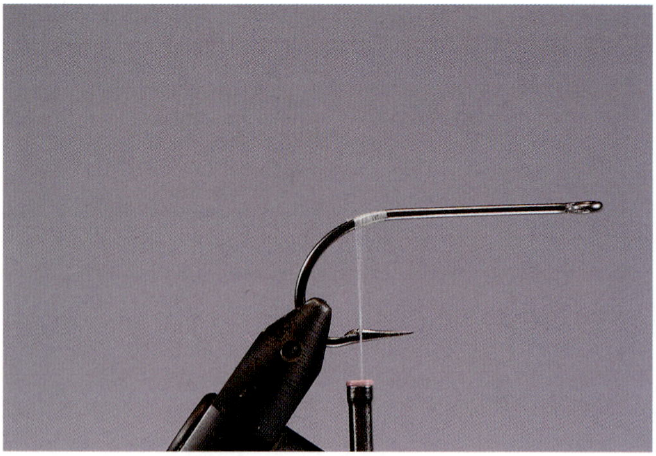

1. Tie in the thread at the hook's bend.

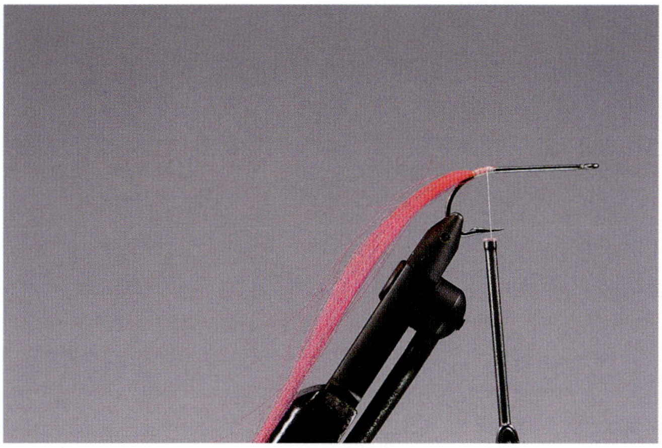

2. First tie in the hot pink Fluoro Fibre, starting at the hook's bend. (Hot orange works too.) The Fluoro Fibre should extend about 4 inches back from the hook's bend.

3. Tie in the lower section of the tail with white Metz Flash 'N Slinky (or Steve Farrar's Flash Blend), extending back about 6 inches. This part of the tail extends about 2 inches beyond the Fluoro Fibre. Colors like white, pink, or tan or blends of several different colors work well. If you're using several colors, layer white, or the lighter color, on the bottom below the Fluoro Fibre. Kinky Fibre is also another excellent choice, but if you use it, add some flash.

4. Then tie in the top section of the tail, also using white Metz Flash 'N Slinky. The top and bottom sections of the tail should surround the Fluoro Fibre in pale blue.

If you're making this pattern with mixed colors, use a darker color on top and make the head a variety of colors. The nature of materials like Flash 'N Slinky, Steve Farrar's Flash Blend, or other translucent blends allows the Fluoro Fibre to produce a glow inside the fly.

5. Tie in a section of white EP Brush materials at the base of the wing. Choose the 2½-inch EP Brush materials for larger flies. Kinky Fibre, used in the original pattern, is still a useful material for this pattern. The newer materials are somewhat easier to use and look better in the water, but Kinky Fibre still makes a fishable fly. Using the EP Brush materials for the body is a change from the original pattern where I used Dan Bailey's Sapp Body Fur. Any material that flares and forms a round, chunky body will work, but the EP Brush is an exceptional material.

6. Begin wrapping the EP Brush materials over the hook shank toward the hook's eye and keep folding the fibers back as you wrap. This prevents the fibers from being crushed down onto the shank.

7. Continue wrapping and folding the EP Brush to just before the hook's eye.

8. Tie off the EP Brush, firmly bonding it to the hook's shaft with at least a dozen wraps before tying off and cementing the thread. I like a pink head for a two-tone fly, but matching the tail color also works.

9. Trim off the EP Brush with cutting pliers.

10. Finish the fly by gluing a large eye above the hook's bend in the center of the tail material. Squid have large eyes, so don't be afraid to use a big eye.

11. The finished fly. I build the Glow Squid in several different colors. But the important features of the fly are the bright strip of Fluoro Fibre that makes the fly glow and the large eye.

Here are several variations of Glow Squids. Other combinations of colors catch fish, but I prefer to use light-colored, translucent wings and tails to enhance the glowing effect.

CHAPTER 13

Barracuda Fly

The Barracuda Fly's long tail gives it great movement no matter what retrieve you use. The glowing color like the Glow Squid is an important feature. Gamefish get excited when any food source becomes frightened. That color change might entice a strike even from a wary cuda.

The design of this fly came on the heels of the Glow Squid, and it uses the same concept, imitating frightened bait. When chased, some fish, both gamefish and baitfish, change colors. It must be a survival mechanism that makes a fish look bigger or helps the fish escape. When barracuda or sharks chase bonefish, they become brighter, as do most baitfish.

After I developed the Glow Squid, the Barracuda Fly was easy. It uses the same tying techniques and similar materials but imitates a lit-up bonefish. It gave me a fly that hopefully will excite a wary barracuda. Cuda are often tough to fool, even with spin tackle—let alone fly tackle—especially in locations with fishing pressure. One way to turn on a cuda is to use a fast-retrieve spinning reel. A fast fly retrieve is not even close. But in the right conditions, a fly that appears frightened can work. The best scenario is a location where cuda are herding bonefish or where a cuda attacks or tries to chase a bonefish or another larger food source like a big needlefish.

While fishing Andros Island in the Bahamas, I had an ideal opportunity to test this fly. My fishing partner Eric Peterson was fighting a bonefish in one of the back bays when a barracuda cut the fish in half. Telling Eric to keep watching the cuda, I quickly tied up a leader with wire and tied on the fly. I cursed myself for not having the leader and fly ready to go because after such a long wait I didn't know how the fish would respond. Eric dropped the fly about 6 feet in front of the fish, and before he was even ready, the fish crushed the fly. It was Eric's first big cuda on fly tackle and a good test for this new pattern.

Also on this trip we discovered a way to neutralize a poor guide without the guide losing face. It was a group fishing week with great friends, and each day each of us fished with a different guide. One guide was bad, and Eric and I drew the wrong card, so it was our turn to fish with him. I told Eric that I had a plan. We told the guide that I was moving out of the country and Eric and I would probably never fish together again. We said that wading each flat would give us more time together and make it a fun day. The guide dropped us off at one end of a flat, and we spread out and fished each section of water. We fished this way all day. It worked great because other anglers reported the guide spooked more fish than he would spot. At the end of the day, we took some decent fish without the frustration that a poor guide can bring. The guide was none the wiser and no one's feelings were hurt.

Because cuda are so unpredictable, they are never a sure thing, but with the right circumstances, this fly works. It seems that when these great fish are around other feeding fish, they are

Here is Eric with his first nice cuda on fly. Often cuda take long looks at flies but seldom strike. They often follow without any real interest. The way this fish rushed and took the fly with no hesitation told me I had a winner. It was a great trip with a great friend.

Not only a barracuda pattern, this fly will take other species like mutton snapper. Southern reef fish will strike a lure or fly that seems too big for them. They see something that looks like food and grab it. I once watched a grouper that could not have been 12 inches long strike a 9-inch streamer fly. The fish was too small to get the hook.

easier to excite. A cast that puts the fly where the fish sees it and needs to respond quickly might work. Sometimes casting behind the fish's tail might catch the fish off guard. It hears the fly land and hopefully turns and takes quickly. But once it follows too long, it is less likely to take.

Fish that follow and refuse to take the fly are most likely curious. You may need a different type of fly—it's almost never because the fly was tied poorly. A badly tied fly might create problems in some clear, shallow water flats, but unless you are dealing with educated fish, when a fish doesn't strike, usually it is the wrong pattern, or the fish is not ready to eat.

Fly speed is often essential when fishing for cuda. The fast speed seems to provoke the fish to strike. You can produce fly speed in two ways. One is to use long pulls with your retrieving hand throwing the line back behind you into the boat. This action produces a fly that moves through the water with 3-foot bolts. This retrieve can excite fish, but it might also cause the line to tangle. A cuda's first run is a burst of speed that will part a leader like a gunshot if you have even the slightest line tangle after the hookup. The second method for producing fly speed is a two-handed retrieve, which has good fly speed and better line control. However, it lacks the long, darting fly action that the single-handed retrieve offers. One way to get long, sharp, surging fly action and still have enough line control is to use a two-handed retrieve that is different than the standard hand-over-hand retrieve. Start with the rod tucked under you casting arm with both hands together just below the rod. Grip the line firmly with your retrieving hand and cup the line with your casting hand. Pull down the line and extend with your retrieving hand behind your back, while forming a loose circle with the thumb and forefinger of your casting hand. Hold the line tight in your retrieving hand and stop behind your body. At the same time pull up with the casting hand, cupping the line and letting the line slide across your palm. Both hands should move, one hand up and one hand down at the same time. This will produce a long, fast strip, making the fly bolt forward.

Once the strip is made, grip the line with your casting hand and bring both hands together quickly. Gripping the line with your casting hand prevents a missed strike. With both hands together, repeat the process, making another strip. It sounds more involved than it actually is, and most anglers pick it up quickly. This is also an effective way to fish a popping bug or to produce fast fly action with long bolts.

This fly catches grouper and snapper along shorelines with structure. Use either a fast-sinking or intermediate fly line, depending on the water depth and conditions. If you're fishing ocean structure with wave action or an outlet flowing into open water, a fast sinker is better. I like the intermediate line when working calmer water along the sound side. Work the holes and get the fly to swim along the coral. This can be tough fishing because a grouper will rock you quickly if you do not turn its head. One advantage with a fly is it lacks other hooks to lodge into structure, but the stopping power of even a 12 weight is nothing compared to a big surf-spinning rod. Unlike normal fly fishing, where you let the fish clear the loose line from the basket or deck, with reef fishing you hold tight and fight the fish holding the fly line until you have stopped the fish away from the structure. Only then try to reel in the loose line. This is challenging but exciting fishing because the strike is often a quick rush right at your feet. For a chunky-looking fish, grouper can rush, strike, and turn in a flash. Snapper also rush with lighting speed, but they usually do not dive into holes in the coral to hide.

BARRACUDA FLY

Hook:	#2/0-1 Mustad 34007
Thread:	Hot orange
Tail:	Kinky Fiber, pearl Krystal Flash, and hot orange Fluoro Fibre
Body:	Braided Mylar tubing
Wing:	Light green Slinky Fibre or Steve Farrar's Blend, and white Kinky Fibre
Eye:	Glue-on, 3-D, soft plastic eyes (small)

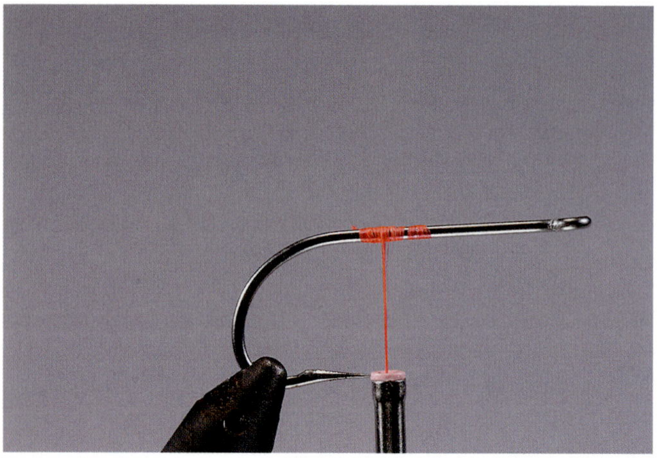

1. Tie in the hot orange or hot pink thread about a third of the way back from the hook's bend.

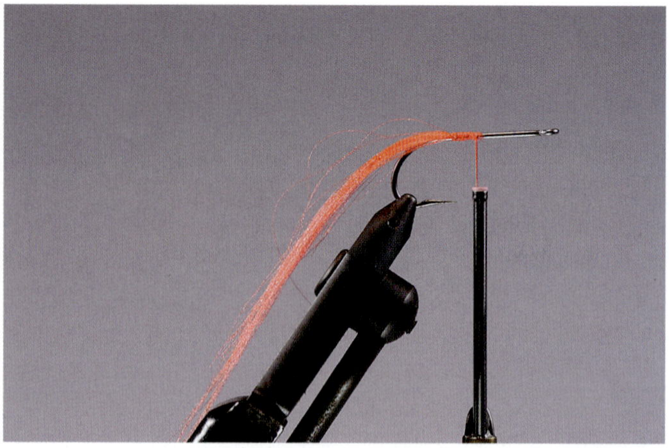

2. Begin tying the tail with a ⅛-inch-wide section of hot orange Fluoro Fibre about 4 inches long.

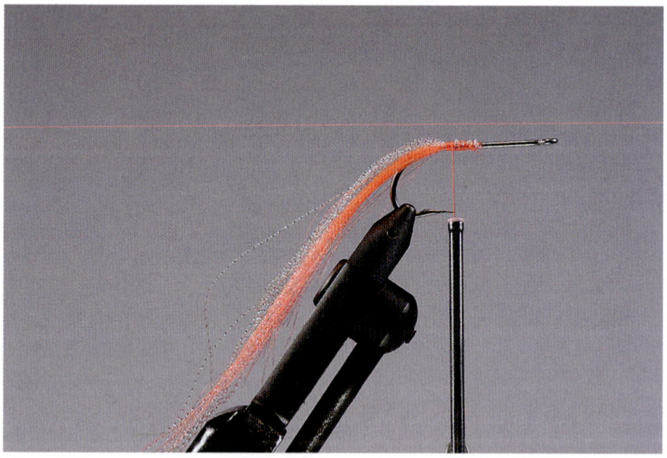

3. Tie in about 10 strands of pearl Krystal Flash of the same length over the Fluoro Fibre.

4. Finish the tail with a section of Kinky Fibre on top of both materials. Natural Steve Farrar's Flash Blend or a blend of Flash 'N Slinky also works instead of Kinky Fibre.

5. Tie off the thread and cut it for the next step.

6. Cut a section of ¼-inch braided Mylar tubing large enough to extend to the back of the hook starting about ½ inch from the hook's eye. A 1-inch-long piece of tubing will work with a standard-size hook. Slip the piece of tubing over the hook's eye, sliding it back so it covers all 3 materials, and let the tubing flare just beyond the hook's bend.

7. Tie off the front section of tubing about ½ inch from the hook's eye. This forms a translucent body with the tail now positioned at the hook's bend.

8. Add a lower wing of white Kinky Fibre extending about 3 inches past the hook's bend.

9. Tie a topwing of light green natural Steve Farrar's Flash Blend on top, extending back about the same distance as the bottom wing.

10. Finish tying the head and nose, building up the tying thread to make a bright-colored, ¼- to ⅜-inch-long orange snout in front of the base of the wing. (This is optional.)

11. Glue on the eye at the base of the wings, in the middle of hook shank. If the tubing covering the body is long enough, the eye should fit right on the edge of the tubing.

12. The finished fly. Just like the Glow Squid, the main features are the large eyes and the bright Fluoro Fibre that makes the fly glow. The fly's long tail and wings add good action and movement.

CHAPTER 14

Pop-Hair Bug

The pink-colored popper has a homemade, single-cell foam head and long saddle hackles for a tail. The yellow bug has a preformed popper head with bucktail for the tail. Using saddle hackle for the popper's tail produces a tail that sinks between pops and adds tail action. A bucktail tail is buoyant, keeping the popper more stable. If using a faster retrieve, both tails will function similarly. Often fish strike popping bugs because the splash excites the fish—they are grabbing a shape that is in motion, and the strike is a reaction. If you move the popper slowly when fishing along a weed bed for largemouth bass, the saddle hackle, feathered tail will make the bug more enticing. Here the tail adds movement, giving the bug more life.

I like to work bugs on the surface when conditions are favorable for topwater fishing. It is one of the great thrills in fishing: watching a fish take a popper or surface slider. Blind casting using sinking lines in low light is fun but does not produce the thrill of watching a fish crush a surface bug. I fished Hair Bugs for years. They were easy to cast, floated fairly well, and produced an ample pop but not the noise that a hard-body popper does. Hard-body poppers produce a splash, but they tend to dance around in choppy water. By putting both designs together, I developed a Pop-Hair Bug—half popper, half Hair Bug. This topwater bug is stable, makes a good splash, and is easy to cast.

I use a small version in fresh water and several sizes in salt water. If you want more splash from the bug, make the head larger with a bigger hollowed cup. For a subtle splash, use a small head and a longer spun body. Because it's easy to make many different versions of this topwater bug, the possibilities are endless. I used to make my own heads from single-cell foam used in boat building or for surfboards, foam that was high quality and strong. But they require special tools to form the bodies and are time consuming. Now you can find many decent preformed foam popper bodies with a center hole, making the bugs easier to build. And the bug's design with a spun body allows the body to lock onto the hook shaft. Once the back end of the foam body hits the body hair, both materials help hold the body in place. For the original Pop-Hair Bug, I used cork and cut a groove in the body before I glued it in place. I was too lazy to drill a hole in the cork bodies.

There are many ways to work a popper. A steady two-handed retrieve produces a constant pop-and-splash action. This is an effective technique in calm water. For fishing around lily pads for largemouth bass, try a stop-and-go action, sometimes letting the bug sit for 20 to 30 seconds. For freshwater fishing, make some bugs with an ostrich herl tail to give them more motion as they sit. (You could call this a Snake-Pop Bug.) When fishing choppy water, use hard, long pops.

If you're using a single-handed retrieve, you can use the rod to add a stronger pop by lifting up the rod at about a 45-degree angle on each pull. A trick that my friend John Posh taught me was to hold the rod under your arm with one hand at the first guide. With each pull of the retrieving hand, lift the rod up enough to produce a load splash. This creates a hard pop while giving the casting hand a rest. Poppers are deadly on calm mornings, drawing fish to their sound. When fish are busting on the surface and taking poppers, the excitement is hard to beat.

In a pinch you can use an intermediate fly line to work a popper, and in fact, this creates better action if you're using a larger popper because it keeps pulling the bug down, not letting it kick around on the surface. But good fishing technique is important; make a straight cast and begin the retrieve quickly before the line drags the popper below the surface. Some intermediate lines settle faster than others, and these lines are designed to maintain their depth once you start the retrieve. After making the cast, begin the retrieve and move the popper at a fast pace. A slow retrieve is difficult unless the popper is

Believe it or not, poppers work on Alaskan silver salmon. I had a ball for several days surface fishing for these great gamefish. By chance I happened to have several small saltwater poppers in my fly box. After catching several on streamers, I tried fishing the little silver bug and had great success. Perhaps I hit fish that were fresh from the sea and still remembered feeding on baitfish.

large. Remember, use a slow-sinking line to fish a popper only out of necessity; floating lines with short front heads are the best tools. I like shorter leaders in the 5- to 6-foot range, and if you need a bite guard, keep it short and light.

Casting big bugs is similar to casting large, wind-resistant flies. Slow the casting stroke down a little so that the line flows out with a smooth loop. If the popper is landing in a pile with the leader and the front section of the fly line, the likely problem is too much line speed. Also try extending another 5 feet of line on your false cast. This might be tough for some casters, but it helps to increase the casting distance and allows the front loop to roll over with more power.

Fly-fishing for school-feeding fish like bluefish, stripers, and jack crevalle is exciting action—there's nothing better than watching a fish take a topwater bug. Remember, many species of gamefish will take a topwater bug, and poppers work well to cover large areas of open water. In locations with heavy weed, over mussel and oyster beds, and around bridges and dock pilings, poppers allow snag-free fishing.

A wake that appears behind your popper is a sure sign of a fish charging the bug. In freshwater also watch for wakes coming from the side. This happens when you're working a popper along shorelines or close to weed beds. In either case, wait for the take; never strike at the splash. Fish miss poppers on the strike or use their head or tail to hit the bug before grabbing it. Try hooking the fish only when you feel the take. If you can't control the impulse to strike too soon, look away and use your sense of touch.

For bugs with longer bodies, use a longer-shanked hook or even a popper hook, which is bent along the shaft for a better bond and hold between the hook shaft and the body. One problem with extra-long-shanked hooks is strength. Use two bunches of spun body hair and a larger popper body. Another option is to build a standard-size bug on a long-shanked hook. Build the bug on the front section of the hook, leaving the bend and hook point just past the bug's body. This makes for a better hook set. When using a long-shanked hook, tie the tail closer to the hook's eye, leaving enough room for spun body hair and the head. A number of precut foam bodies are on the market in many sizes and shapes. You can always cut the body down, so oversize is better.

If you make your own popper bodies, cut enough of the body to allow a tight fit. I use a hacksaw blade to make a groove in the bottom of the body ¼ inch deep. A hacksaw blade is also ideal for trimming the body. For producing a hollow-faced bug, use a small, round grinding bit in a small hand drill to hollow out the foam cylinder. Remember, if the bug creates enough noise and a splash, it does not need to be beautiful.

POP-HAIR BUG

Hook:	#3/0-2 Mustad 34011
Tail:	Yellow bucktail
Body:	Spun deer or elk body hair, chenille, popper body
Head:	Five-minute epoxy

Note: You can substitute the Eagle Claw 66SS for the hook. The head has a tapered body and a hollow, round, cupped face. If you have limited experience building poppers, choose one of the preformed foam heads. Ones with predrilled holes are easier to work with, or cut a groove in the bottom of the bug with a hacksaw blade. If the bug is too long, cut off the tail with the same tool.

1. Before beginning to tie the fly, make a cut in the body about a third of the way into the body from the bottom.

2. The cut should run end to end.

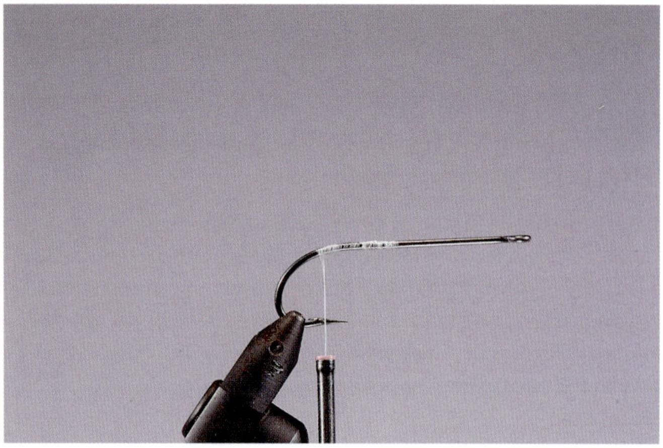

3. Tie in the thread at the hook's bend. For longer popper bodies, use an extra-long-shanked hook and tie in the tail so that you leave in enough room for the bunch of body hair and the foam popper body.

4. Put the popper body in place to be sure it will fit in the planned space.

5. Tie in the tail at the hook's bend using yellow bucktail about 3½ inches long. For a longer bug, use saddle hackle feathers. Also, try ostrich herl on freshwater bugs.

6. Spin on one ample size bunch of yellow body hair right in front of the bucktail.

7. Tie in a section of thin chenille next to bunch of spun body hair. In this case I'm using yellow, but any color will work because it will be covered.

8. Wrap chenille over the bare section of the hook shaft where you will glue the popper body. This body will fill the entire space, so wrap the chenille all the way to the hook's eye. This coating is a much stronger bond for the popper body to the hook shaft.

9. Again, check the selected popper body to be sure it fits between the hook's eye and the spun body hair. If necessary, cut more off the popper body's tail to fit the space. It's always better to have a body that is too long.

10. Slide the body off the hook shaft. Apply the epoxy, being sure to use enough to form a strong bond. Put it along the wrapped hook shaft and at the end of the popper body. After testing different glue, I found that five-minute epoxy bonds the best for preformed soft bodies. Epoxy bonds the best for single-cell boat-building foam and cork too. Goop is easier to use and works, but it gives a soft hold. Epoxy is messy and requires mixing, but it cements the popper body to the wrapped hook shank much better than several other glues I tried. Another glue choice is Zap-A-Gap, which Bob Clouser suggests for tying his EZ Popper.

11. As you slide the body onto the wrapped hook shaft, it will form an extra blob of epoxy. This blob will bond the popper body's tail to the spun body hair. If you have too much epoxy, fill any gaps along the cut in the bottom of the bug and then remove the extra and be sure to clear the epoxy from the hook's eye while it is soft. When using five-minute epoxy, glue three poppers at one time. This saves time and epoxy.

12. To finish the bug, trim the bottom of the body hair along the bottom of the hook shaft and trim around the top to form a neat-looking bug.

13. The finished bug. Poppers can be any color, but if watching the bug is important, then make it bright.

Several different versions of the Pop-Hair Bug. The two bugs on top are splashing bugs. The bottom bug is a slider that makes a slight pop.

CHAPTER 15

Bonefish Fry

The Bonefish Fry should be about 1¼ to 2 inches long with a medium body width. This fly can be tied with any number of wing materials; just keep the fly small and bright with a light green hue. The key to this fly is a bright-colored wing that looks like a small baitfish. The eye painted with a Sharpie is not fancy, but below the surface in clear water it stands out and is important. The wing should be about ⅜ to ½ inch wide with enough flash to give the fly a little action. If you're casting to cruising fish, place the fly 10 to 15 feet in front of the fish to allow the fly to settle. This is as simple as fly building gets.

I have witnessed bonefish feeding on small baitfish for years but never really experimented with using a fry pattern to fish for them. After spending more time in bonefish country and getting a chance to fish on my own, I learned that a baitfish fly could be a fish-getter. This is especially true with spooky, hard-to-take fish.

There is a little corner on a flat I fish in one of the Out Islands of the Bahamas. This location is hit hard with many inexperienced anglers, and the fish are tough. One day the usually slow-moving, spooky fish were acting differently. I watched as a group of six to eight fish raced onto the flat, feeding aggressively on 2- to 4-inch-long baitfish. Putting on my tiny pattern, I waited until they appeared again and placed a cast 10 feet in front of the fish to avoid spooking them off the flat. As the fly hit the water, four fish attacked it on a dead run. And for the next five days, I took fish when they were pushing bait. The following year, about the same time of year, this happened again, and that year the bonefish several times were busting on top like bluefish. This behavior shocked me. It did not happen often, but it was surprising to see fish that could be at times so hard to take feed so recklessly. It has happened each year, and I'm sure it occurs in many locations. With this pattern I have taken fish in other locations even when fish were not chasing baitfish, and other anglers experienced the same thing with this pattern. This fly will take fish in many conditions and is worth a try especially on flats that get heavy pressure.

If bonefish are acting unusually, moving too quickly or racing across a flat at high speed, they are often feeding or looking for baitfish. If the fish are hot to take, casting this fly within 5 to 10 feet of fish will usually produce a response, and often they will rush the fly at full speed. If you see a dozen fish, you will never be able to get the fly back—they will pounce on it. The hard part is getting the fly far enough ahead of the fish so you can be ready for the strike. In normal fishing conditions, bonefish look down toward the bottom for their food, not up in the water column as bonefish feeding on baitfish do.

When casting to bonefish using shrimp or crab patterns, let the fly settle to the bottom as the fish approaches. The fly should land well in front of the fish so it can sink down to the fish's sight range. If everything works, the fish will take the fly either from the bottom or dropping to the bottom. Really spooky bonefish do not like a fly that moves too much. In some of these

This little fly never ceases to amaze me. For the last five years, it continues to work even without heavy concentrations of baitfish. I have taken fish on a number of different flats, and if I'm fishing a new location, this fly is often my first choice. Bonefish feed on baitfish like scaled sardines. I have seen selective, tough-to-catch bonefish feed aggressively on baitfish up to 4 inches long. These fish were surface feeding, rushing a fly from 10 feet away. It doesn't happen often, but when bonefish turn on to baitfish, fishing is excellent.

hard-hit places, a single strip is the limit, and at times simply dropping the fly near the fish will send them bolting off the flat. Yet if they are feeding on baitfish, you can move the fly with a steady retrieve or even faster.

Fish that are feeding on baitfish act in several different ways. When they race around, a fast cast is important. Getting the fish to see the fly before they leave the flat is the key to success. If you are not ready, you will miss opportunities. I like to take a position between the bait and the deeper water. When the fish first appear along the flat's edge, begin casting and try to land the fly at least 10 feet in front of the fish. This gives you a shot at the fish both coming and going. They usually rush the bait, picking off baitfish as they scatter. Some days they move on and off quickly with the speed of albacore racing into bay anchovies.

On several other mornings, I watched fish cruising along the outside of the school of bait. Not being able to see the fish clearly, I started blind casting, working the fly to the locations where the fish kept appearing. Sometimes I could spot several fish and tried to get the fly into position. To prevent spooking fish, I only cast to locations when I could see clear water. I even moved to one side to a better slot where the fish were easier to see. I cast when the location was clear and then let the fly settle and used a slow stop-and-go retrieve, which kept the fly in the location longer, and it worked. I only spooked a few fish and was able to hook up five fish in a short time before they moved off. It seems when these fish feed, they are not in one location long.

Another way they feed is to cruise the flat, swimming along the edges of schools of baitfish and trying to pick off any bait that strays from the pack. These fish are tougher to take because they are not as reckless. Here you need to line up the cast, delivering the fly at least 5 to 10 feet in front of the fish. Try to get the fly to swim out of the school in front of the cruising fish.

When the bonefish are hot, they are easy to take. On several occasions when the fish were on, even when the fly landed behind the fish because I misjudged their speed, they turned and took the fly almost before I was ready. And the takes are not subtle—they hit like a freight train.

BONEFISH FRY

Hook:	#4 Mustad C68S SS
Body:	Bill's Bodi-Braid
Wing:	Olive Fluoro Fibre mixed with pearl Krystal Flash
Head:	White tying thread
Eye:	Permanent black marker

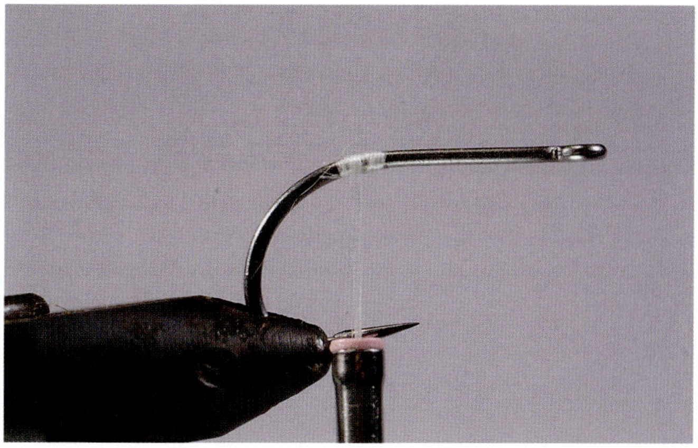

1. Tie in the thread at the hook's bend. (You can use a short-shanked stainless steel size 2 as well.)

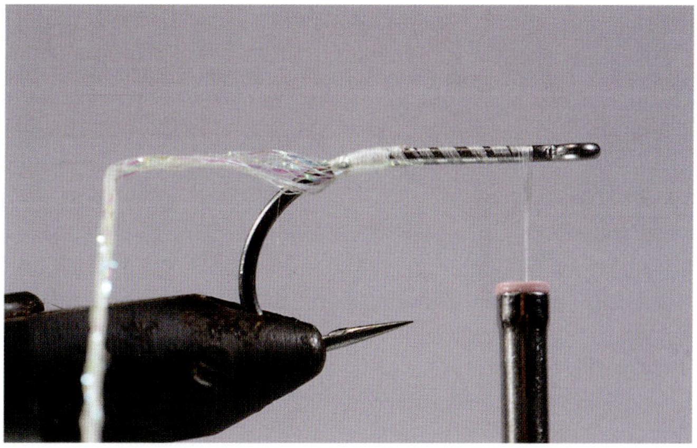

2. Tie in a section of pearl Body Braid at the hook's bend.

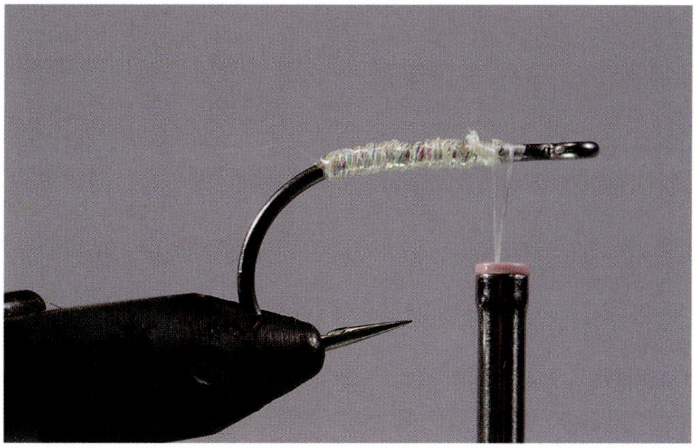

3. Wrap on the Body Braid to build up a ⅛-inch-thick body along the hook shaft. Leave enough room to tie in the wing.

4. Tie in a small section of olive Fluoro Fibre (or light green) about 1¼ inches long. The wing should be sparse. Other synthetic materials also work, but be sure that the wing is thin.

5. On top of this, add 6 to 8 fibers of pearl Krystal Flash and build up a small head with tying thread. You can also use Holo Fusion or Steve Farrar's Flash Blend in the same colors, but the body will be wider.

6. Paint on a black eye with a permanent black marking pen.

7. Coat the head with epoxy to illuminate the eye. (This is optional.)

CHAPTER 16

Wide-Eyed Shrimp

The fly as it settles on a flat in the Bahamas is in perfect balance. This fly looks alive and natural. Flies that settle or lay on their sides do not look right to a smart, shallow-water fish. This pattern lends itself to many options, both different materials and any number of colors. When you experiment with different materials and sizes, test the fly in water to achieve the proper balance to make it settle and sit upright. Remember, the most important feature of an effective bonefish fly is that it is always balanced both when settling and when sitting on the bottom.

I have tied bonefish flies for years. I never gave much thought to how the small flies with a wing and tail and weighted eyes acted once they hit the water. I threw the fly to a fish, and it would take or refuse. Did the fly settle to the bottom and sit on the bottom as live crustaceans would? I didn't give it a thought. Most locations I fished were not virgin, but they were not always fished hard either. When I started fishing locations with heavy fishing pressure, I found that a fly that acted unnaturally was like throwing a brick in the water. Permit anglers want a crab that drops to the bottom at an angle. The basic design of a crab fly, a flat disk, allows it to sit on the bottom like a natural. However this is not the case with some bonefish flies.

In hard-fished places, a fly must remain upright when it drops to the bottom and continue to sit upright on the bottom as you fish it. During the retrieve the fly must move forward and keep landing in an upright position. Tidal flow, wind speed and direction, and line drag, as well as the design of a well-balanced fly, influence how the fly acts in the water. Casting angle in relation to the wind also influences how the fly acts. But first and foremost, is the fly balanced and stable when both dropping and sitting on the bottom?

Getting a fly to remain upright requires both wing and tail materials that control how the fly settles along with a properly placed weight to prevent the fly from rolling on its side. Adding outriggers or arms and legs to keep the fly balanced on the bottom adds to the fly's effectiveness, keeping it erect even on flats with water movement. I have developed several patterns that remain balanced in most conditions, but this concept is still a *work in progress*. I still need to test so many combinations of materials, weights, hook types, and ways to stabilize the fly on the bottom. For this book my goal was to develop a pattern that would match several important food types by changing the color and size. I believe that a buggy-looking fly with active materials in the right size and color will work in many locations for bonefish as long as the fly is in balance during the presentation. With a basic blueprint, most anglers can develop patterns that will work no matter where they fish.

This pattern took some hard work to come up with the proper balance. First I tried to add weight to the head or tail using small dumbbell eyes and Sili Legs for outriggers to keep the fly balanced on the bottom. The fly settled OK but did not always stay upright on the bottom. Some combinations of tail and wing materials work better than others to stabilize the fly on the bottom, but because of the weight's position, the fly's balance was never consistent enough. Adding a strip of lead weight to the underside of the hook shank and removing the dumbbells produced a balanced fly that dropped properly, but the fly was not stable on the bottom. Only after adding the mono crossbar

Here is Eric Peterson and our guide with a big bonefish. Fish of this size require a fly that looks and acts like a natural food source, not an imitation.

Melting Mono Eyes

Melted monofilament eyes are fairly easy to make and can be tailored for each pattern. Use a piece of clear mono 1 to 1¼ inches long. For larger eyes, use 60- to 80-pound-test; for smaller eyes, use 30- to 40-pound-test. Grab the small section of mono in the middle with forceps, and melt each end over a lit candle, letting the round ball of mono retreat toward the jaw of the forceps. The mono will form into a ball or an eye right near the jaw of your forceps. To make wider eyes, use a piece of mono that is about ¼ inch longer. Remove it from the heat before the ball gets too close to the jaw, leaving a larger space between both eyes. To make darker eyes, keep the mono closer to the tip of the flame—for a light amber eye, hold the mono about 1 inch above the flame.

Melt the eyes from a single piece of mono so the eyes are about ⅜ inch from center to center. The eyes should look like a square horseshoe with two blobs at each end. I like to make several dozen mono eyes at once.

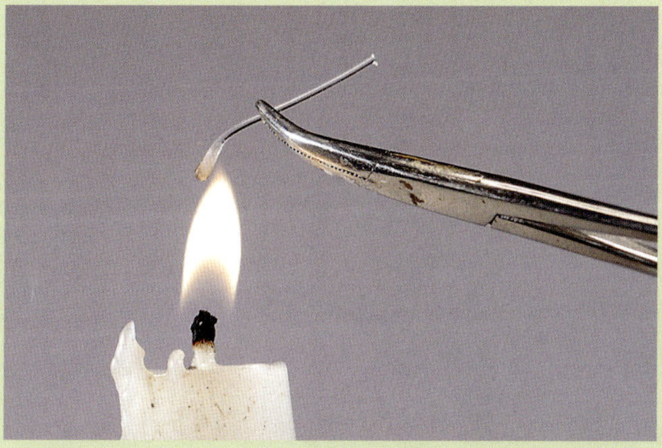

1. Hold the end of the mono over the candle flame and allow it to melt forming a blob at the end of the mono.

2. Once the eye is formed remove it from the heat quickly. Try to get the eyes even, and if one eye needs more heat, apply it from a distance and be careful because too much heat will ruin the eyes.

3. Melt the second eye on the other end of the mono to match the first eye.

4. Dipping the eyes in a small cup of water will set them quickly, preventing the eyes from deforming. It might take several tries until you find the right technique, but you can customize eyes for many different patterns using this technique. ■

to the tail and the wide, reversed mono eyes at the fly's head did I get a stable fly.

It's good to spin on a hackle feather and trim the bottom flat on a bonefish pattern. The spun hackle helps keep the fly stable on the drop, and the wide webs of the feather act like legs holding the fly upright. Not only that, but if you spin the hackle at the fly's head, it looks like the legs, feelers, and antennae found on many species of shrimp in the South. The spun hackle also softens the fly's entry noise. The only downside is a slower sink rate.

The simplest addition to this shrimp fly was the head and wing. I'm a fan of rabbit fur and other furs like fox or raccoon, so I only had to decide which combination I wanted to use for the wing and tail; any of these furs give enough action and come in a variety of colors. I chose light tan rabbit fur for a tail with tan-cream arctic fox fur for the wing. I added a little pearl Krystal Flash, and the fly came to life. If I could only fish one shade of fly, it would be light tan. That seems to match the food types in many locations in the different bonefish flats I fish. It might not fit the bill on grass flats or dark coral flats, but it would cover most locations.

At one time I made a fly with tan rabbit fur tail and body with a tan spun hackle head that Bob Popovics called the Paprikash Fly. Not that the fly was the color of the red Hungarian spice, but rather it was not tied with great care. After looking at the fly's unsightly appearance, he marveled at its ability to catch any fish. (Both Bob and I are of Hungarian descent, and we never stop razzing each other.) Even when you're fishing a well-balanced fly, you need to get the proper casting angle for the right presentation. A fly dragged along the bottom does not look right. In low-pressure locations, it might work, but not in spooky bonefish country.

A crossing wind is difficult for three reasons. It often prevents the fly from reaching the bottom, or by the time the fly reaches the bottom it is out of the fish's range. Or the wind drags line, which moves the fly along the bottom, keeping it off balance and preventing you from fishing the fly properly. When you can, try to use the wind to your advantage by casting into the wind or downwind. In both cases the wind has less effect on fly presentation.

In most hard-fished locations, if it's possible, I prefer to wade. I can keep adjusting, moving to get a better casting angle. The downside of wading is not being able to spot fish at a greater distance. Fishing from a boat allows you to spot fish at a much greater distance. Also, the boat gives you more mobility. Wading allows for better casting angles and, because you are lower to the water, shorter casts. Most anglers are more accurate placing a fly at 35 feet versus 65 feet. But the big advantage with shorter casts is having less fly line to control. Less fly line on the water means that the wind has less effect on the fly's movement. One advantage of wading on windy days is the ability to get even closer to fish. You usually can't get so close when boat fishing because waves slapping on the boat's bow can spook fish. However, the choppy surface often disguises your movements.

WIDE-EYED SHRIMP

Hook:	#2-6 standard stinger or short shank stainless steel
Tail:	Tan rabbit fur
Body:	Lead wire, 40-pound mono, and pearl body wrap
Eye:	Melted mono eyes
Wing:	Arctic fox fur with pearl Krystal Flash
Collar/Head:	Saddle hackle feather

Note: Although this fly is inverted and fished with the hook point up, begin tying the fly like a standard pattern with the hook point facing down in the vise. The hook sizes are small, and the back section of this fly is intricate, with three parts crammed into the tail. With the hook shaft up, it's much easier to get this section right. Once you have worked to the front section of the fly, spin the hook around in the vise so the hook point is up. This gives a better perspective of how the fly will look sitting on the bottom.

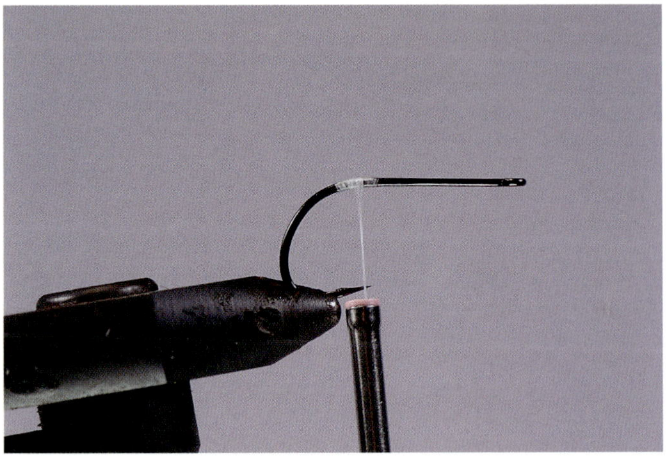

1. Tie in the thread at the hook's bend. I use a size 4 Stinger right out of the box—no bending required. Standard or short-shanked stainless steel hooks in sizes 6 to 2 also work.

2. For the tail, tie on a small section of tan rabbit fur without the skin about ¾ inch long at the hook's bend.

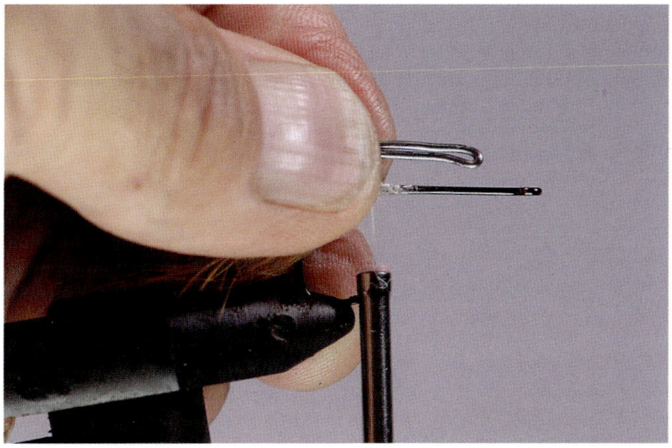

3. Cut a section of lead wrap about 1 inch long and fold it in half. Place the lead, leaving a small space between the lead and the tail.

4. Tie in the lead using tying thread to the top of the hook shaft, which will be the bottom of the finished fly. When placing the lead, leave enough room toward the front section of the fly to tie in the wing, eye, and spun hackle. About ⅜ inch is an ideal space. This weight, although light, helps balance the fly as it settles to the bottom.

5. Between the rabbit fur tail's base and the section of lead, tie in a piece of 40-pound mono about 2 inches long to the underside of the hook. Position the mono onto the hook shaft in the space between the lead and tail.

6. This view is from the bottom of a finished fly showing the proper position of the section of mono. The mono should form a T on the hook shaft. This section of mono will help stabilize the fly on the bottom.

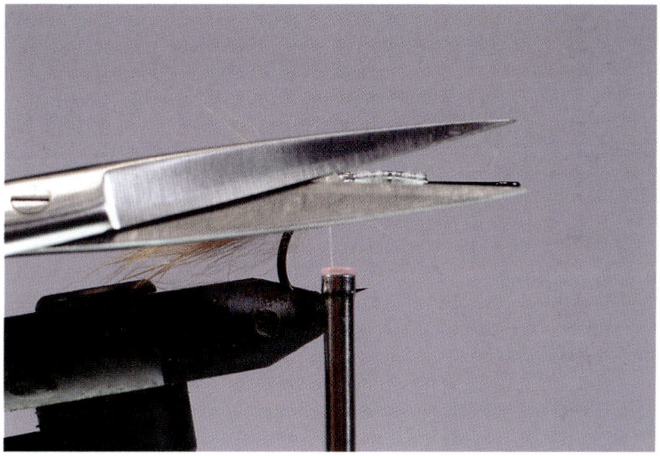

7. The mono is too long and needs to be trimmed. Use scissors or a pair of nail clippers to cut the mono. Leave the mono about ¼ to ⅜ inch long on either side. You can wait until after the fly is finished to trim the mono.

8. Tie a section of pearl body wrap at the base of the mono T.

9. To form the body, wrap over the lead and the hook shaft with pearl body wrap. Stop the wrap right where the lead ends, leaving enough room to fit the wing, spun hackle, and eyes.

10. Once the back section of the fly is finished, turn the fly over in the vise with the hook pointing up.

11. Tie in the mono eyes behind the hook's eye, placing them face down, hanging below the hook shaft, and bring the thread back to the base of the lead. The best technique is to have the eyes droop down below the hook shaft. Using eyes made with one piece of mono makes the fly sit better. The eyes, like the mono T, act as landing gear, and the flared hackle is like wings, adding even more balance to the fly. The fly will balance without the mono eyes, but they add stability. A shrimp sitting on the bottom often has its eyes raised, so if you want a more realistic fly, leave the eyes up. If you are careful to put glue on just the front section of the tying thread, the eyes can rotate either up or down.

12. If you want to cement the body with the mono T bar, do so now. (This is optional.)

13. For the wing, tie in a section of light tan to cream arctic fox fur, extending about ½ inch past the hook's bend close to the end of the tail. Position the wing just in front of the lead-covered body. Fox fur is more stable for building a larger fly with a longer wing. For building smaller flies, rabbit fur is a fine choice for the wing.

14. Blend in several strands of Krystal Flash over the top of the wing. The Krystal Flash should extend past the hook's bend close to the end of the tail.

15. Tie in a saddle hackle butt end to the hook shaft just behind the mono eye.

16. Spin the hackle onto the hook shaft, making the collar about ¼ inch wide between the melted mono eyes and the wing.

17. Tie off the hackle feather, tie off the head of the fly, and finish with a drop of glue.

18. Trim the bottom of the flared hackle, leaving two side wings of spun hackle feathers behind the eyes. The wings should form a shallow V on the underside of the fly. Use the tip of your scissors to trim the spun hackle for the fly's final touch.

19. A front view of the fly shows how to trim the hackle to form a shallow V and how the eyes should sit to support the fly on the bottom. Remember, the eyes can also be turned to face up or out when the fly is sitting on the bottom. Having the eyes resting on the bottom makes the fly more stable. If you did not trim the mono stabilizer bar before, do it now. Trim the mono so it extends out at least ¼ inch from the hook shaft on both sides.

CHAPTER 17

Blue Lady

This lady crab version of the Blue Lady has active materials that keep moving. If the fly is sitting motionless on the bottom, and there is any water flow, this fly remains active. Both arctic fox fur and rabbit fur keep breathing, and the EP Brush and bucktail maintain the body shape. The rabbit fur claws bend back when the fly is swimming through the water and reach up when it sits on the bottom. The Blue Lady is effective fished along the bottom or when retrieved up in the water column.

The Blue Lady was one of the most frustrating patterns for me to build. I tried using EP Brush as a shell first, with one piece on the bottom and another on top. Then I tried to use different feathers to form a shell like the ones on duck wings and pheasant back feathers. Some of these flies looked good sitting on the bench but did not perform well in the water. They did not land right or were not suited to retrieving. The tail was fine and the rabbit fur claws and eyes made the fly look alive, but the midsection made the fly unpredictable. Once I started wrapping the EP Brush onto the hook shank, the fly started to become a working pattern. But the clear caulk along the fly's underside added the action I wanted and stabilized the fly on the bottom, making it come to life.

Blue claw crabs are plentiful in estuaries from Cape Cod south into the Gulf of Mexico. I have seen them while fishing in the Bahamas and along the east side of Mexico. The adults are fairly large and quick, strong swimmers. Their rapid growth diminishes their value for fly anglers as a long-term major food source in many colder water locations. You might have a window of about three weeks to a month when you can match their size with a fly before they become too large. But in Southern waters that length of time can double. And some locations could have several spawnings. Also down South, four or five other species of crabs resemble the blue claw, so a fly that matches this species of crab should be a winner.

Lady crabs, also called calicos, are plentiful and a key food source on flats in New England. They range farther south to Florida, and similar species are found in the Gulf of Mexico. Unlike blue claws—which develop in areas of soft mud, weed, and sea grass—lady crabs are found along beaches on open flats and areas with pure salt water. They also live in pure saltwater estuaries, but these crabs do not venture into brackish water. The speckled crab, a close cousin to the lady crab and another surf-dwelling crab, lives in the South. Stripers and red drum feed on these crabs along beaches and on open flats.

It can be hard to tell different species of crabs apart. Many crabs are similar, and even the same species will look different in various environments. Most crabs have similar body shapes, some are good swimmers, and most can crawl quickly along the bottom. When approached, crabs defend themselves by raising their claws up to fight. With one pattern in two colors, a light blue-green fly and a tan fly mixed with light pink to reddish brown, you could match many crabs.

Match the colors of crabs where you fish. In the waters in New England, for example, green crabs are plentiful in some locations. Here an olive or dark olive matches this crab to a tee. These crabs are fast crawlers and burrow into the sand

The blue crab inhabits estuaries from New England to the tropics.

Green crabs are mostly a New England dweller. Found inside estuaries, they also live along sandy outflows where they burrow into the sand quickly when approached.

quickly. Another example is a crab I often see in the Bahamas along the rubble shorelines of flats and on coral flats. They are cream colored with a dark brownish to blackish, blotched shell about the size of a quarter. They move quickly and vanish in the blink of an eye.

When I developed this pattern, I focused on building a fly that sat on the bottom with raised claws that would move with each strip. If fished like a swimming crab up in the water column or along the bottom, the fly would take on a swimming posture with the legs and claws trailing behind. I wanted to get as much movement as possible because crabs are active creatures. They either sit still raising their claws to fight, or they swim or crawl quickly. When a crab is moving, every part seems to have motion, even though it has a hard shell. This fly does not have a hard-top, shell shape like many other crab patterns, so the fly does not look crabby until it hits the water. Here the fly comes to life, whether it is moving, settling down, or just sitting on the bottom.

When you use short, slow pulls with this fly, it will crawl along the bottom, and with each pause the claws raise up in a fighting position. When the fly is on the bottom, it looks like a crab facing forward, but when you retrieve the fly, it imitates a crab swimming sideways. All the materials trail backward like the legs on a side-swimming crab. Even though the eyes are in front when the fly is swimming, I believe that a fish looks at the action, the movement, much more than each detail of the fly. A fish approaching a fly sitting on the bottom is more aware of detail. If the fishing location requires a fly that quickly dives to the bottom on an angle, use a heavier, weighted eye on the tail.

Depending on the species of fish that you are targeting, try fishing this fly with different actions. In hard-fished locations, you often need a more subtle approach. And when bonefish flats are hit hard, too much fly movement can spook fish. This is also true when fishing for stripers on popular shallow-water locations. On flats with spooky fish, I like to let the fly sit and if necessary make one strip when a fish approaches the fly. When sight-casting, place the fly in front of a fish, letting it drop to the bottom. If the fish is moving toward the fly, wait for the take. If you think the fish does not see the fly, move it and look for the fish's reaction. Also, try several strips once you think that the fish sees the fly. If the fish are not affected by fly movement, retrieving the fly usually works, and it's much easier to hook the fish. Remember, many of these crabs move a lot, and fish often need to act quickly before they disappear. If fish are rushing the fly, you are in for an exciting day.

This is an early version of the Blue Lady along a coral shelf on the edge of a flat in the Bahamas. The saddle hackles were originally planned as back fins. The body is spun hackle, and the tail is short. It's a decent-looking crab but did not always settle to the bottom properly.

This lady crab version of the Blue Lady has lighter-colored claws. Note that the claws are straight up in a fighting position.

If you're fishing along a beach, cast at an angle to the beach so the fly swims along the edge of the shoreline. Let the fly swing with the flow, looking like a crab that is caught by the wave. Some species of crabs swim freely at certain times of the year or swim along the surface during mating season. Crabs are more active during full moons in the spring and early summer, depending on the location. One effective way to fish is blind casting a crab pattern during outgoing tide below bridges and at the mouths of outflows. Some anglers use crab patterns to fish blind, moving the fly along the bottom. Several friends of mine in Maine take stripers with green crab flies, fishing them slowly along the bottom. This pattern is suited perfectly for this technique: use an intermediate fly line to work the fly along the bottom, using short pulls with a pause between pulls. The fly has good movement and balance, so it slips along the bottom, and the materials keep moving even when the fly is stopped.

THE BLUE LADY

Hook:	#1/0-2 standard stinger hook
Eye:	3/16-ounce weighted dumbbell eyes
Tail:	Arctic fox fur
Body:	EP Sparkle Brush
Wing:	Tan bucktail
Claws:	Two strips of thin rabbit fur with skin
Head:	Melted mono eyes
Bottom Shell:	Silicone

Note: This fly should sit or ride along the bottom with the hook point facing up and the claws reaching up. Tie the fly inverted once the back section of the fly is completed, but begin with the hook in a normal position in the vise. Make this pattern in light blue, green, or tan. For matching a blue crab, use a mixture of blue and green. To match a lady crab, mix tan with light pink and yellow. To match a green crab, use medium or dark olive. The EP Sparkle Brush in pink blends with other colors to make both the blue and lady crabs.

1. Pre-trim two strips of thin rabbit fur with skin for the claws. Be sure to cut both corners of the skin of the rabbit fur to form a V. The rabbit fur claw on the left is trimmed properly—the right claw needs trimming. This makes tying in the claws much easier.

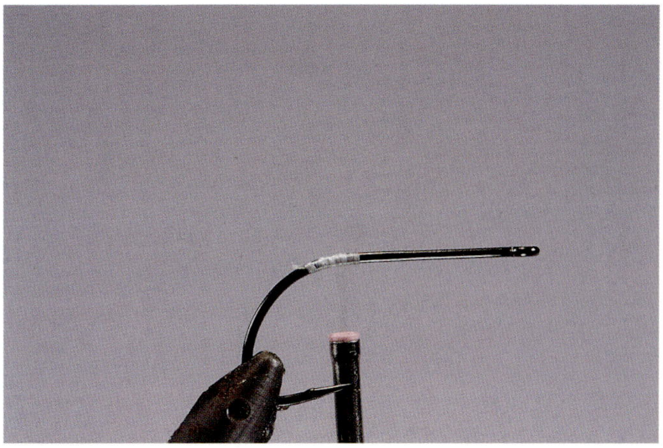

2. Tie in the thread behind the hook's bend.

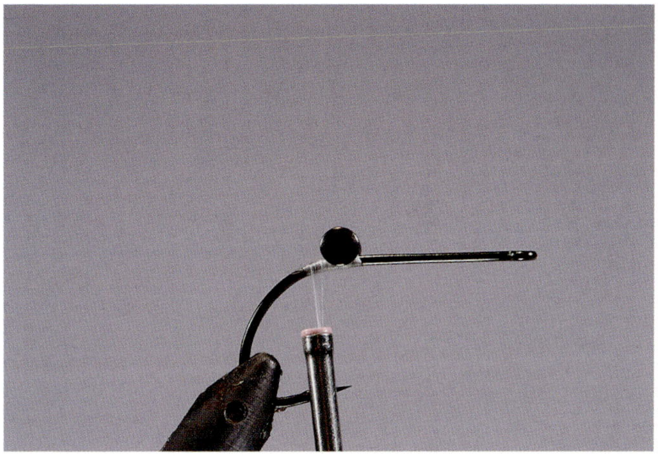

3. Tie in the 3/16-ounce weighted dumbbell eyes, leaving enough room for the tail. A painted eye is unnecessary. Choose the proper eye weight depending on your fishing location. I like 3/16 or 1/4 ounce. If you need more weight, add it, but be sure that you can still cast the fly.

4. Against the eye at the hook's bend, tie in a 1½-inch-long clump of arctic fox fur for the tail.

5. Next tie in a section of EP Sparkle Brush between the dumbbell eye and tail and move the thread, wrapping it close to the hook's eye. Enrico makes these brushes in many different sizes and colors.

6. Begin wrapping the EP Brush along the hook shaft using the same technique of folding back the fibers as you did when forming the head of the Glow Squid. Use the thumb and forefinger of one hand to pull the fibers on the EP Brush back to prevent the fibers from wrapping onto the hook shaft. The fibers should flare up and not be pinched under the wire core that holds the fibers on the EP Brush material.

7. Tie off the EP Brush material, leaving enough room for the wing, claws, and mono eyes. (at least ⅜ inch, but ½ inch is better). I'm not a smart planner and often need to crowd this section of the fly. Be smart and leave enough room.

8. Cut the wire in the center of the EP Brush material with cutting pliers.

9. Now invert the fly hook up in the vise, and tie a tan bucktail wing to lie on top of the EP Brush material. The wing tip should extend a short distance past the hook's bend. This acts as a shell to hold down the spun brush material.

10. Put the mono eyes behind the hook's eye and tie them in firmly.

11. Tie in the first claw so it extends back at about a 45-degree angle over the wing, angling out to form a V shape when you look at the fly from the top. Use the pre-trimmed rabbit fur sections shown at the start of the tying instructions.

12. Tie in the second claw to match the first. Both claws should be at a 45-degree angle to the hook shaft and form a V.

13. Add several drops of superglue to the eyes and the base of the claws to give them a firm hold on the hook's shaft.

14. Turn the fly back over, and with your thumb and forefinger, grab the fibers of the brush material to feather and pull them, forming a flat, bottom shell. Do this to both sides. This is not so much for looks as to make the fly's bottom flat.

15. Apply silicone to the bottom of the fly in front of the dumbbell eyes to the base of the claws. Create a smooth shell, and if needed, pull both sides of the brush fibers with your thumb and forefinger to keep the fibers flat. A smooth surface on the underside of the fly will help it sit and slide along the bottom better.

16. Smooth the silicone with your finger to flatten the bottom. If you wet your finger with saliva, the silicone will not stick to you.

17. After smoothing the silicone, pull the edges of the EP Brush to be sure that the bottom is flat. If the spun-on EP Brush fibers make the crab too large, trim them to create a smaller crab-shaped shell.

18. See how the claws angle outward.

Several different variations of the Blue Lady. The center fly is a blue claw, and the two outside crabs are lady crabs.

CHAPTER 18

Glow Sand Eel

Using epoxy for this fly makes it look lifelike and keeps the profile thin. The mix of materials produces lifelike color with a slight glow in clear water with good light. This sand eel pattern has also taken bonefish when they are feeding on baitfish. Small versions of this fly hold their shape well. The offset to that is less action. I like using sharp, short- to medium-length pulls when retrieving to keep the fly moving.

The Glow Sand Eel uses epoxy to enhance the fly rather than as a coating to protect the fly. Some of my early sand eel patterns from the mid-1960s were coated with epoxy to protect the fly and add weight. Back then I never saw the potential that this clear glue would have to produce a lifelike pattern. I made a fly called a Sinking Sand Eel in the early 1980s with a silicone-coated body, but I lost interest in the pattern, and it wasn't until the epoxy craze hit that I saw the need to develop an epoxy sand eel.

The Glow Sand Eel's shape is easy to form and simple to make. I don't have the patience that some fly tiers have to put on two or three coats to form a perfect body, so most of my epoxy flies have one coat. I started with basic epoxy sand eel flies and then added Fluoro Fibre to make it glow. The fly requires very little epoxy, so the epoxy doesn't drip. You can build three flies at once with a small amount of material—my type of fly. With little effort, I build a fly that looks alive in the water.

I mainly used this pattern for stripers in shallow water in the Northeast, but I was pleasantly surprised that it was effective on bonefish when they were feeding on baitfish. Even though the fly did not match the size or color of the bait that these bonefish were feeding on, they rushed the fly.

When fishing the flats, the fly must move in front of the fish rather than swim at the fish. And the fly must be in the fish's line of sight. When stripers first move onto flats, they continue their normal feeding habits, looking ahead or up, but when they frequently visit shallow water to feed, they mostly look down. Stripers learn quickly that most foods like sand eels and crabs hide in the bottom because escape is difficult. The fly must be in the striper's line of sight or right below it. I don't know how many times a striper has swum right under my fly because I misjudged the speed of the fish or the current flow. On shallow flats, it's not as difficult, but when fishing along drop-offs or when walking a high bar and fishing a 4- to 6-foot flat, a long lead is important.

Bonefish always look down, except when they are feeding on baitfish. A bonefish's demeanor changes when it's feeding on small fish; then it looks like an aggressive predator, not the careful, calculated feeder we see most of the time. When bonefish feed on baitfish, I often fish a medium-speed retrieve with 6-inch pulls. If the bonefish are moving quickly, then I go to a faster retrieve with longer strips.

When fishing this fly for stripers around schools of thick baitfish, work the fly under or to the side of the baitfish using a steady retrieve. Also try letting the fly drop to the bottom

My wife, Barb, casting to a pod of stripers on an incoming tide in late June. When casting to a group of fish, get the fly in front of several fish. If two or three fish see the fly, it often creates competition, bringing a rush to the fly.

and giving it one quick pull like a baitfish trying to gain the safety of the school. An interesting note: when bonefish are swimming along the edges of a baitfish school, I do the same thing—let the fly drop, and then give it more movement to imitate a crippled baitfish. All predators are looking for an easy pick, a baitfish that is hurt or that strays from the school's protection. A fly swimming in the middle of a thick school of baitfish is one in many thousands—poor gambling odds. But your odds increase and that fly becomes a target when it stands out from the school.

In locations with sand eels, sometimes these small baitfish die at low tide, and as the flats begin to fill stripers, look for dead bait on the bottom. An effective technique is to cast at least 10 feet ahead of a cruising fish and let the fly sit on the bottom. If the fish sees the fly, don't move it because they will often take the fly off the bottom. If you think the fish will miss the fly, then give it several short pulls, like a bait trying to recover.

When fishing stripers on most flats, I like an intermediate fly line with a 9-foot leader. Many Northern flats have gullies and pockets, or you are fishing along the edge drop-off and need to get the fly down quickly. For bonefishing most flats, a floating fly line with a 9-foot or longer leader is the best combination. Anglers who want perfect flies need a drying wheel or a rotary vise to control the epoxy as it dries. Five-minute epoxy is ideal for a rotary vise. Thirty-minute epoxy may be better for a drying wheel, but I have no experience using one.

Epoxy can be messy, so be aware of dripping onto any work area. The room should have adequate air circulation. Use a fan or air conditioner if you frequently use toxic materials. And read the labels on all packaging before using any product. I have caught enough fish, even bonefish, on flies with epoxy bodies that were far from perfect—actually some of them looked unfinished. Surprisingly, this pattern in small sizes catches bonefish even when they are feeding on larger, thick-bodied baitfish.

GLOW SAND EEL

Hook:	#2 Mustad 34007
Body:	Pearl Krystal Flash
Wing/Tail:	White bucktail, pearl Krystal Flash, and hot orange and purple Fluoro Fibre
Body:	Epoxy
Eye:	Permanent marker

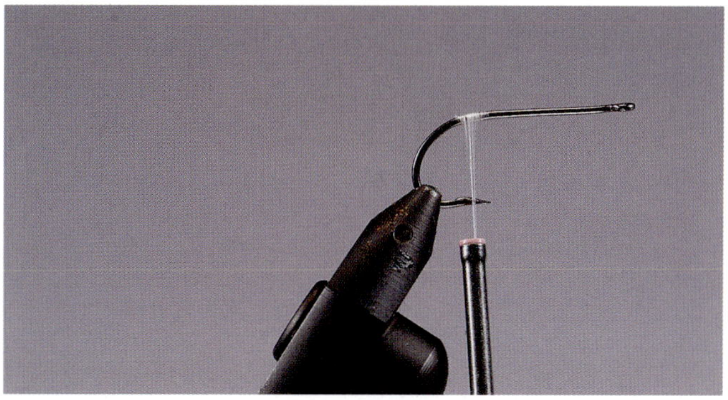

1. Tie in the thread at the hook's bend. Any standard, stainless steel hooks in sizes 4 to 1 will work.

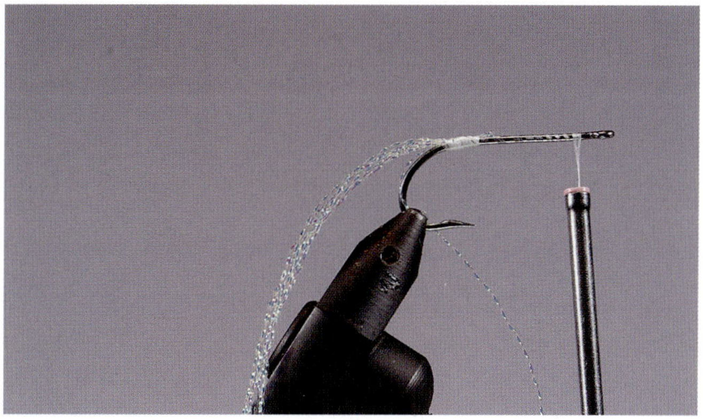

2. Next tie in a small bunch of pearl Krystal Flash. Separate a single strand of the Krystal Flash, and drape it around the hook point. This will be used to wrap the wing to the body.

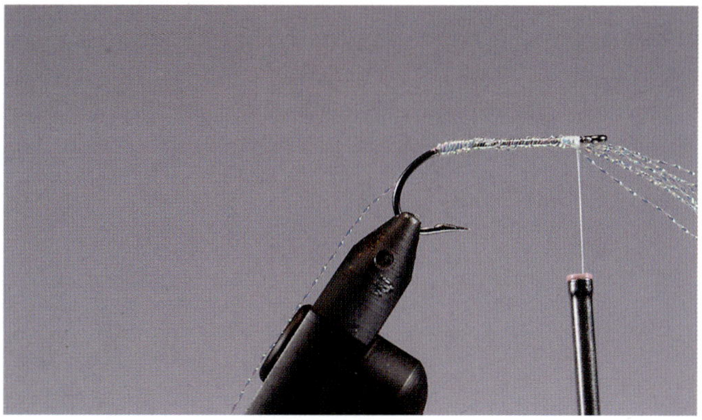

3. Wrap the bunch of Krystal Flash over the hook shank, forming the body. Tie the Krystal Flash behind the hook's eye, and leave the remaining Krystal Flash facing forward.

4. Tie a small bunch of thin white bucktail, about 3 inches long, for the wing and tail. (When you thin out bucktail to produce a long tail, keep the smaller hairs for flies that require thin, short hairs.)

5. Next, fold the Krystal Flash back over the bucktail, and tie it as the second part of the wing and tail, keeping it the same length as the bucktail.

6. For the third part of the wing and tail, tie in hot orange (or hot pink) Fluoro Fibre over the Krystal Flash. Keep the tail thin and the Krystal Flash the same length as the other materials.

7. Tie in purple Fluoro Fibre for the top of the wing and tail. Other color combinations also work for the wing.

8. Now wrap the single strand of pearl Krystal Flash over the entire wing. Keep this wrap loose so all the colors project through the epoxy. If you want a thicker body, wrap the strand loosely or leave the wing unwrapped.

9. Build up a decent-size head to have room for the eye.

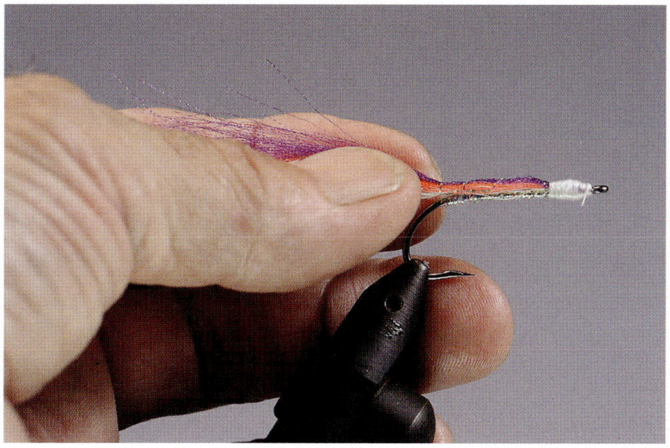

10. If you need to adjust the wing, give it a soft pull with your thumb and forefinger.

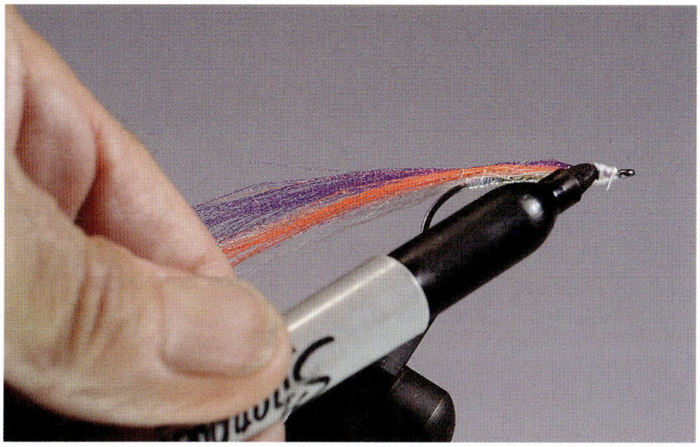

11. Add the eye with permanent marking pen. Alternatively, you can use stick-on, 3-D, soft plastic eyes.

12. Mix up a small batch of epoxy, and coat the fly using a bodkin or a wooden skewer. I use one-minute epoxy for making one fly in the vise. Keep working the epoxy until it sets. I like to do only one coat. If this is your first time using epoxy, you might want to use five-minute epoxy because it gives you more time to shape the fly. If you want the fly to look symmetrical or you want a larger body, then use several coats. If you need to remove runs or drips on the hook or vise, do it before the epoxy hardens—you have time, even with one-minute epoxy.

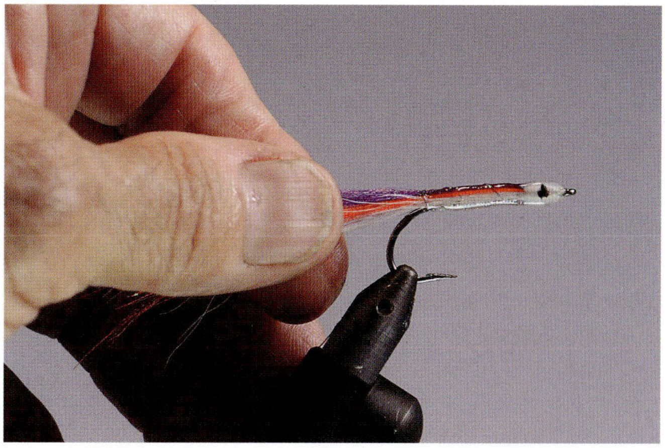

13. Once the epoxy is beginning to set, grab the tail between your thumb and forefinger to keep it thin. If you want a slightly thicker fly, skip this step.

14. The finished fly is ready to fish. Note the slim profile and how the color blend makes the fly look lifelike.

CHAPTER 19

Sea Rat

The Sea Rat has a cigar shape like a mullet, spearing, or many juvenile gamefish. It breathes well and is an attractor pattern with a weighted eye that gives it a hopping action when you fish it with long pulls, pausing between pulls. Building the fly with a smaller body-hair head or a heavier eye will enhance this hopping action.

I tied the Sea Rat many years ago, had decent success, and then forgot about the fly. The Sea Rat is really a version of a Long Saddle Snake Fly with a larger head and a weighted eye. When writing the second edition of *Inshore Fly Fishing*, I found this squid fly, thought it was a good-looking pattern, and added the fly to one of the fly plates, writing that the tier was unknown. Only after digging through boxes of flies did I realize that I had built this fly as an offshoot of the Sea Rat, only with a long nose. I prefer fishing the Glow Squid because it is so effective, but this Rat Squid made me realize what a fine concept the Rat-style fly is. I had fished Sea Rat patterns for years, but somehow placed them on the back burner. I had too many other patterns to fool with, and never saw the potential of this pattern. Only after I gave several friends chunky Sea Rats to fish in Florida did I realize how useful it would be to match shrimp, finger mullet, and small minnows; in Southern locations it became a go-to fly. I also discovered that another version of the pattern catches trout and large- and smallmouth bass. Too many times we overlook flies and never realize how effective a pattern might be in another environment. Flies designed for salt water are also great freshwater patterns and vice versa.

This pattern has some of the action of the Snake Fly but with a chunky, rounder build. The weighted eyes give the fly a slightly nose-down movement. The basic shape could match any number of baits, from squid to mullet to a small, chunky mummichog or even a shrimp. One reason I like the fly is its simplicity: it is easy to tie and produces great action in many fishing environments.

In smaller sizes, it matches small foods in many different locations. The head design allows you to tie in a weedguard, which is one of the keys to producing a fly for fishing around weed beds. Then one day I looked at the head and the nose that spawned the Rat Needlefish (see page 177). That beak with eyes produced a good, easy-to-tie, long baitfish. And once I saw the potential in fresh water as a short, stocky fly to match such baits for bass and trout, the Rat Series was born. The design of a short Rat gave the fly a nose-down action when you use a sharp, hard pull during the retrieve.

When fishing the original Sea Rat, most often I used a steady retrieve with pulls of different lengths to make the fly bolt, stop, and then nose forward again with a slight hopping action. When fishing in flows, cast across current and work the fly so it swings across the flow and then turns upstream at the end of the retrieve. One of the keys is using a hard pull to make the fly jump forward, which causes the feathers to pull together and then puff up when you pause. This breathing action is deadly with any fly with active materials.

SEA RAT

Hook:	#1/0 Mustad 34007
Tail:	Eight light orange saddle hackles
Wing:	Two tan marabou feathers
Eye:	Red pewter dumbbell eyes (3/16-ounce)
Collar:	Spun light tan deer or elk body hair
Head/Nose:	Yellow chenille

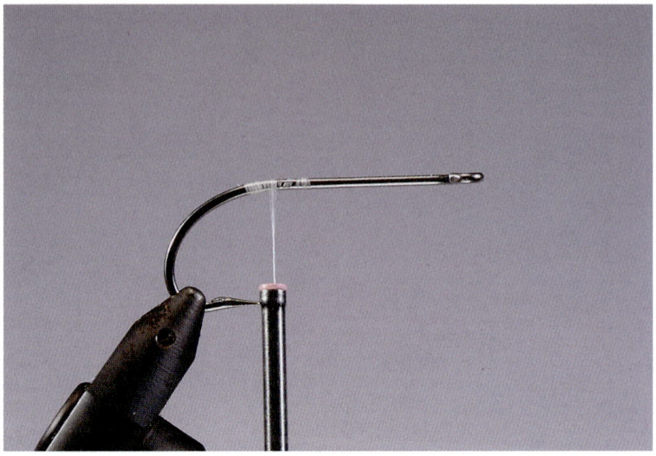

1. Tie in the thread at the hook's bend. (Use any standard, stainless steel hook in sizes 1 to 3/0.)

2. Tie in eight light orange saddle hackles about 5 inches long for the tail. Use hackle feathers with a wider web because the fly's silhouette should be chunky.

3. Tie in two tan marabou feathers in front of the saddle hackles about half the distance between the hook's bend and the hook's eye.

4. Tie in a red, 3/16-ounce pewter dumbbell eye between the hook's eye and the wing, leaving enough room to form the rat nose.

5. To form the collar, spin light tan body hair tight to the dumbbell eyes. Remember, as with any body hair, always point the tapered ends of the hair toward the fly's tail. On big flies, you might need two bunches of body hair.

6. Tie in yellow chenille in front of the dumbbell eyes.

7. Start wrapping the chenille behind the dumbbell eyes, and then crisscross the wrapping over the base of the eyes. This will lock in the eyes and tighten the collar. Keep wrapping in front of the eyes to form the rat-shaped nose.

8. To finish the fly, trim the short sections of body hair to form a smooth collar, leaving the long tapered hair to flow back over the wing.

CHAPTER 20

Trout Rat

This is the perfect short pattern for trout, large- and smallmouth bass, and in salt water to match small baits like shrimp or mummichog-type foods. Being a short, chunky pattern with weighted eyes, it has a good hopping action, and using different furs or marabou adds to the action. It's a fly that I'm still developing and a fun pattern to play with.

This fly started out as a freshwater bass fly, looking like any of the food fish that those bass eat. All pond and lake fish will feed on any number of small, chunky baits, from small perch, juvenile suckers, and chubs to small frogs. Many of these baits also live in rivers and streams and are food for trout. And it was only after looking at underwater photos that I realized the Trout Rat also copied a sculpin. After fishing with Chauncey Goodrich in Wyoming, I learned the best approach to fishing most streamer patterns and how important this small, ugly baitfish can be.

What's neat about the Trout Rat is its ability to match any number of small baitfish that have a big head or a wider middle that tapers to a smaller tail. The fly is easy to tie and cast, and by using different tail materials, you can match most small, chunky baits. Depending on the water's size, the flies should be 2 to 3 inches long. Build it with a medium to fat head, and vary the tail materials to produce different-size bodies. For a realistic sculpin pattern, tie a tan head with the rest of the fly being mottled brown, black, or black and brown. For chubs, use lighter colors mixed with white and add some red flash, or make them all white with silver or pearl flash.

In most streams and small rivers, Chauncey fishes straight down the flow. When fishing a good-looking hole, fight the temptation to make a long cast into the best-looking water. Keep the first several casts shorter, working the closer water. It's surprising how often you will take fish holding in the tail of the pool. Then, keep working up the pool to cover all the water. Often, several bigger fish are in the better sections, and it's possible, even in small water, to take two or three nice fish from one section of water. If the pool is small, cast to the head and work the fly down the middle.

Also cast quartering upstream at different angles to the flow. Retrieve the fly down the flow in smaller waters and midsize streams because the fish face into the current so you are less visible to them. If a fish follows but misses the fly, let it settle down and make another cast. Try to see the spot where the fish relocates and then adjust the casting angle and distance to swim the fly down the flow several feet from the fish.

This technique works in bigger water, but also try casting across the current and then mending downcurrent, working the fly so it swims down the flow, crosses, and turns upstream. A cast aimed straight across or that quarters downcurrent is

The Trout Rat is ideal in small streams but also performs well in big rivers. The beauty of this pattern is that so many different variations are possible. This brown trout took a Trout Rat in a tiny Idaho creek in late spring. This fly is ideal for many of the pocket-size creeks out West. Many of these creeks are fishable right after runoff and might keep flowing all summer. Build some flies with lightweight eyes for creeks with shallow pockets.

also effective; work the fly as you would for stripers holding in a flow.

Stripers, trout, smallmouth bass, snook, and weakfish hold near structure, undercut banks, piles of debris, or seams. All of these fish hide and wait to ambush food in a flow. And whether it is a freshwater stream that usually has a constant flow or an outflow that changes with the tide, fish take up feeding stations. Anglers who understand where the holding locations are know how to fish them, whether for trout, stripers, or snook. Even anglers new to trout fishing can use their knowledge of fishing other species to locate decent holding water. I constantly use striper techniques when fishing for trout, and experienced trout anglers should have no trouble finding stripers in a flow.

Fishing with streamer flies for trout can be action-packed. When you turn a fish on, it often travels some distance to take the fly. You don't see the usual, casual look and sip of a trout taking an aquatic insect imitation. If you are a saltwater angler, this is your type of fishing.

TROUT RAT

Hook:	#1-4 Mustad 34007
Tail/Wing:	Mottled marabou and gold flash
Eye:	Yellow pewter dumbbell eyes (3/16-ounce)
Body Collar:	Elk body hair
Head:	White chenille

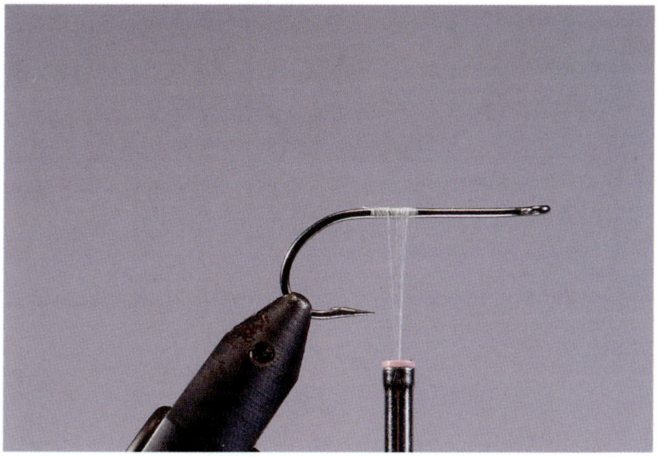

1. Tie in the thread at the hook's bend.

2. Tie mottled marabou to match the tail of a sculpin. Other good materials are raccoon, fox, or rabbit fur or standard marabou feathers or blends of two materials. When using two different materials or colors, put the second bunch of material over the first bunch, leaving room for the collar. The possibilities of different blends are endless. I prefer natural blends, but synthetics would also work. Build the tail size to match the fly size. I make standard Sea Rats from 5 to 7 inches long, but for Trout Rats, I make the flies 2½ to 3½ inches long. Larger patterns for freshwater bass should be about 4 inches long.

3. Tie in gold flash on top of the wing, and then move the tying thread to the eye location and coat the hook shank with thread. Place the dumbbell eyes about ¼ inch back from the hook's eye.

4. Tie in the dumbbell eyes about ¼ inch behind the hook's eye to allow space for the collar and nose.

5. Next tie in a section of body hair for the collar, with the tapered ends toward the rear. This tan elk body hair with a white base gives a two-tone color to the head. For smaller flies, do not try to spin on the hair, but tie in a small clump behind the eye. Usually hook sizes 2 or higher have enough room for spinning, but you be the judge. If you're tying a fat, chunky-bodied fly, then make the tail and collar fuller.

6. Tie in white chenille in front of the eyes.

7. Wrap the chenille around the dumbbell eyes, first wrapping behind the eyes and then crisscrossing the base of the eyes. Then wrap in front of the eyes to the hook's eye, making the nose tapered, like the nose of a rat.

8. To finish the fly, trim the head, tapering the back and sides, and cut the bottom square.

9. The finished fly. In clear water, lighter colors are often more effective, but I also like to try darker colors. Many Western streams contain darker baitfish, like sculpin.

Here are a few different possibilities of Trout Rats. I like the mottled marabou Rat (the fly used in the tying sequence) because its many colors can match different types of food.

CHAPTER 21

Winged Weedless Rat

The materials used for this fly keep breathing even when the fly is not being retrieved. It was designed to match small, chunky foods found in Southern backwaters. If fishing over weed beds, over oyster beds, or along mangroves, use a snag-resistant fly—this one rides with the hook up with a weedguard. Keeping the hook up so the back of the fly bumps along the bottom avoids most obstacles.

The Winged Weedless Rat fills a gap between the original Sea Rat and Rat Chovy. This weedless fly is designed to ride hook up, and with the proper balance of materials, it is fairly stable. Its blended tail lends itself to a variety of different materials with longer wings. The basic pattern has a tail of fox fur or Finn raccoon with marabou or a mixture of these materials, similar to the Trout Rat but larger. Using marabou for the wing tied over the fox or raccoon fur keeps the two tails from wrapping around the hook. Extending the fur past the marabou makes the tail wiggle. I also like a strip of rabbit fur with a marabou wing. My goal was to build a fly that imitates a shrimp or one of the many small minnow baits found in estuaries and back-bays in the South. The term "mud minnows" refers to a number of small, stout-bodied baits like killifish and mummichog, but the fly also resembles a juvenile mullet before it reaches finger mullet stage, or any number of small gamefish.

Getting the fly to ride hook up took many tries, and I'm still trying to develop an even better pattern. This is a complex pattern, requiring more tying steps than I usually use. However, getting the fly to flow in a controlled manner takes more time, but I believe the effort is worth it. And this pattern seemed to perform better using a loop knot.

Inside many estuaries, redfish, spotted sea trout, black drum, snook, and even tarpon feed on a number of small baits 3 to 4 inches long. In some locations, you can expect to find larger grass beds, and depending on the locations you fish, you may need to build most flies with a mono weedguard. This pattern will also work on freshwater bass that feed on small panfish, frogs, and other small baits. The tail action mimics a frog's swimming kick. With the inverted hook and weedguard, this fly is ideal for casting into and around lily pads.

The weedless features also are ideal for casting along mangroves, around docks, or when working bridge pilings. Try casting as close as possible to the structure. One trick to use when fishing around overhanging mangroves is to cast sidearm, making the loop roll out parallel to the water. Make the last forward casting stroke with the rod level with the water and sidearm. Another casting technique is to drive a low cast right above the surface of the water below the mangroves. This requires a hard casting stroke with a strong double haul. The loop needs to be small and tight. For most anglers, the sidearm cast is a better choice.

Fish the fly near the bottom or just above weed beds using short pulls to hop the fly. Fish the fly like you would most

Use this fly in tight locations when there are many tangles. This snook was tucked along a wall of mangroves. It would have been tough to cast a fly that wasn't weedless into the mangrove pockets where this fish was holding. This design is also ideal when fishing among tree stumps and fallen trees or other obstacles that the will foul the hook.

This largemouth bass was taken on an early version of this pattern. I was testing the fly's action, fishing it along a weed bed. I didn't even trim the knot. This early pattern was an imitation of a weighted Snake Fly. It had a much longer tail and was not as chunky as today's Winged Weedless Rat, but the fly rode hook up with a weedguard. Once I began to develop the fly as a Southern estuary pattern, it took on a different shape. I made the fly shorter and chunkier with different materials, and its whole demeanor changed, but it's still an effective freshwater bass pattern.

attractor patterns to cover sections of water in open locations that don't have enough cover to hold fish. Work the edges of mangroves or along mussel and oyster bars. Often, bars form flows. Be sure to work moving water that might hold fish. I like to cast so the fly swings across the current. If you're sight-fishing, cast the fly so it settles in front of the fish and work it slowly away as if it were retreating.

When redfish are tailing in weed beds, it's often a tough sell because with their heads buried in the weeds, they seldom see the fly. When sight-casting in open-bottom locations, let the fly drop to the bottom and then hop it along the bottom with short pulls.

For fishing fresh water, build some patterns with lightweight eyes to work around lily pads and along shallow shorelines. You'll need to use a much slower retrieve when fishing for largemouth bass. And because the fly is weedless, you can cast into lily pads or other weedy locations with few hang-ups. For most flats and sight-fishing, a floating line works fine. Even when you're not casting to sighted fish, a topwater line works to fish along bars, near shorelines, or over weed beds.

Night fishing is one of the best ways to catch snook. You have to cover the water with a steady retrieve. Even when fishing around lights, you often don't see the fish until the strike. Unless the water is clear, a $7\frac{1}{2}$-foot, tapered leader is a good choice. When blind fishing slightly deeper water, an intermediate line is effective. Work the fly with a steady retrieve using short pulls.

I believe this pattern would work for laid-up tarpon with a few changes: Use a strong tarpon hook and eliminate the weedguard. The stinger hook can be used for other fish, but I would not recommend it without testing it on tarpon first.

The combination of materials gives the fly movement that allows it to walk along the bottom or drift just off the bottom, looking like a shrimp or baitfish. Excellent Florida fishing guide and longtime friend Frank Catino gave me some great information about how he wanted a fly to perform. This helped me to better understand how to design a fly that would work in a different fishery. Getting Frank's expert advice was a big help. Tan, pink, and white or a mixture of these colors is a good choice for many Southern locations. Frank referred to these shades as shrimpy.

For a fast retrieve or when you need a steady, flowing retrieve, the two-handed retrieve is hard to beat. Using two hands, you have so many options and a much better feel for how the fly is performing. In conditions where fast-swimming gamefish take the fly and keep moving toward you, a two-handed retrieve allows for a faster take-up for setting the hook.

Building Weedless Flies

Putting weedguards on flies takes more time, but it's often worthwhile when you're fishing in locations where fish are feeding in and around weedy areas like grass beds. Tie in a section of 60- to 80-pound-test monofilament so it stands up off the hook shaft, blocking the hook point. A straight section of line will work, but a bent section of mono is easier to tie in. Take a section of mono about three inches long and pinch both ends between your thumb and forefinger to form a rounded U. Hold the U close to a flame from a candle or lighter. When the mono changes shape, forming a teardrop, quickly remove it from the flame and stop pinching. The bend should be about 75 to 90 degrees, but it depends on the fly design and hook size. You be the judge. Do not get the mono too close to the flame or you will melt it into two pieces or weaken the mono. It does not take much heat to bend the mono.

Tie the mono in using enough thread so it does not move and bond it with superglue. If you want to ensure that the weedguard will never move, cut the mono a little longer than the hook's eye on the section where you'll tie it into the fly's head. Melt that end, forming a tiny ball, and while the mono ball is still hot, put several turns of tying thread over the ball. This will bond the weedguard to the tying thread. Then use a strong wrap of tying thread and glue, and it will never move. Weedguards prevent most bottom snags, unless the weeds are thick. Using a shiner or stinger hook and putting a slight bend behind the hook's eye makes a weedguard more effective and easier to tie in. ■

My first attempts at this pattern produced flies that didn't always ride perfectly upright. The early flies hopped along, at times rolling on their side. They didn't have the lead wrap, and the two wings were tied inverted, with a shorter body hair collar. They caught fish, but I thought the action might bother some anglers. The bigger wings and lead wrap with lightweight eyes keep the fly fairly stable, and the new flies remain upright and bounce along the bottom, riding hook up. However, I didn't mind the fly rolling because it looked like a crippled bait bouncing along the bottom, trying to hide. This pattern can be tied with $\frac{1}{4}$-ounce eyes or $\frac{5}{32}$- and $\frac{3}{16}$-ounce eyes for a slightly heavier pattern.

WINGED WEEDLESS RAT

Hook:	#1/0 Gamakatsu Stinger B10S
Tail:	Light orange arctic fox fur and two tan marabou feathers
Wing:	Long tan elk or deer body hair or bucktail
Collar:	Deer or elk body hair
Weight:	Lead wire
Head:	Yellow Crystal Chenille or Sparkle Chenille
Eye:	Pewter dumbbell eyes ($\frac{5}{32}$- or $\frac{3}{16}$-ounce)
Weedguard:	60-pound mono

Note: Even though this fly is fished inverted, start tying it with the hook shaft upright in the vise. Tying the first steps is much easier that way. Once you tie in the eyes, then turn the fly over for a better perspective on how the fly will look in the water.

1. Bend a 1/0 stinger hook along the shaft about $\frac{3}{8}$ to $\frac{1}{2}$ inch behind the hook's eye; when you're finished, the hook shaft should be on the same plane as the hook point to maintain the best hook set. Don't use a standard hook because a bend like this will affect the hook set. The stinger hook is effective for this application. Sizes 1 to 2/0 work for the weedless fly. Because the weedguard and buildup of material somewhat reduce the hook gap, I like to use larger hooks. The closest hook, the one pictured here in the vise, has the proper bend.

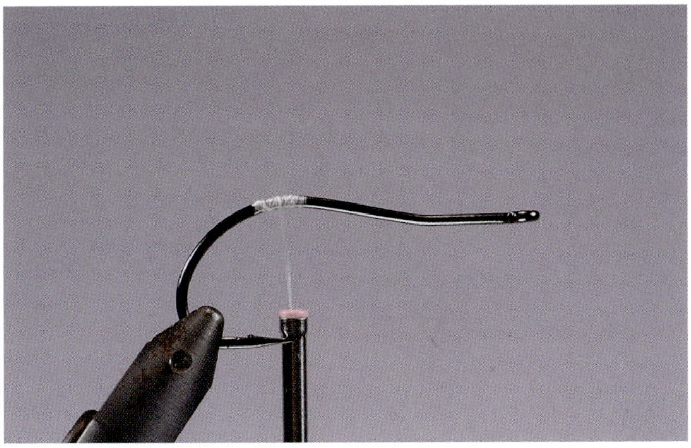

2. Tie in the thread at the hook's bend.

3. Tie in a tail of light orange fox fur about 2½ inches long at the hook's bend above the shaft. Remember, this will be on the underside of the fly when it is inverted. Raccoon fur is longer and better for larger flies. If you want a longer fly (instead of larger) use a strip of rabbit fur.

4. Tie the first of two tan marabou feathers on each side of the fox fur. The tan feathers should extend about ½ inch short of the fox fur.

5. Tie in the second feather on the other side of the fox fur. The marabou feathers should envelop the fur. The marabou helps stabilize the fur, which is supple. For larger flies, the fur should extend about an inch beyond the marabou.

6. Next make about five tight wraps of lead wire on the hook shaft. The lead should butt up to the tail's base. About 1¼ inches of lead wire is ideal.

7. Then cover the lead with tying thread, making a firm bond to the hook shaft. Cover the lead with Mylar tubing. (This is an option for looks only.)

8. Tie in the pewter dumbbell eyes to the crook of the bend you made in the hook shaft. Tie them to the top of the shaft, which will be the underside of the fly when you're finished.

9. Now turn the fly over so the hook is inverted in the vise, leaving the eye on the bottom of the fly, and tie in the first of two bunches of long, tan body hair over the lead wrap. These wings should form a V shape on either side of the hook point, extending about an inch past the hook's bend. This should leave space to spin in the collar between the lead and the eye.

10. Tie the second wing onto the lead wrap on the other side of the hook point. These wings stabilize the fly and keep it upright as it settles to the bottom. If you want a thinner profile, use bucktail. Face the tapered hairs toward the tail of the fly.

11. Between the wings and the dumbbell eyes, tie in the collar, spinning in a section of shorter, finer tan body hair. If it looks too bulky, trim the top to open up the hook point.

12. Tie in a string of yellow chenille in front of the eyes.

13. Wrap the chenille behind the eyes, crossing over the dumbbell eyes' base. Do not finish wrapping the chenille nose. Tie off the chenille using a loose wrap behind the frame of the vise.

14. Make the weedguard with a piece of 60-pound mono. Form a bend in the mono, and hold it near the flame of a small lighter or candle. Make up to a dozen of these at one time if you plan to make a number of flies.

15. Use the premade mono weedguard, and tie the bend of the mono to the base of the dumbbell eyes. An effective trick to make the weedguard nonslip is to melt the end of the mono, forming a molten ball. While the ball is still hot, wrap the ball with tying thread. The soft mono will bond with the tying thread. Then, continue to wrap the thread over the mono from the dumbbell eyes to the hook's eye, locking in the weedguard.

16. Melt the end of the guard before tying it onto the nose of the fly.

17. Finish wrapping the chenille. Cover the mono and hook shaft with chenille around the eyes and to the hook's eye. Then cut the weedguard off above the hook point.

18. To finish the fly, trim the collar, leaving the longer tapered ends that lay back over the fly.

19. To reinforce the weedguard, add some superglue to the chenille wrap where the mono sticks up from the chenille, and on the thread at the fly's head.

20. The finished fly. When tied properly, the fly should flow through the water with the hook point up. The breathable material gives the fly great action.

Several different versions of this fly. Like the snake fly, this "rat" can be tied in many colors. If using this pattern for well educated flats fish, tie flies that match the bottom color.

CHAPTER 22

Rat Chovy

Anchovies have shiny bodies with a light green, blue, or pink tint. Depending on the water clarity and sunlight, their color can vary. In some locations where fish feed on smaller baits, the fly's size is critical. The eye is important for two reasons: appearance and weight. I want enough weight to make the fly drop after each pull. Hardtails often pick off baitfish that are swimming below the dense school. A fly that is hopping below the main school of bait offers an appealing target.

Bay anchovies, also called rain bait, appear in mid to late summer in New England. This baitfish is a favorite of both false albacore and Atlantic bonito. However, many other fish also feed on these small, 2- to 3-inch-long baitfish. Other members of the anchovy family range from the Northeast into Florida. Anchovies range along the entire East Coast, from New England to the Gulf of Mexico and south into the Caribbean. They vary in size from 3 to 6 inches. The Bahamas have a 4- to 5-inch-long baitfish locals call pilchard, and Spanish sardines that look similar.

Most anchovies are small, and flies that match them should be 3 to 4 inches long. They are chunky baits with a deep body for their size. I started building these small flies to fish for the ocean speedsters that can drive anglers nuts. Farther south when fish feed on larger anchovies, you can catch them more consistently. What I tried to do was build a small fly that would drop when you pause during the retrieve, and then dart forward with each pull of the retrieve.

Anchovies have a light tan to light pink appearance with a shiny side. Tan or pink is my first choice of color, but I think light green or light yellow would also be effective. I like to mix in tan body hair and tan chenille. It seems any light color works. I believe that fly placement and size is more important than color, as long as the color used is not much different than the naturals. Flies in different light conditions can take on several colors.

When casting anchovy patterns to hardtails, you need to get the fly under the thick schools of bait. Both the small size of the bait and density of the schools make it necessary to present the fly so it stands out. A fast-sinking line will make the fly settle down quickly below the school. You can then start the retrieve sooner. A fast-sinking line also casts more quickly and fights the wind better. I like a bolting action, giving the fly short, fast pulls, or try longer pulls. A faster moving fly is usually the best technique for hardtails. These fish are fast swimmers and feed quickly. Their speed when they take the fly can make feeling strikes difficult, especially if the fish is swimming toward you when it takes the fly and if you are using a slow retrieve. A fast retrieve gives you a better chance to feel the take.

Remember, even if these fish are busting on the surface, getting the fly down is often the best technique. When fish are feeding, moving quickly, try to get the fly ahead of the feeding fish, not into them. One of the problems with fly fishing is that the time it takes to make a 60-foot cast, get it to the proper depth, and then begin retrieving might put the fly behind the fish. If you can determine the direction that the fish are moving, cast ahead of the feeding fish. Often, fish are looking for

False albacore can be tough to take when they are on small baits. Here is Capt. Dan Marini with a big Rhode Island albie. The key to taking fish on this day was size—2½- to 3-inch patterns fished below the schools. Usually it is better to fish below thick schools of any baitfish.

Tying Flies with Built-in Bite Guards

What follows are instructions for making a haywire twist in solid trolling wire. To illustrate this knot properly, I used thick lead wire to produce clear photos, and a large hook and thread for winding guides on a spinning rod to show how to tie the wire onto the hook shank. For more information on tying a haywire twist and other valuable knots, see Lefty Kreh's excellent knot book *Fishing Knots*.

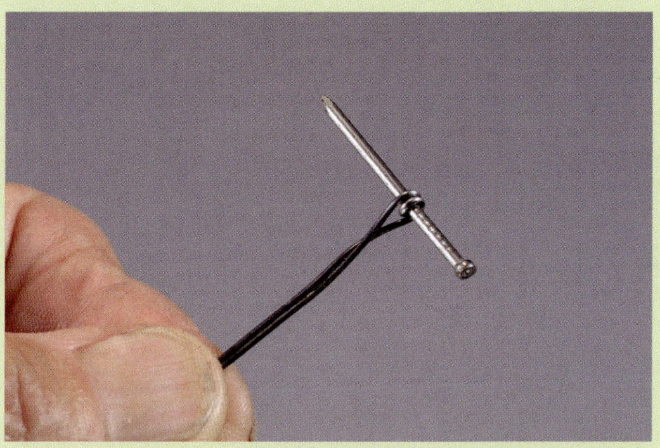

1. Cut a piece of 38- or 56-pound solid wire about 10 inches long. Bend the wire in the middle, and wrap the wire around a small finish nail or the shaft of a fly-tying bodkin to form a double loop. This will be the end of the bite guard where you will tie the leader when attaching the fly.

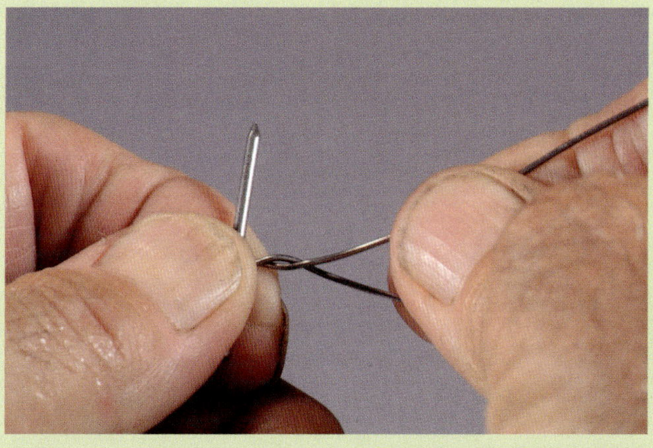

2. Pinch the double loop between your thumb and forefinger, forming a V in the wire below your thumb. Hold the V and twist the wire one half turn. This will put a twist just below the double loop.

3. Continue putting twists in the wire until you have five to six turns in it. Be sure they are tightly wrapped. Twist one after the other.

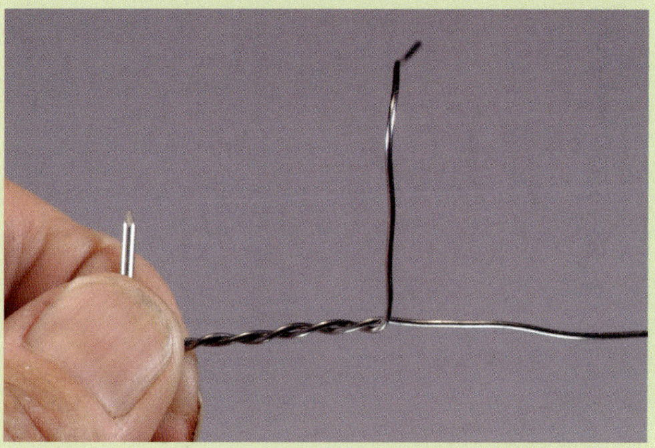

4. Bend the tag end of the wire to form a 90-degree angle off the standing wire, and form another 90-degree bend to make a handle off the first bend.

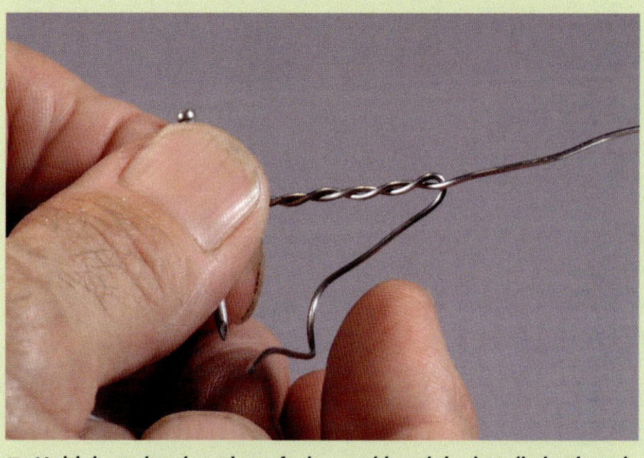

5. Hold the twisted section of wire, and bend the handle back and forth along the standing wire. This will flex and then produce a clean break, removing the tag end of the wire. Do not cut the wire because it leaves a burred end that will cut your fingers.

(Continued)

6. Done properly, the haywire twist leaves a clean wire connection for a bite guard.

7. Bend the hook's eye up enough so the wire can slide through the hook's eye and lie flat along the hook shaft. Tie in the tying thread about ¾ inch behind the hook's eye.

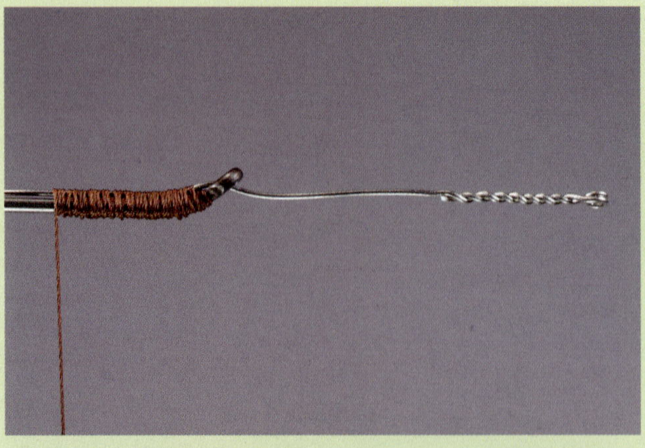

8. Slide the wire into the hook's eye, extending the wire with the double loop about 2 to 3 inches beyond the hook's eye, and wrap the wire and hook shaft back to the end of the thread, bonding the wire to the hook shaft.

9. Bend the wire back over the section of wire on the hook shaft, and cut the wire with cutting pliers behind the hook's eye.

10. Wrap over the same section of wire again, covering the doubled wire and hook shaft. This puts a double bond over the wire, and folding the wire back over the hook shaft gives it extra strength.

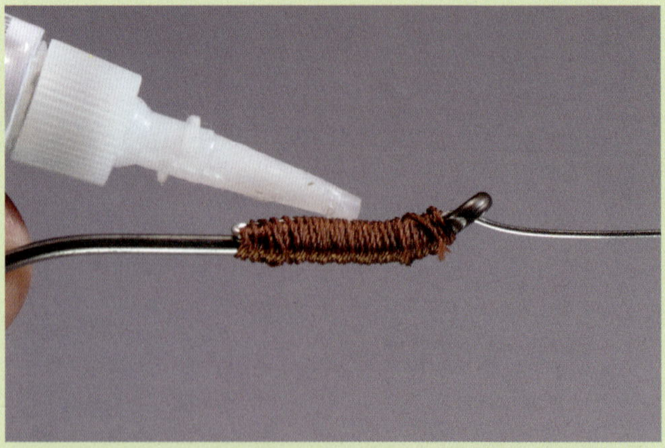

11. For even more strength, put a drop of superglue over the wrapping.

Tie any fly pattern to the hook. If you're using this system for bigger flies, use heavier wire. I usually use 38-pound wire if I'm fishing in clear water because the smaller diameter is less visible. If visibility is not a problem, the heavier, stronger wire will kink less and hold up better. ■

Here is Roger Swiderski with a nice school bluefin. From a drifting boat, try to cast at a right angle to the boat's path, or behind the boat so the boat's forward motion keeps the line tight. Anglers who cast in the same direction as the boat's flow often miss the strike because the boat's forward movement creates slack. A fly that acts crippled under the mass of bait should attract attention. But even with all the planning and special flies, getting albacore and bonito to strike consistently in the Northeast is tough. Albies and bones are truly fish that leave anglers muttering to themselves.

bait ahead of the surface-feeding fish, and these fish will single out a fly. Many times I have hooked up by casting before the fish start breaking.

When chasing fish from a boat, don't run straight into breaking fish. The chance of putting the fish down is much greater, but also the boat will drift forward a distance. If you make a cast in front of the boat as it drifts forward, you can't fish the fly or feel the strike. The boat will overrun the line and fly. It's better to make a 90-degree turn and cast off the side of the boat. As the boat drifts forward, the movement helps to tighten the line.

I learned this when running other anglers into breaking hardtails. The anglers in the bow would cast first, sometimes rushing the cast. Unless they cast at a 90-degree angle to the moving boat, there would be slack line. I would wait and cast after the bow angler. By then the boat's movement had slowed, and its direction was easy to calculate. Often I hooked up first, and the bow anglers missed because feeling strikes and retrieving the fly was difficult there. One day while fishing with two anglers for small bluefin off Rhode Island, I learned a lesson about waiting. The angler in the bow did not listen to my instructions and rushed his cast on every school we approached. But the guy in the stern waited until I said to cast. He took three fish; the bow angler never had a strike. Making a quick cast is important, but timing and fly placement are equally important.

RAT AND GLOW CHOVY

Hook:	#1 Mustad 34007
Tail:	Light pink arctic fox fur
Body:	Polar Flash
Eye:	Red pewter dumbbell eyes ($^3/_{16}$-ounce)
Wing:	Polar Flash
Collar:	Fine tan elk body hair
Head:	Thin tan chenille

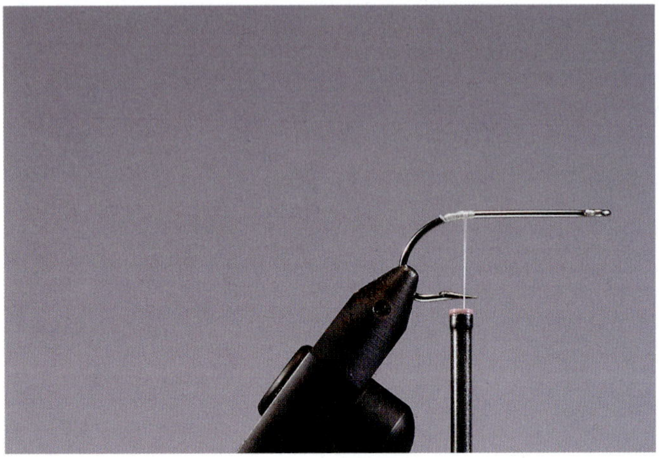

1. Start by tying the thread at the hook's bend. Any standard, stainless steel hook in sizes 4 to 1 will work.

2. Tie in a tail of arctic fox fur, extending back about $2^1/_2$ inches. This will make a fly about $3^1/_2$ inches long. Depending on the hook size, you can build flies from $2^1/_2$ to over 4 inches long. For longer flies, Finn raccoon fur is better. If you want to make a Glow Chovy, tie in a small section of hot pink or hot orange Fluoro Fibre, first at the hook's bend, and then tie in the fox or raccoon fur at the hook's bend around the Fluoro Fibre. (Here I used light pink arctic fox fur, but tan or light green would work too.)

3. Tie in a long section Polar Flash in front of the tail's base, and wind the thread to the front of the hook shaft. The Polar Flash serves as both the body and one wing.

4. Tie on the dumbbell eyes about $^3/_8$ inch behind the hook's eye.

5. Wrap on the Polar Flash to form the body, stopping before the dumbbell eyes and leaving enough room for the collar.

6. Use the remaining Polar Flash for the top wing. Fold back the Polar Flash and tie the top wing in place.

7. Tie in a thinner bottom wing of Polar Flash. Both wings should be about the same length.

8. Spin in a small section of fine, tan elk body hair with the tapered ends facing toward the tail, just behind the dumbbell eyes. It should flare on top and behind the dumbbell eyes, forming a good collar.

9. Tie in a thin section of tan flash chenille, wrapping it in front of the dumbbell eyes.

10. Begin wrapping the chenille by bringing it first behind the eyes. Make several wraps. This will lock in the eyes and tighten the collar. Then, keep wrapping around the eyes and continue to wrap in front of the eyes to form the ratlike nose. Tie off the thread. Because the fly is small, the nose does not have the longer taper of the bigger Sea Rat.

11. Trim the body hair to form a smaller head.

Three different variations of this pattern. Anchovies are small baitfish. In the Northeast, they range about 2 to 3 inches long, but as you travel south, they can be up to about 5 inches. I make these flies 2½ to 4 inches long and keep the colors to a light tint. Their general color is light tan to light pink or light olive with flash.

CHAPTER 23

Rat Needlefish

This Rat Needlefish is dropping between strips near a coral outcropping in the Bahamas. The long tail matches the movement of a needlefish. These long, thin baitfish kick their tails when chased—it's the tail movement that gives this fly life. Needlefish either sit, holding just below the surface, or they swim at high speed. An effective retrieve is to use long, fast pulls with a slight pause in between.

I thought the shape of the Sea Rat's head was perfect for a needlefish fly. The long nose and eye placement were similar to a needlefish, and the head and nose are easy to tie. The profile of the Snake Fly also fit needlefish, but it would require too much trimming to get the head thin enough. The Rat Needlefish fly did not require much trial and error. It is easy to make, and you can tie a number of different versions. The fly swims well in the water, and depending on the weight of the eye, it will either glide with a slight dip to the nose, or the nose will drop down after each pull.

Needlefish and halfbeaks are long, thin fish with slender noses. They are important bait in Southern waters for cuda and offshore species and are a favorite bait for stripers along outer beaches. They are often seen in small groups and are common in Florida and the Bahamas, holding along the edges of flats and into deep water. Needlefish can be a nuisance when they are present on bonefish flats. When you reel in a bonefish fly to make another cast, a needlefish might chase the fly and grab it. If its teeth catch the leader, it will either cut the fly off or damage the leader. If you see a needlefish around your fly, even if you do not feel it grab the fly, check the leader for damage.

In Southern locations I see needlefish everywhere, ranging from 3 to 4 inches up to 12 inches long. Similar species like houndfish grow to over 3 feet long. All these baits are similar: they are long and thin with no dorsal fin, have long noses, and hold near the surface. They jump, sometimes greyhounding along the surface with great speed. When frightened, needlefish swim, almost bolting through the water as if jet-propelled, giving hard tail kicks. When you fish a needlefish fly in Southern locations, try using a fast retrieve. Use a two-handed retrieve, or try long, fast pulls with a single-handed retrieve. You can't match the speed of these baitfish using fly tackle. Even with spinning tackle it's difficult. However, they do at times feed on small fish near the surface. This is the best opportunity to match their erratic action. Try fishing a floating fly line, working the fly near the surface, and getting it to bolt with sharp pulls. Also try a long, gilding action with a steady, two-handed retrieve to keep the fly moving. Try moving the fly along near the surface with short pulls to make it look like a feeding baitfish. For this type of fishing, build some flies with lightweight eyes.

I like fishing with an intermediate fly line along beaches for stripers, working the fly like a needlefish plug. Needlefish lures used with surf tackle are real fish-getters, and depending on the lure design, they generally run 1 to 3 feet below the surface. An intermediate line will get the fly down and tracks effectively in light surf. Fish the fly using long pulls with a short pause. This gets the fly to glide and then dip down on each pause. Make some of these flies all black for night fishing in the North. Yellow is also another popular color for early morning striper fishing. This fly also matches a large offshore sand eel, which looks like a needlefish without the nose. Offshore sand eels differ from the small, thin, inshore sand eels. Offshore sand eels average about 6 inches long but can be over 8 inches and have a much thicker body.

I think that sometimes in these Southern waters, a fast retrieve can trigger a response that will excite some fish to strike. I've had success fishing for reef fish like snapper and grouper or the tough-to-fool barracuda when I get the offering to move as fast as possible. Speed turns most reef fish on, as it does with many offshore species. Yet fish that feed in back-bays, flats, and along sandy beaches seem to prefer a slower fly (except for bluefish and jacks).

RAT NEEDLEFISH

Hook:	#2/0 Mustad 34007
Tail:	Long, thin light green and white saddle hackles and pearl Krystal Flash
Eye:	White dumbbell eyes (3/16-ounce)
Wing:	Sparse marabou feathers, to match tail
Collar:	Chartreuse elk or deer body hair
Head/Nose:	Green chenille

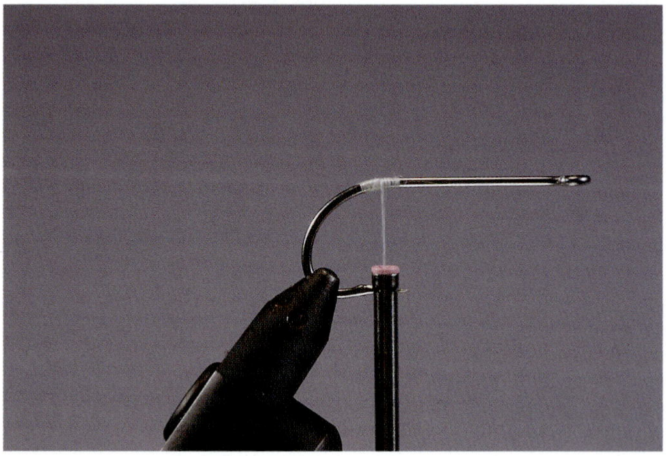

1. Tie in the thread at the hook's bend. Other standard, stainless steel hooks in sizes 1 to 2/0 will work as well.

2. As with all needlefish flies, keep the tail thin, using six or seven thin feathers. Start with three thin, white saddle hackle feathers tied at the hook's bend. This pattern works well in many color combinations. For daytime fishing, the colors in this fly match most needlefish that I see.

3. Tie in three light green (or light blue) hackles over the white hackle.

4. Over the hackle feathers, tie in about ten strands of pearl Krystal Flash. (Any flash with a light blue or light olive tint will work.)

5. Tie in the dumbbell eyes about $\frac{1}{2}$ inch behind the hook's eye. Remember, a drop of superglue will secure the eyes better.

6. For the wing, tie in thin marabou feathers behind the eye that match the tail color. Thin Bird Fur feathers also work, but be sure that they lay flat and don't make the fly's silhouette too fat.

7. Spin on a thin section of chartreuse body hair behind the set of dumbbell eyes.

8. Tie in thin green chenille in front of the eyes. (The color should match the tail.)

9. Wrap the chenille to build it up around the eyes, and then form a thin nose, ending at the hook's eye.

10. Trim the body hair collar to make a tight head to fit the fly's profile.

11. The finished fly is ready to fish.

CHAPTER 24

How to Set Up a Fly Box

These three fly boxes are set up for a variety of fishing. The two boxes at the top will catch fish in the North to blue water to Southern locations. These boxes match Northern foods like squid, sand eels, spearing, and herring and will also match Southern foods like mullet, pilchards, and shrimp. These boxes hold both a mixed bag of attractor flies and some patterns that match different baitfish. Remember, some bait types are found in many locations. The box on the bottom has mostly bonefish patterns, including some crabs for permit or redfish. Some of the larger bonefish flies also work on stripers and weakfish.

I'm perhaps the last person to tell anyone how to arrange flies in a box. Some anglers I fish with have systems that keep their flies visible and always ready for use. On one bonefish trip with Eric Peterson, a professional fly tier and one of the best anglers I know, I noticed he kept each pattern in a section. He had rows or blocks of flies with like patterns together. If he had a pattern in three different colors, each color was in a row. He also had flies of different sizes in separate boxes. He once gave me a box of small baitfish patterns, and each fly type was neatly arranged in its proper section.

Dave Skok is another professional fly tier and great angler who keeps each fly organized at his fingertips. He uses both boxes and plastic bags to keep flies in order. Dave makes several large patterns that he stores in bags rather than stuffed in a box. Dave makes a point about keeping flies in a safe package to prevent them from being crushed. You can ruin some fly patterns if you don't store them properly.

Bob Luce, the dean of fishing the rips between Monomoy and Nantucket on Cape Cod, looked in my fly box and laughed. First he picked out each fly that still had the leader knot left in the hook's eye, and then he pulled out the flies that were not properly hooked into the box. He delighted in giving me a hard time about the disarray of my fly boxes. His fly box was in perfect order, and usually his flies were in small plug boxes, with each fly in a plastic envelop. Each season Bob took me and my wife, Barb, fishing on the rips from Monomoy to the north and east of Nantucket. His untimely passing at the end of 2012 was a reminder that nothing lasts forever. We will miss those trips, but even more, we will miss his entertaining, dry humor. The most important advice I can give any angler is to keep your fly box neat. Have the patterns that fit the fishing conditions, and be able to find them when you need them. And store each fly to protect it from harm. Nothing is worse than needing a fly and realizing that you can't fish it.

Setting up a Beginner's Fly Box

Anglers must choose patterns that fit their fishing needs. A small selection of popular fly patterns in a few colors and sizes is the way most novice anglers begin fly-fishing the sea. You might have two each of a dozen different flies, a scattering of mostly attractor patterns. This is a smart way to start; keep the fly selection simple. As you develop and learn more about the sport and begin to gain experience in the waters you fish, your selection will become more sophisticated with six to twelve flies of patterns that work for you, sometimes in several sizes. Once you have an ample supply of all the basic baitfish patterns, then it's

Stripers, even large ones, will lock into a worm hatch, even going up into small backwater to find them. No matter where or when I'm fishing in the Northeast, I always carry a few worm hatch flies. I have seen hatches of these small baits in many locations at different times throughout the season.

I am different from most bonefish anglers. I have a number of small baitfish patterns in my box. I still have many other patterns, but I will never be without small flies that match small baitfish.

time to add some precise flies of the most popular baitfish. Southern anglers need to include a selection of larger shrimp and some crab patterns, along with baitfish flies. Trout and bass anglers in fresh water have fewer baitfish patterns to choose from and even fewer frog and mouse flies. Not until the trout angler gets to dry flies and nymphs does it get bewildering. Fresh water usually has fewer bait changes in one location, and some places might have the same foods all season. In sweet water, matching fly size to fish size is more important when you move from small creeks to big rivers. Remember, several frog and mouse patterns will catch largemouth bass anywhere they swim.

Saltwater anglers also need special patterns—small crustaceans, crabs, shrimp, or worm hatch flies. Again, the choice of flies depends on the location. As you gain experience, you will learn which flies to use for specific fishing conditions. Though you won't often need these special patterns, when you do, they are important. What usually happens, and it has certainly happened to me, is you jam more and more flies into the box until you can't find what you need. I constantly develop new fly patterns; it's fun and keeps fly tying interesting. However, what often happens is you stop fishing with old, reliable patterns.

If you find a fly box cluttered with too many flies, start by removing all of them. Then put the flies in like categories. Place the flies in groups or rows where they can be seen. A good way to position the flies is by food types. Work out a system to keep the fly box in order. But, as I mentioned, I am perhaps the worst person to give advice about keeping an orderly fly box.

Your fly selection should have the basic attractor patterns that work all season, several types of precise, lifelike flies, and some special flies that might change throughout the season. Some of the precise and special flies might only catch fish for a month or less, or they may not even be useful when the bait they represent is not prevalent.

How I Set Up My Fly Box

Usually I use a system with three fly boxes: one box for larger patterns and poppers, one box for general baitfish, and a third for small baitfish, crabs, shrimp, and worms. The box of larger patterns consists of thin to wide-bodied flies that are 7 to 9 inches long. Flies that copy wide-bodied baits like spawning river herring that occur in spring will fill most of the big fly box. Poppers are often great fish-getters and fun to fish. Carry several larger, three to four midsize, and two to three small poppers. If you fish offshore rips where squid are abundant, carry a decent selection of squid flies. When stripers are on squid, they feed near or on the surface, even when holding in deep rips. Remember, rod and line size and your casting skills might limit the number of bigger flies and poppers you can use.

The next box is for general use flies, go-to flies that catch fish in most locations and conditions. I carry a few each of perhaps six special patterns and add more as needed. The go-to box should have a mixture of thin to midbodied attractor flies from 4 to 7 inches long. Have a good selection of colors. All black, all white, all yellow, and light olive are good choices, as well as some flies with blends of light colors. Include flies both with and without flash. Most patterns I use catch fish in many locations. This box would also work well in many freshwater locations for largemouth and smallmouth bass, trout, Alaskan salmon, or pike and pickerel. For trout I would use the same patterns, but the sizes would be smaller, 3 to 5 inches, and I'd include some chunky patterns 2½ to 4 inches long. The trout box would also be useful for other freshwater species.

The last box is for small flies like sand eels, small fry patterns, worm flies, shrimp and crab patterns, and any special flies that might only be useful for a short time. If I'm planning to fish for offshore species, I could convert a section of this box for bay anchovy patterns and tuna flies. Some years, this box might get less use, but when you need special flies, it can save the day. Many of these small patterns also work for fresh water.

In these boxes some sections never change—my seasoned veterans, the workhorse flies that catch fish under many conditions. These are the attractors that work along the coast of the Northeast and are also effective when I travel to the Carolinas, Florida, the Bahamas, Mexico, or Puerto Rico, and they worked in Alaska and for big, early- and late-season trout fishing. Some of these flies catch fish in places where they don't seem to match the local food, but they work because their action excites the fish.

Fly Boxes for the South

Once you get down South, fly types change because the baitfish are smaller and shrimp and crabs are a much more dominant food source than in Northern waters. For fishing Southern

Here is Capt. Curt Jessup, from Cape Cod, who took this big albie while fishing in North Carolina. These albies were feeding on larger anchovies than what we see up north. Curt found that using bigger flies in slightly discolored water made the albies feed way more aggressively than when he fished for them in his local waters. WARREN MARSHALL

You can use a smaller fly box for bonefishing compared to other types of fishing. First off, the flies are smaller, and once you are familiar with a location, you often select from less than a dozen patterns—sometimes less. However, when traveling to new areas, the right selection of flies is important. Here is where that small fly-tying kit can save a trip.

waters, you need a box for 2½- to 4-inch swimming shrimp patterns, a box for general baitfish 3 to 6 inches long, and a box of small, special flies. I might include a number of the same patterns I use for fishing the Northeast, but with thicker bodies or altered to match larger shrimp or local baitfish. And some portion of these patterns should be designed with weed-guards or built to slip through the weeds with less hang-up. Remember, shrimp, crabs, and midbodied to wide-bodied, small baitfish are more abundant in Southern waters. Inside estuaries, at certain times of the year, shrimp and crabs might be as important as baitfish. And bonefish and permit are a whole other story: you need many different small patterns. One fly type I will never be without when bonefishing is a 1½- to 2½-inch-long baitfish fry pattern.

Rearranging Your Fly Box

Rearranging your fly box to coincide with changing food types is wise. Never totally remove one group of fly types; just keep up with dominant bait types. I always carry one box of mixed fly types that cover baits for the entire season, except for very large flies. This is a smart way to arrange your fly box as the season unfolds and a good standard to follow to keep your sanity.

I always carry a few big patterns, but in the spring when fishing the estuaries, I have a much larger assortment of bigger, full-bodied flies. Have a few tiny flies in the box at all times, also, but have a wider selection in the summer and early fall for hatches of crabs and small baitfish like butterfish, anchovies, tiny whiting, and other baits. Most of these flies should range from 1½ to 3 inches long. Be aware of the times that juvenile foods appear and begin to develop where you fish. They can create a windfall of excellent fishing, but it might not last for long. Remember that in different locations the times that big baitfish arrive, young of the year develop, or when hatches occur is different.

Flies for Ocean Fish

Anglers who fish for ocean species like bonito, false albacore, or bluefin and blackfin tuna need a special box of flies tailored to match the different conditions of offshore fishing. Some of the patterns might be similar when these fish move close to shore, but the fly's construction is different. Even when bluefin are feeding on small baitfish, 3 to 4 inches long, I tie small flies on bigger hooks. Normally, 3-inch patterns are tied on size 2 or 1 hooks; however, for species like bluefin tuna over 30 pounds, I like to use an extra-strong 2/0 to 3/0 hook. The same is true when fishing for tarpon: a strong hook provides better hooking qualities.

I like to put bigger eyes on flies for pelagic species. In clear water the eyes of a baitfish stand out and even look bigger than they actually are. Eyes and the fly's size are important for offshore fishing when the fish are being picky. In some locations these fish seem to examine each fly like a diamond dealer checking a gemstone. Often the baitfish are small, 2 to 4 inches long, with bay anchovies being a major bait in the Northeast. It's amazing to see 50-pound tuna feeding on 3- to 4-inch-long baitfish.

Each angler must develop a system to keep the fly box neat. Mine looks fine until I start fishing, and then it becomes messy. Every so often I take the time to rearrange it, but I'm not like other anglers who have perfect rows of neatly tied flies. One problem is the game I play to see how many different fly patterns will work if I get into feeding fish. I keep changing flies after catching several fish. It's surprising how many different types of flies will catch fish even when they are not in a feeding frenzy. I should learn to put them back in their proper space, but that never happens. One trick is having a separate section of the box for each food type or a section for like patterns. Some fly patterns might copy several food types.

Another simple way to organize flies for ocean fish is by size. When you're using only fly one box, pick one with three sections: one for small, thin patterns; one for large herring-type flies and poppers; and a section of mixed flies ranging from thin to chunky, 4 to 7 inches long. If you use three boxes, have a box for each category and then break the flies into sections. The box of small flies needs the most work because it might hold five to six times the number of flies compared to the box of bigger patterns. Never mix small flies into a box with large patterns; the smaller flies get buried.

Except for those carrying big herring and bunker patterns, I like fly boxes that have soft material on the top and bottom, so each fly can be held in place by securing the hook into the bottom or top of the box. This way the flies don't fall or blow out. And the small flies are easier to find.

Index

Page numbers in italics indicate photographs.

Adams, Aaron J., 5
alewives, as food source, 35
anchovy
flies, *169*
as food source, 28, 32, 170
patterns for, 175
Rat Chovy, 169–76
arctic fox Zonker, 47

Badger Sand Eel, 93–96
recipe for, 95–96
baitfish, 27–37
anchovy as, 170
appearance of, 2
Bonefish Fry, 123–26
color patterns of, 18, 21
cycles of, 29
example of, *3*, *27*
fish feeding on, 124–25
flies to match, 5
ballyhoo, as food source, *31*
Barracuda Fly, 111–16
color in, *19*
example of, *18*
recipe for, 114–15
Bird Fur, 47
bite guards, 171–72
Blue Lady, 135–42
example of, *135*, *138*, *142*
recipe for, 139–42
bluefish, as food source, *36*, 37
bobbin, fly-tying, 41
bonefish
color of, 112
feeding patterns of, 37, 124–25, 144
fishing techniques for, 11, 14, 18
flies for, 1–2
patterns for, 52, 55–57, 60
sand eel patterns for, 144
shrimp patterns for, 124
sight-fishing for, *94*
Bonefish Fry, 14, 123–26
Fluoro Fibre used for, *50*
recipe for, 125–26
bucktail hair, 43
butterfish, as food source, 35

casting
anchovy patterns, 170
for barracuda, 113–14
Bonefish Fry, 124–25
large fly, 76, 99
poppers, 118–19
sand eel fly, 94–95
shrimp or crab patterns, 124–25, 128–30
Slab Fly, 86–87
Snake Fly, 60–61
squid fly, 106
in surf, 87
trout streams and rivers, 83, 154–55
weedless flies, 160–61
weighted flies, 7
Worm Hatch Snake Fly, 70
Catino, Frank, 161
cement, for fly building, 54–55
Clark, John, 25
color, of flies, 17–25
crab
blue, 136
as food source, 28, 35–37, 136
green, *137*
lady, 136
crustaceans
action of, 128
as food source, 28, 35–37

deer hair
  fly building with, 45
  spinning of, *59*
deer tail, 43
Dunaway, Vic, 5

eyes
  dumbbell, tying on, 88
  for fly building, 11–13, 54
  melted monofilament, 129
  weighted, 13

feathers, for fly-tying, 45–47
Finn raccoon Zonker, 47
flash, fly-tying, 50–51
flies
  active materials in, 6–7
  balance of, 14–17
  with bite guards, 171–72
  body shape of, 2
  color of, 17–25
  crab, 136–42
  critical features of, 2
  crustacean, 128
  eyes for, 11–13, 88
  large, fishing with, 99
  to match baitfish, 30–37
  monofilament eyes for, 129
  movement and action of, 6–13
  organization of, in fly box, 181–86
  shape of, 2–6
  sink rate, 14–17
  size of, 2–6
  for Southern fishing, 184–85
  supplies for, 39–55
  water testing of, 9–10
  weedless, 163
Fluoro Fibre, 17–18, 48, *50*
fly box, 181–86
  example of, *181*
  for ocean fishing, 185–86
  for Southern fishing, 184–85
fly building
  bite guards, 171–72
  natural materials for, 42–48
  supplies for, 39–55
  synthetic materials for, 48–51
  tools for, 40–41
  weedless flies, 163
Fly Fisherman's Guide to Salt-Water Prey (Adams), 5
Fly-Fisher's Guide to Saltwater Naturals and Their Imitations (Roberts), 5
fly fishing
  with anchovy patterns, 170–73
  with Barracuda Fly, 111–14
  with crab flies, 137–39
  with crustacean flies, 128–30
  with eel-like flies, 76–77
  with Glow Sand Eel, 144–45
  on grass flats, 66–67
  with large flies, 76–78, 99
  in mangroves and weed beds, 160–63
  with Mole Nose Bunker, 98–100
  with Mullet and Whitefish Snake Fly, 82–83
  with needlefish patterns, 178
  with poppers, 118–19
  in sand eel school, 94
  with Sea Rat, 150
  with Slab Fly, 86–87
  in surf, 60–61, 87
  with Winged Weedless Rat, 160–63
  worm hatch, 70–72
Fly Fishing in Salt Water (Kreh), xvii
food, types of, 27–37
Fournier, Steve, 41

Gilkes, Cooper, 23
Glow Sand Eel, 143–47
  example of, *143*
  recipe for, 145–47
Glow Squid, 10, 105–9
  color of, 17
  example of, *109*
  recipe for, 106–9
Goodrich, Chauncey, *82*, 154

herring, as food source, 35, *98*
hooks, 51–52

Inshore Fly Fishing (Tabory), xvii

Jessup, Curt, *184*
Johnson, Paul, 25

Kinky Fibre, 50
Kreh, Lefty, xvii, 24

Laszlo, Pete and Ann, 11
Leiser, Eric, xvii, 60
line
  for poppers, 118–19
  for surf fishing, *87*
Long Saddle Snake Fly, 75–79
  example of, *75*, *79*
  recipe for, 78–79
Luce, Bob, *76*, 182

marabou, 45
Marini, Dan, *170*
menhaden
  as food source, 28, *34*
  large flies for imitation of, 100

Mole Nose Bunker, 97–103
  example of, *97*
  recipe for, 100–103
mullet, as food source, 32, 82
Mullet and Whitefish Snake Fly, 81–83
  recipe for, 83–84

needlefish
  as food source, *31*, 178
  patterns, 178
night fishing, 2, 13, 87, 106, 161
  color patterns and, 17, 23–24
  for snook, 161
  worm hatch and, 70

ostrich herl, 47

Paprikash Fly, 130
Peterson, Eric, 112, *128*, 182
pike, fishing for, 77
pilchard
  example of, *12*
  as food source, 35
Pop-Hair Bug, 117–22
  example of, *117*, *122*
  recipe for, 117–22
Popovics, Bob, 130
poppers, 117–22
  bodies, 52–53
  fishing with, 11
Posh, John, 118

Rat and Glow Chovy
  example of, *175*
  recipe for, 174–75
Rat Chovy, 169–76
  example of, *169*, *176*
  recipe for, 174–75
Rat Needlefish, 177–80
  example of, *177*
  recipe for, 178–80
Reenen, Paul, 48
river herring, as food source, 29, *98*
Roberts, George V., Jr., 5

saddle hackle, 45
sand eel, *4*
  as food source, *29*
  imitation fly, 93–96
Sand Eel Snake Fly, 65–67
  recipe for, 67–68
sardine, as food source, 28–29
scissors, fly-tying, 41–42
sculpin
  as food source, *37*
  Trout Rat as copy of, 154

Sea Rat, 7, 149–51
  example of, *149*
  recipe for, 150–51
Sea Rat Squid, 10
shad, as food source, 35
shiner
  as food source, 32
shrimp
  as food source, 28, 35–37
  patterns, 128–30
sight-fishing, 5, 11, 13, 66–67, 82–83, *94*, 161
silverside, as food source, 28–29, 32
Skok, Dave, *8*, 77, 182
Slab Fly, 85–92
  example of, *92*
  recipe for, 90–92
smelt, as food source, 28, 32
Snake Fly, 57–63
  action of, 58
  example of, *63*
  materials in, *6*
  recipe for, 61–63
  surf fishing with, *87*
snapper, as food source, *36*, 37
Sosin, Mark, 25
spearing, *32*
Sport Fish of Fresh Water (Dunaway), 5
squid
  body color of, 17
  color patterns of, *105*, 106
  as food source, *34*, *105*, 106
  stripers feeding on, 34, 106
striper
  crab as food source, 136–37
  feeding patterns of, 37, 76, 99–100
  fishing techniques for, 66–67, 86–87
  Glow Sand Eel for, 144
  needlefish as food source, 178
  poppers for, 119
  sand eel as food source, 144–45
  squid as food source, *34*, 106
stripping basket, *87*
Success Fly Fluoro Fibre. *See* Fluoro Fibre
surf fishing, 60–61, 87
Swiderski, Roger, *173*

Tabory, Barb, *144*
thread, for fly building, 55
Trout Rat, 153–57
  example of, *153*, *157*
  recipe for, 155–57

Van Reenen, Paul, *19*
vise, fly-tying, 41

weakfish, *4*
whitefish, as food source, 82
Wide-Eyed Shrimp, *15*, 127–33
  example of, *127*
  recipe for, 130–33
Winged Weedless Rat, 159–67
  example of, *159*, *167*
  recipe for, 163–67
Worm Hatch Snake Fly, 69–73
  example of, *69*
  recipe for, 72–73
worms, as food source, *31*, 37, 70